THE COMPLETE BOOK OF
CATS

THE COMPLETE BOOK OF
CATS

JUDITH A STEEH

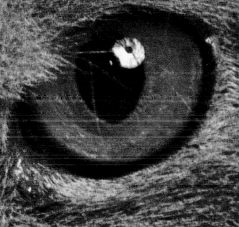

GALAHAD BOOKS

A Bison Book

Contents

Page 15 **Introduction**
17 Cats in History
17   Origins
17   Ancient Egypt
18   Europe
18   The New World
18   The Orient
20 Cats in Folklore and Myth
21 Cats in the Arts
21   Literature
23   Art
23   Music
24 Cats Today

27 **Anatomy**
28 Skeleton
30 Hair and Skin
30 Senses
30 Eyes
30 Ears
30 Nose
31 Tongue
31 Whiskers
32 Nervous System
33 Respiratory System
33 Circulatory System
35 Digestive System
35 Reproductive System

37 **Catalog**
39 Colors and Patterns
50 Encyclopedia

209 **Cat Care**
210 Choosing Your Cat
211 Daily Care of the Healthy Cat
211   Grooming
212   Hazards
213   Feeding
213   Nutrition
214   Essential Nutrients
215   Other Pets
215   Sanitation
216   Training
219   Travel
219   Vaccinations
220 Diseases and Other Ailments
220   Signs of Trouble
222   Feline Enteritis (Distemper)
222   Rabies
222   Toxoplasmosis
224   Pneumonia
224   Cystitis
224   Anemia
224   Eclampsia
224   Cancer
224   Ear Ailments
224   Eye Ailments
225   Skin Ailments
226 Parasites
226   Fleas
226   Defleaing the Cat

© Copyright 1978 by Bison Books Limited
All rights reserved
Library of Congress Catalog Card Number: 77-79967
ISBN 0-88365-397-4
Printed in Hong Kong
Published by arrangement with Bison Books Limited

Printed in Hong Kong
Galahad Books,
New York City
ISBN 0-88365-397-4

226	Defleaing the House	232	Choking	237	Breeding for Various Characteristics	
226	Defleaing the People	232	Convulsions	237	Breeding Abnormalities	
226	Ticks	232	Drowning		Choosing a Mate	
227	Ear Mites	232	Electrocution		How to Mate Your Cat	
227	Mange Mites	232	Eye Injuries	239	Terms Commonly Used in Genetics and Breeding	
227	Lice	232	Fractures			
228	Ringworm	232	Heat Stroke	240	Reproduction in Cats	
228	Favus	233	Poisoning	240	Behavior of the Female	
228	Roundworms	233	Shock	240	Behavior of the Male	
228	Tapeworms	234	Daily Care of the Sick Cat	241	Mating	
228	Hookworms & Whipworms	234	The Sick Room	241	Contraception	
229	Protozoa	234	Taking the Cat's Pulse	241	Pregnancy and Birth	
229	First Aid	234	Taking the Cat's Temperature	243	Care of the Kittens	
229	Artificial Respiration	234	Giving the Cat Its Medicine			
230	How to Lift and Transport an Injured Cat	234	Feeding	244	*Photography*	
		235	Special Care for the Incapacitated Cat	250	Index	
230	A First Aid Kit and Medicine Chest for Cats	235	Giving the Cat an Enema	253	Picture credits	
230	Automobile Accidents	235	The Elizabethan Collar			
231	Bites and Stings	236	Care of the Older Cat			
231	Bleeding	236	Genetics and Breeding			
232	Burns	236	Cat Genetics			

Below : Tabby Persian kittens

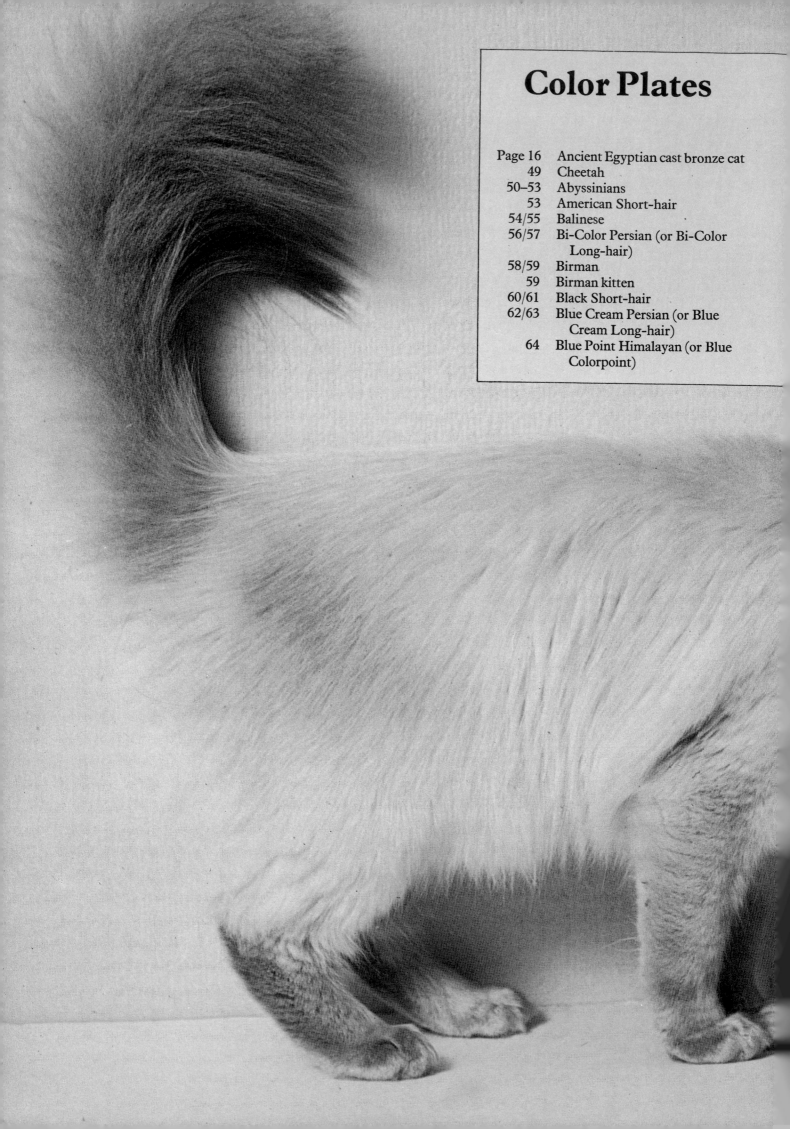

Color Plates

Page 16	Ancient Egyptian cast bronze cat
49	Cheetah
50–53	Abyssinians
53	American Short-hair
54/55	Balinese
56/57	Bi-Color Persian (or Bi-Color Long-hair)
58/59	Birman
59	Birman kitten
60/61	Black Short-hair
62/63	Blue Cream Persian (or Blue Cream Long-hair)
64	Blue Point Himalayan (or Blue Colorpoint)

65	Blue Persian (or Blue Long-hair)
66/67	Bobcat with flicker
68/69	Bobcat chasing deermouse
69	Bobcat on hillside (inset)
70/71	White British Short-hair
72/73	Sable (or Brown) Burmese
74	Siamese kitten
74/75	Blue Burmese
76/77	A Pair of Burmese cats (Sable and Blue)
78/79	Blue Burmese
80	Oriental Lavender (or Foreign Lilac) queen and kittens
81	Oriental (or Foreign) Smoke
82/83	Calico
84/85	Smoke Cameo
85	Shaded Cameo
86/87	Caracal Lynx
88/89	Chartreux
90/91	Cheetah
92–95	Chinchillas
96–97	Chinchilla kittens
98/99	Clouded Leopard
100	Himalayan (or Colorpoint Long-hair)
101	Lynx Point (or Colorpoint Short-hair)
102/103	Cornish Si-Rex
104	Cream Persian (or Cream Long-hair)
105–107	Cream Short-hairs
108/109	Devon Rex

Below : Blue Point Balinese

110/111	Devon Rex kittens	130/131	A pair of Jaguars
111	Devon Rex adult	132/133	Jaguarondi
112	Bronze Egyptian Mau	134	Jungle or Swamp Cat
113	Silver Egyptian Mau	135	Oriental Lavender
114/115	Egyptian Mau	136–139	Leopard
116/117	Scottish Wild Cat	140	Leopard Cat – Adult
118/119	European Wild Cat	141	Leopard Cat – kitten
120	Oriental (or Foreign) White Short-hair	142/143	Pride of Lions
		144	Lionesses in tree
121	Cinnamon Oriental (or Foreign)	161	Pallas' Cat
122	Rex Kitten	162	White Persian (or White Long-hair)
123	Havana Brown (or Chestnut Brown)	163	Peke-Face Persian (or Peke-Face Long-hair)
124/125	Havana kittens		
126/127	Chocolate Point Himalayan (or Chocolate Colorpoint)	165	White Persian (or White Long-hair)
128	Ocelot	166/167	Puma (or Mountain Lion or Cougar)
129	Indian or Asiatic Lionesses		

168/169	Solid Red (US) or Red Self (UK)	196/197	Bengal or Indian Tiger
170/171	Rex	198	White Tiger (top)
172/173	Russian Blues	199	Sumatran Tiger
174/175	Sand Cat	200	Tortoiseshell and White Short-hair
176/177	Scottish Folds		
178/179	Serval	201	Tiger Cat (bottom right)
180/181	Shaded Silver Persian (or Shaded Silver Long-hair)	202	Tortoiseshell Short-hair
		203	Tortoiseshell Persian (Long-hair)
182/183	Seal Point Siamese		
184/185	Lilac Point Siamese and kitten	204	Turkish Van Cat
186	Seal Point Siamese kitten	205	Blue-Eyed White Persian (Long-hair) kitten
187/188	Smoke Persians (or Smoke Long-hairs)		
		206/207	Lynx and kitten
189	Snow Leopard (or Ounce)	208	Veterinarian applys drops to cat's ears
190/191	Silver Spotted Cat		
192	Brown Tabby Persian (Long-hair) kitten		
193–195	Brown Tabby Short-hair		

Above : European Lynx

Introduction

Cats are extraordinary animals, and reactions to them run the gamut from fear and loathing to adoration and worship.

Although few people are true ailurophobes, and even fewer would go to the same lengths as the ancient Egyptians, shaving their eyebrows and mourning for months over the death of a kitten, it is still worth considering how a small, relatively insignificant animal like the domestic cat can inspire such strong reactions. (Big cats, too, are often feared or revered, but in their case the reasons appear to be at least understandable.)

The most common reason given for disliking cats is their cool, independent, aloof attitude. They seem silent, predatory creatures, accepting sustenance and affection from the misguided humans who keep them, and offering nothing in return. The fact is, of course, that cats *are* mysterious – and it is part of human nature to fear that which we do not understand.

But cat lovers, on the other hand, would point out that it is entirely possible to win a cat's affection and even devotion – and that if companionship with a cat is harder to achieve, that makes it even more valuable. Cats communicate far less with their voices than do dogs, but anyone who takes the trouble to learn their 'body language' will soon discover that they are not nearly so inscrutable.

Left: Abyssinian mother and her kitten

16

This ancient Egyptian Bronze figure was cast in the Saite Period about 600 BC. It resides now in the Cairo Museum.

Cats in History

Origins

Cats, or *Felidae*, are found throughout the world, but all – big or small, wild or domesticated – have so much in common that scientists have not formally subdivided them. This and other evidence strongly suggests that all cats had a common ancestor.

The first cats appeared in the Oligocene era, about 20 million years ago. There were two types: one, *Holophoneus*, produced *Smilodon*, the saber-tooth tiger and the other, *Dimictis*, eventually evolved into the modern day cat.

Dimictis was smaller than *Holophoneus*, faster, more agile, and much more intelligent. This, then was the ancestor of the almost 40 different cat species recognized today.

No one knows how or when domestic cats appeared on the scene. They are almost certainly mixtures of several species of wild cat (in scientific terms they are of *polyphyletic origin*). The earliest records state that domestic cats came from Egypt and are only about 5000 years old (dogs have been domesticated for at least 20,000 years). Short-haired cats were exported from Egypt to the European continent by the Phoenicians and to the New World by European colonists.

Ancient Egypt

The heyday of the domestic cat was certainly in ancient Egypt, where the pets were not only useful members of society, but for almost 2000 years were deified as well.

The fertile Nile Valley was the granary of the ancient world, and rats and mice must have caused severe damage before the cat appeared on the scene. In addition, cats were trained to hunt snakes, birds, and other small mammals, and even to retrieve ducks for hunters.

No one knows exactly why or when the Egyptian cat came to play such an important role in religion, but probably the reason for its deification was a complex mixture of respect for its hunting abilities, love of its beauty, and awe of its mysterious 'magical' personality. Paintings, sculptures, and tomb decorations portray a short-haired elegant cat very similar in size and shape to today's Abyssinian.

The cat goddess Bastet (or Bast or Pasht) was the daughter of Isis (goddess of the sun, moon, and earth) and Ra (god of the sun and the underworld). Worship of Bastet (and her representative, the cat) reached its peak around 950 BC. Beginning as the goddess of sexuality and fertility, she became the sun, moon, motherhood, and love goddess as well, in addition to protecting the dead, decreeing the success or failure of crops, making rain, and helping heal the sick, especially children.

More than 700,000 pilgrims traveled by boat to Bubastis each spring for her festival which was the gayest of the year. The appearance of the boats loaded with singing, dancing people was a signal to those who remained at home in cities along the way to begin their own festival.

Although there are several accurate accounts of the pilgrims' journey to Bubastis, no one seems to know exactly what went on when they got there. Some historians limit the attractions to good music, food, and wine while others describe the festival as a huge drunken sexual orgy. There were, at any rate, many parades, and the atmosphere was probably very like that at Mardi Gras or Oktoberfest.

Egyptian cats had either short ears and blunt noses or long ears and sharp noses. Most were short-haired and ginger-colored with black markings. They were spoiled and pampered by peasant and pharaoh alike; mummified cats have been found wearing necklaces, earrings, and even nose rings. When they died cats were given elaborate funerals, and the household where the death occurred was plunged into deepest mourning. Even poor families held a wake for their pet, and the bereaved owners shaved their eyebrows to demonstrate their grief.

For a long time it was illegal to harm a cat in Egypt, and the crime was punishable by death. Herodotus, who was usually quite accurate about things he saw firsthand (if a bit credulous when it came to believing other travelers' stories), gives a graphic description of an unfortunate Egyptian who happened to witness the death of a cat – trembling, bathed in tears, loudly proclaiming to all and sundry that he had had no part in the matter. Perhaps there was good reason for this extreme behavior – one Roman soldier was literally torn to pieces by an infuriated mob in Thebes after he accidentally killed a cat.

By about 100 BC cat worship was in decline and Phoenician traders, who had been trying for years to smuggle cats to a rodent-ridden world, were finally able to export them in quantity. The best days had come to an end.

Europe

*Below: In contrast to the photograph on the preceding page is this picture of a living Bronze Egyptian Mau. This breed and the Abyssinian share the dubious distinction that their ancestors were the cat deities of ancient Egypt.
Inset: A short-haired white cat of Foreign or Oriental type. The Foreign type is said to have originated in Egypt.*

By the end of the fifth century AD the domestic cat was well established in the Middle East and Europe. As the barbaric invasions brought rats and plague sweeping across the continent, cats rose in value. In several countries in fact (including Wales and Switzerland), there were laws governing the sale and protection of cats.

Unfortunately, during the Dark Ages the cat became an outcast. Cats never quite lost the supernatural, pagan reputation they had acquired in Egypt, and they were soon caught up in a wave of witch-hunting and persecutions. There are horror stories by the dozen of cats – hundreds of thousands of them – being burned, flayed, crucified, and thrown from the tops of towers, usually under the auspices of the Church.

Paradoxically, the cat was saved by the Black Death. Returning Crusaders brought with them the Asiatic black rat, carrier of the bubonic plague. With so few cats left the rats bred unhindered, and in only two years in the middle of the fourteenth century three out of every four people in Europe died of the disease. Those who had sometimes literally risked their lives to keep cats now came into their own; their homes and farms were relatively free from rats. Gradually the authorities saw the light and ended their persecution.

By the end of the Renaissance cats were again valued members of society. Cardinal Wolsey in England insisted on taking his cat with him to the cathedral and to royal conferences. In France Montaigne, Richelieu, and Mazarin all doted on their pets, and Moncrif wrote his charming *Histoire des Chats*, the first cat book as we know it.

The Victorian Age found the cat prized not only as a useful pet, but as a thing of beauty. Cats were fashionable; the first cat show was held at Crystal Palace in

London in 1871. In 1895 an American version was held at Madison Square Garden, and the success of these shows began a tradition that continues to this day.

The New World

Domestic cats probably arrived in the Americas with Columbus or shortly thereafter – there were certainly only wild cats in the New World before it was colonized by Europeans.

In the early part of the eighteenth century cats traveled with the Jesuits as they moved up the west coast of Mexico. There were cats on the *Mayflower*, and in the middle of the seventeenth century many more were imported to help defeat a horde of black rats who were battling the colonists for their grain supplies.

Cats traveled with the French voyageurs on the great Midwestern waterways, and pushed westward with the wagon trains. As the Indians discovered the cat's hunting abilities the animals became valuable trading items, and later western miners paid as much as fifty dollars for a good mouser.

The Orient

Domestic cats probably arrived in China early in the Han dynasty (206 BC–221 AD) and were soon firmly entrenched in Chinese society.

The first known litter of kittens in Japan was born on 19 September 999 in the Imperial Palace in Kyoto. It was the Emperor Ichijo's thirteenth birthday and he was so completely entranced by the small animals that he ordered the kittens to be given the same care that royal infants usually received.

For several centuries cats in Japan belonged exclusively to royalty. But around the fourteenth century the growing silk industry was threatened by mice. Cats, who were by then more numerous, became even more valuable and closely guarded. Finally the authorities were forced to decree that all cats were to be set loose, and that it was forbidden to buy or sell them.

Today cats are highly regarded in both China and Japan – in the former, more for their prowess in hunting rodents, and in the latter perhaps more for their beauty and charm.

Cats in Folklore and Myth

The larger members of the cat family appear in the myths and legends of almost every country in the world, and the domestic cat too, has a place in that tradition.

There were no domestic cats in Eden – only lions, tigers, panthers, and leopards – and in fact the Bible does not mention cats at all (perhaps because they were being worshiped as pagan gods in nearby Egypt at roughly the time the Bible was being written). But legend has it that during the long weeks afloat in the Ark the rat and mouse population increased so alarmingly that the rodents soon threatened the safety of the entire ship. Noah, rising to the occasion, passed his hand three times over the head of the lioness, and she obligingly sneezed forth a cat who soon dealt with the problem.

The ancient Greeks had another story of the cat's creation – one of the few times the animals are mentioned in their literature. Apollo, it seems, created the lion and sent it to frighten his sister Diana. The Huntress was not so easily intimidated however, and promptly created the domestic cat as a parody to poke fun at her brother's monster. Diana was also goddess of the moon, an association cats had held earlier in Egypt and retained for centuries thereafter.

According to an old Norse legend, Utgard-Loki, king of the giants, had a giant cat; and of course Freyya, goddess of love and marriage, rode in a chariot pulled by two cats.

Cats hold a special place in the Arab world, as Selema held a special place in Mohammed's heart. It is written that once in Damascus the prophet cut off his sleeve rather than disturb his sleeping cat when it was time for prayers. A Sultan in Cairo was the first man known to have left a legacy for stray cats. Cats figure in several tales in the *Arabian Nights*, and Burton claims that the word 'tabby' comes from a quarter of Baghdad called Attabi that is famous for its watered or streaked silks.

Every country has tales of cats that take human form or vice versa. In Japan, cats with long tails were said to have this power – which may either account for or be accounted for by the fact that the native cats of Japan have very short tails. In Japan too, black cats were considered good luck as they were thought able to cure disease especially in children, but red or

Above: Cream Persian.
Below: The lucky (or unlucky) but always mysterious black cat.

pink cats were thought to have supernatural powers and were avoided.

During the fourteenth century the black cat was well known as either a witch or a devil in disguise, and these poor creatures took the brunt of the feline persecutions during the Dark Ages.

Today, however, whether or not one avoids black cats depends on where one lives. In the United States and Ireland the old superstitions persist, and a black cat crossing one's path always means bad luck.

But in England and Scotland black cats bring good luck. English sailors purchased them for their wives, believing that as long as the cat was contented the weather would be fair, and in Scotland a black cat in the house ensured that the young ladies who lived there would have plenty of beaux.

Black cats are also considered good luck in the Orient. Chinese sailors carried them aboard ship to bring favorable winds.

Cats in the Arts

Cats in Literature

Cats and writers seem to have an affinity for each other, and the list of famous writers who owned, were fond of, and in many cases, wrote about cats would be long indeed. From Lord Byron to Mark Twain, from Henry James to Ernest Hemingway, Dickens, Wordsworth, Baudelaire – the names span the history of poetry and prose on every continent.

During medieval times animal stories were very popular, as they had always been – and still are today. Many of these stories were collected into *Bestiaries*, collections of descriptions of the habits of various animals, each followed by a 'signification' that derived a Christian moral from the story. One of the few fragments remaining of the Anglo-Saxon *Physiologus* is the story of the Panther, and the more complete Middle English *Beastiary* contains 'The Lion.'

The first text devoted entirely to the domestic cat appeared during the latter half of the sixteenth century. Chaucer mused on the cat's preference for mice over milk in *The Manciple's Tale*.

Cats pop in and out of literature for the next three centuries, gradually becoming more likeable as time goes on. Cervantes has Don Quixote accuse a group of cats of witchcraft – a reference to the horrors of the Middle Ages, as is the witches' invocation of Graymalkin in *Macbeth*. In John Gay's fable 'The Rat-Catcher and Cats' the two factions eventually arrive at a working agreement. There are three rather important cats in Dicken's *Bleak House* (1852), belonging to Krook, Mr Jellyby and Mr Vohles. And who could forget Dinah in *Alice in Wonderland* or the Cheshire Cat in *Through the Looking Glass* ?

Cats play starring roles in many more modern works by famous writers. Even the briefest list would have to include Kipling's *The Cat That Walked By Himself*; Poe's masterpiece of horror, *The Black Cat*; Hemingway's short story, *Cat in the Rain*; *The Cat* by Collette; and *The Malediction* by Tennessee Williams; not to mention *archy and mehitabel* by don marquis; and a number of excellent books by Paul Gallico.

Poets have been no less inspired by their pets: Thomas Gray wrote *Ode* in 1742; Horace Walpole's unfortunate cat Selima drowned in a tub of goldfish; Edward Lear

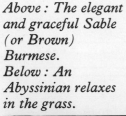

Above : The elegant and graceful Sable (or Brown) Burmese.
Below : An Abyssinian relaxes in the grass.

Above and Below:
This sublime
Abyssinian looks
as if it could
adorn the walls of
an ancient tomb.

immortalized the marriage of *The Owl and the Pussycat*. Wordsworth, Blake (The Tyger), Yeats, Swinburne, and Hardy are just a few of the many others whose cats moved them to poetry.

The poetry of T S Eliot is justly famous for its erudition and social consciousness, but not often for its humor. In *Old Possum's Book of Practical Cats*, however, he reveals an entirely new side of his character in a witty, but always thoroughly sympathetic and knowledgeable series of poems about cats.

The poems address two very important topics, *The Naming of Cats* ('. . . a difficult matter, (that) isn't just one of your holiday games') and *The Ad-dressing of Cats*.

We are then introduced to a number of cats, all of whom are immediately recognizable. There is the Gumbie Cat, the tabby 'on whom well-ordered households depend . . .' and the Rum Tum Tugger, a perverse animal who '. . . will do as he do do and there's no doing anything about it!' The rather small, black and white Jellicle Cats rest up all day so that they can dance all night; the Great Rumpus Cat single-handedly routs a whole army of Pekes and Pollicles; Mr Mistoffelees, the original Conjuring Cat, not only spirits away various household items, but magically produces seven kittens. Maccivity, the

'Napoleon of Crime' baffles Scotland Yard while Gus the theater cat reminisces about his past triumphs on the boards. Bustopher Jones saunters toward one or another of his clubs in St James's and Skimbleshanks rides the Midnight Mail. And last, but never least, is Growltiger, a bargee known as 'The Terror of the Thames' who is finally forced to walk the plank by a gang of dastardly Siamese.

Furthermore, one of the best examples of indirectly using cat images to establish a mood is a stanza in T S Eliot's *The Love Song of J Alfred Prufrock*.

The study of cat literature *per se* can be a time-consuming but rewarding occupation. Anyone seriously interested in pursuing the topic would be well advised to consult Claire Necker's *Four Centuries of Cat Books, 1570–1970*, published by Scarecrow Press in 1972 – an annotated bibliography of cat books published in English.

The range in cat literature is enormous. There are adventurous cats like Dick Whittington's friend or Puss in Boots, and there are long-suffering cats as in Susannah Patteson's *Pussy Meow*. There are musical cats (*The King of Cats* by Stephen Vincent Benet), talking cats (*Tobermory* by Saki) and even cats who are FBI agents (*Undercover Cat* by The Gordons).

The largest number of cat books are written for children; the next largest subdivision covers cat care. There are also many general cat books (of which Agnes Repplier's *The Fireside Sphynx*, first published in 1901, is an excellent example), fiction, anthologies, picture books, cartoon books, and scientific books – anything in short, that strikes a reader's fancy.

Cats in Art

People have been drawing, painting, and sculpturing cats since the time of the ancient Egyptians. Often they were symbols of freedom and independence; cats appeared on the shields of Roman soldiers, on the coat of arms of the Dukes of Burgundy, and as symbols of freedom both in Holland during the Dutch struggle for independence in the sixteenth century, and again during the French Revolution.

During the thirteenth century the example of St Francis of Assisi led to many sympathetic portrayals of cats especially by Italian painters. Around 1450, the philosopher St Jerome was depicted with a feline companion by Antonello da Messino. But just as often cats represented evil. Ghirlandaio, Luini, and Cellini all painted Judas accompanied by a cat; St Ives, the patron saint of lawyers, was often shown with a cat said to represent all the evil qualities associated with that profession. In Dürer's engraving *Adam and Eve* (1504) the cat is a cruel symbol. Da Vinci's study of the cat however, reveals a scientific exploration of the cat's form.

In 1523 Guilio Romano would paint a threatening evil cat in *Madonna della Gatta*, but by the end of the century Federico Barocci was showing cats in a much more naturalistic manner – in, for example, *Holy Cat With Family* (1574) and *Annunciation* (1584). Cats were residents of the Garden of Eden in Breughel the Elder's *Paradise* in the early 1600s.

From that point on, the treatment of cats in western painting became increasingly sympathetic and naturalistic. Some of the most charming portrayals of cats include Jan Steen's *The Cat's Reading Lesson* (1650), Jean Baptiste Greuze's *The Wool Winder* (1759), Renoir's *Woman With A Cat* (1880) and Mary Cassatt's *Children Playing With a Cat* (1908).

Several artists in both east and west have achieved a certain measure of popularity by drawing or painting cats.

Gottfried Mind, a Swiss artist, became known as the 'Cat Raphael' in Europe at the beginning of the nineteenth century for his drawings and water colors that are almost photographic reproductions of the animals he loved.

During the mid-1800s, a Japanese artist named Kuniyoshi produced many portraits of cats that show both understanding and humor. His cats range from anthropomorphic representations (*The Cat Family at Home*, c.1840) to demons (*The Cat Witch of Okabe*), to realistic studies (*Cats for the Fifty-Three Stations of Tokaido Road*, 1848).

In England at the end of the century Louis Wain was an enormously popular illustrator whose drawings of cats appeared in countless children's books, magazines, and newspapers on both sides of the Atlantic. Unfortunately he went mad and was committed to an asylum in 1924. His popularity continued, but gradually his style changed until his drawings became more concerned with patterns than with accurate representations of cats. Today he is remembered by many for the way in which he helped popularize cats, and is also famous in psychiatry for the manner in which his growing schizophrenia expressed itself in his art.

Cats in Music

Cats have appeared in western music for many centuries. Songs about cats abound – children's songs, famous cat poems that have been set to music, and others like that most popular cat song of all, 'The Cat Came Back.'

Many instrumental pieces have been inspired by cats. Scarlatti and Liszt both composed pieces titled *The Cat's Fugue*, while Chopin produced the *Cat Valse*. Stravinsky wrote *Lullabies for the Cat*. Prokofiev used sensuous woodwinds to denote the cat in *Peter and the Wolf*, while Zey Confrey imitated a cat running over the piano in his jazz classic, *Kitten on the Keys*.

Tschaikovsky's famous ballet *The Sleeping Beauty* contains a famous scene in which two dancers, Puss in Boots and White Cat, imitate feline movements; there are many other dances inspired by cats, and ballet has even named one of its most difficult steps – the *pas de chat* – after them.

No one knows how much cats like human music, but some have certainly been active in the music world. Jenny Lind, for example, used to sing to her pet cat. Saint Saens was a noted cat lover, and Albert Schweitzer was seldom seen without a feline companion.

Cats Today

In many ways many cats lead better lives today than ever before. As the human standard of living rises, so does that of those pets lucky enough to have secured a seat on the gravy train. In America or Europe today, a domestic cat who has a home is likely to have a very comfortable one. The usefulness of cats in advertising and the enormous number of books about them published each year mirror the important place they hold in society's affections. The ever-increasing number of pet boutiques, specialist shops and cemeteries, also indicates their growing status in the eyes of their owners.

Unfortunately this happy picture only applies to a very few of the world's cats. In America alone more than 50 million kittens are born each year – but only a very small number live more than a few months. Millions die of cold, hunger, disease, or injuries. Millions more are put down in one of the nation's 2000 public shelters or pounds, simply because there are no facilities to keep them for more than 48 or 72 hours. Some will even be sold to laboratories in a desperate attempt to raise money to provide shelter to others. The fate of the kittens who are born strays is hard enough to contemplate. The thought of those callously abandoned in rubbish cans or on the roadside by their owners – who thought it cruel or found it inconvenient to have their pets neutered – is horrible.

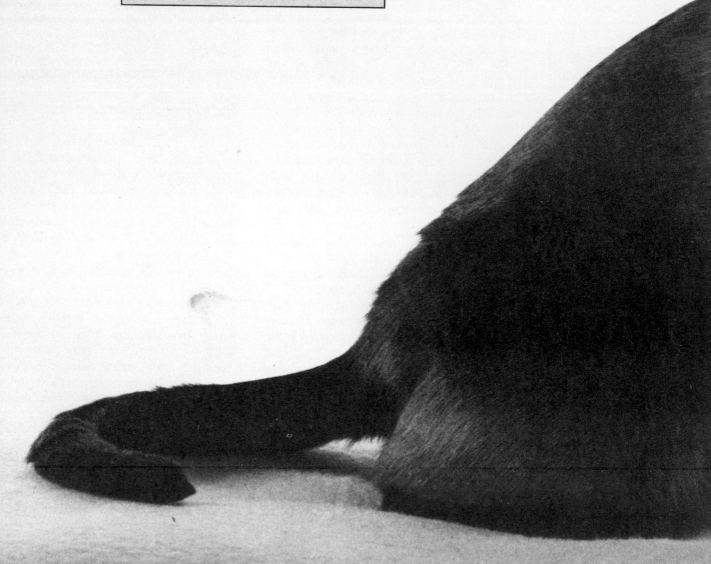

Wild cats find themselves in an equally unhappy though opposite situation. There is scarcely an entry for a wild cat in Section 3 (the Catalog Section) of this book that does not note that the species is in grave danger of extinction – either from intensive hunting, or from more impersonal threats such as the destruction of the animals' habitat through war or the encroachment of civilization. Zoos labor manfully to prevent the total extinction of many rare breeds, but all too often the end result is that the number of animals of a given species becomes restricted to but a few kept in captivity.

Cat lovers, then, have two battles to fight: overpopulation on the domestic front and declining population in the wild. Neither will be won easily, or quickly, or cheaply.

Left inset : Turkish Van Cat.
Above : A young White Short-hair.
Left : The Seal Point Siamese is perhaps the most popular pedigree house cat in the world today.

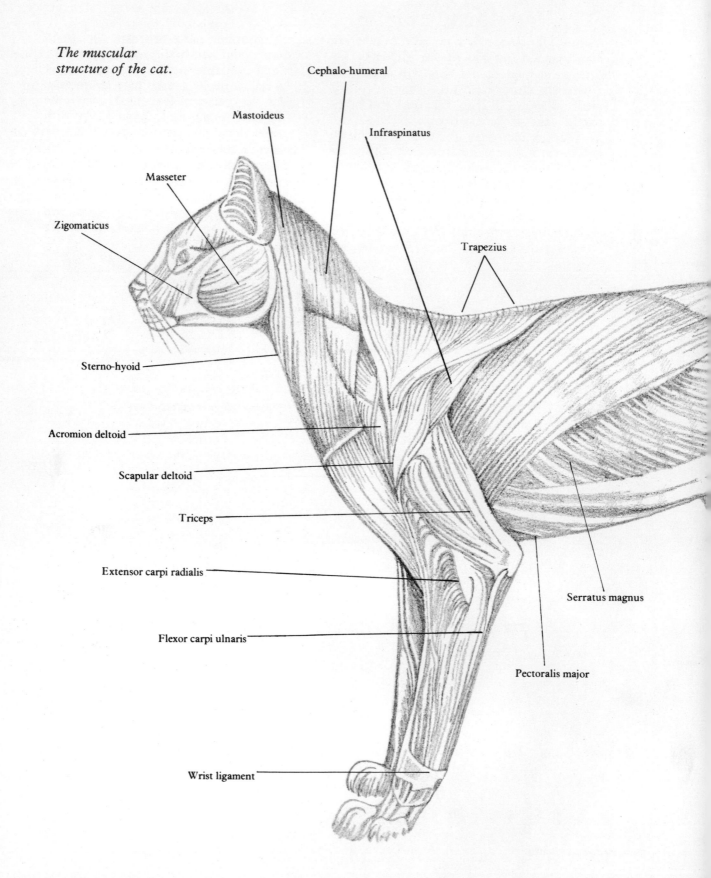

*The muscular
structure of the cat.*

Cephalo-humeral

Mastoideus

Infraspinatus

Masseter

Zigomaticus

Trapezius

Sterno-hyoid

Acromion deltoid

Scapular deltoid

Triceps

Extensor carpi radialis

Serratus magnus

Flexor carpi ulnaris

Pectoralis major

Wrist ligament

Anatomy

Some knowledge of how cats' bodies are constructed and how they work is vital for every cat owner. Not only will it help an owner to understand his cat better, but it will be useful in daily care and will be of great value if the cat becomes ill.

Cats are mammals and thus share many common anatomical features with the other higher animals including man. All mammals have a backbone, mammary glands, a four-chambered heart, a muscular diaphragm, and vital organs such as lungs, spleen, liver, intestines, etc. Cats have hair – a feature scientists believe has helped

many mammals adapt to drastic changes in climate – and bear their young alive. The fact that the babies depend on their mother for a relatively long time may be another reason the species has survived so well; the young have time to learn how to cope with a hostile world instead of relying solely on instinct to survive.

There are many other similarities between cat and human bodies. For example, only the cat's hind legs have knee joints. The front legs are jointed like elbows, and are attached to the shoulder bone like human arms.

Great oblique

Latissimus dorsi

Gluteus medius

Gluteus maximus

Fascia lata covering deeper muscles

Biceps femoralis

Semi-tendinosus

Gastrocnemius

Sartorius

Extensor digitorum longus

Extensor tendons of the toes

Skeleton

The purpose of the skeletal system is to support the body, to protect the soft inner tissues and organs, and to provide levers for moving body parts. As mentioned earlier, there are many similarities between cat and human skeletons, but there are several important differences too. Cats, for example, do not have opposable thumbs nor do they have collar bones. They have thirteen ribs compared to man's twelve, and tailbones.

Cats have from 230 to 290 bones; as with humans, younger animals have more separate bones, some of which fuse together with age.

The cat's skeleton is a strong framework that is flexible enough to provide great freedom of movement. Ball and socket

The skeletal structure of the cat.

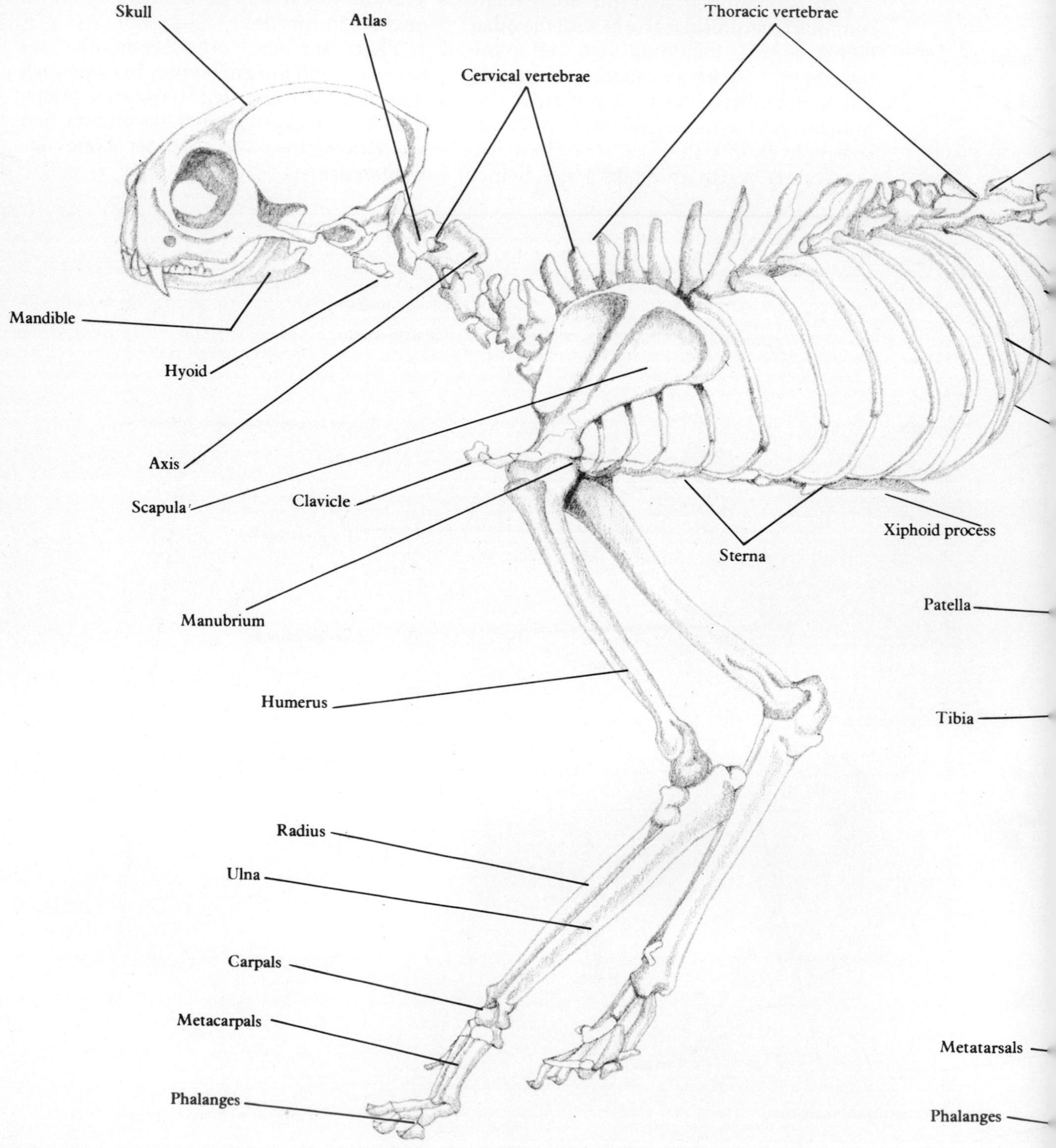

Skull

Atlas

Thoracic vertebrae

Cervical vertebrae

Mandible

Hyoid

Axis

Scapula

Clavicle

Manubrium

Sterna

Xiphoid process

Patella

Humerus

Tibia

Radius

Ulna

Carpals

Metacarpals

Metatarsals

Phalanges

Phalanges

joints, like the hip joint, permit a wide range of movement and give the cat its agility in jumping and climbing. Hinge joints (for example, at elbow, knee, and jaw) and pivot joints (like the neck) which allow side-to-side movement are also useful.

The tail is an extension of the spinal cord and consists of 21–22 bones if the cat has a full tail. It is used primarily for balance in climbing and jumping. Many experts believe that the cat also uses it to help right itself when falling, by whipping it around to help turn the body in air. In addition, it is useful for communicating either pleasure (held stiff and straight) or anger (lashing from side to side or thrashing up and down).

The cat's smooth, gliding walk comes from the fact that unlike most other four-legged animals, it moves both right and both left feet forward at the same time.

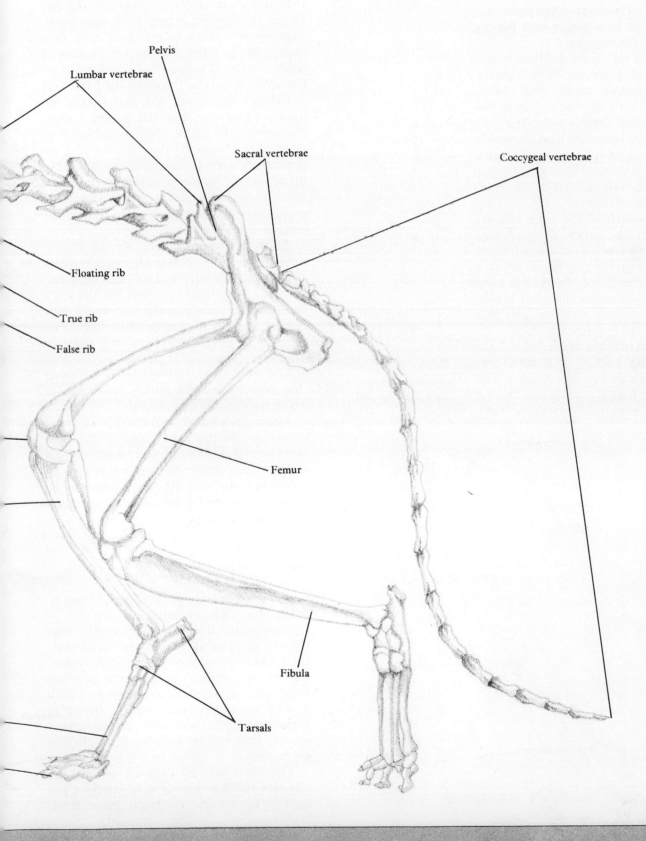

Pelvis

Lumbar vertebrae

Sacral vertebrae

Coccygeal vertebrae

Floating rib

True rib

False rib

Femur

Fibula

Tarsals

Hair and Skin

Cat hair acts as insulation by trapping a layer of air next to the body. By growing more hair in cold weather or by shedding it in warmer seasons, the amount of insulation can be partially controlled. It also protects the cat from insect bites, thorns, and many disease organisms. Thus the hair must be kept in good condition.

When a cat is frightened its hair stands upright. This is a protective mechanism to make the animal look larger and fiercer, and to frighten the attacker.

The cat's skin is a tough, flexible, water-proof membrane made up of two layers: the *epidermis* (outer layer) and *dermis* (inner layer). It contains sweat glands that help regulate body temperature; the cat's body is cooled by radiating heat, however, while human sweat glands cause inner cooling. The skin also has glands that secrete *sebum*, the oily substance that coats the hairs to protect them.

The pads on each of the cat's feet are composed of thick layers of specialized skin that can take a lot of punishment. There is a pad under the bones of each foot and one for each toe (*digit*); the front feet also have pads under the wrist bones. The foot pads contain sweat glands that discharge fluids to the outside.

Claws are also made of special skin cells, like human finger- and toenails. In all cats but the cheetah they can be retracted into folds above the digital pads when the cat is not using them to fight, climb, or hunt.

Below : Cat's paw showing the dew claw and carpal pad.

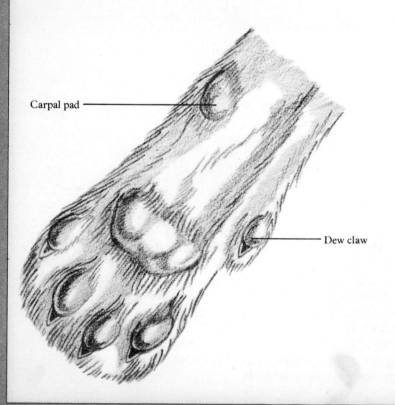

Carpal pad

Dew claw

Senses

Eyes

Cats' eyes, which have long fascinated people because of their shape and ability to see in the dark, are in fact very similar to human eyes.

The eyes are large, round globes protected by the skull; their movement is controlled by six different muscles. In the center of the eye a tiny hole, the *pupil*, expands or contracts (in most cats, to a linear slit) to allow the proper amount of light to enter. The pupil is surrounded by the colored part of the eye called the *iris*.

Behind the pupil, the *lens* bends the light rays so that they fall on the *retina*; the nerve cells in the retina send impressions to the brain via the *optic nerve*. Cats apparently cannot see colors (in fact, only birds and the higher primates have a color sense); a cat sees the world in shades of gray, like a black-and-white television image.

A special layer of cells on the retina, called the *tepetum*, acts as a mirror to collect all the available light and reflect it back into the eye. This helps account for the cat's exceptional eyesight, especially in the dark or even in regions like the ultraviolet. The tepetum is what makes cats' eyes shine in the dark.

The eyes have a transparent covering (the *cornea*) around which is a ring of white tissue called the *sclera*.

There is a third eyelid (the *nictating membrane*) in the lower part of the cat's eye for further protection. It is either pale pink or very dark, and can sometimes be seen when the animal is frightened or ill; veterinarians find it valuable for detecting some diseases or parasites.

Ears

Cats' ears, like human ears, contain mechanisms for both hearing and balance.

Most adult humans hear sounds that vibrate at around 20,000 cycles/second; mice hear at the rate of 100,000 cycles/second. A cat hears somewhere between 30,000 and 100,000 cycles/second – which is why most cats will respond better to higher-pitched voices, and can hear many sounds that are too faint or high-pitched for humans.

The outer ears are cupped, and the cat can aim them at a source to conduct the sound. Inside the eardrum three small

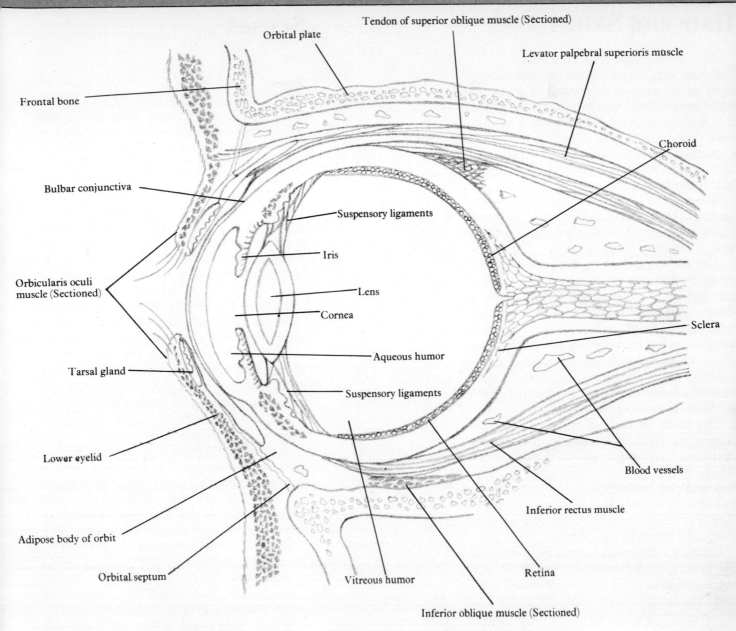

Tendon of superior oblique muscle (Sectioned)

Orbital plate

Levator palpebral superioris muscle

Frontal bone

Choroid

Bulbar conjunctiva

Suspensory ligaments

Iris

Lens

Orbicularis oculi
muscle (Sectioned)

Cornea

Sclera

Aqueous humor

Tarsal gland

Suspensory ligaments

Lower eyelid

Blood vessels

Adipose body of orbit

Inferior rectus muscle

Orbital septum

Retina

Vitreous humor

Inferior oblique muscle (Sectioned)

bones (the *hammer*, the *anvil*, and the *stirrup*) transmit sounds into the *cochlea*, which contains the *auditory nerve*.

Nearby, the three horseshoe-shaped *semicircular canals* help the cat keep its balance. The canals are lined with nerve cells and filled with fluid. As the head moves, the fluid flows over the nerve endings with varying pressure which the brain is able to translate.

Nose

The cat's nose is small and can be any color or colors from pale pink to black. It is made up of several very tough layers of skin.

Cats have a more sensitive sense of smell than humans, but do not smell as well as dogs. Instead cats tend to rely more on sight and touch when hunting. They tend to dislike most of the same smells that humans do.

Above : The structure of a cat's eye. Cat's eyes have always been fascinating to mankind – not without reason.

Tongue

The most important tasting mechanism is the tongue which has taste buds that operate much like those in man. Like humans, cats have distinct and often idiosyncratic preferences and dislikes for certain tastes.

Whiskers

Whiskers grow on the cat's cheeks, above the eyes, and on the lip, extending out to about the width of the shoulders. When the tips of the whiskers brush an object they stimulate a nerve at the base of the hair, thus helping guide the animal through tall grass, shrubs, or perhaps even through dark rooms or tunnels.

Nervous System

The cat's nervous system is much like that of the dog, but it is more intricate, and the cat is usually more nervous and highly strung.

There are two basic parts to the nervous system: the central system (brain and spinal cord) and the peripheral system (sensory fibers gathered together in bundles called nerves). The cat's brain, like man's, is divided into the *cerebrum*, which controls conscious actions, and the *cerebellum*, which controls reflex and motor activities.

A cat's skull.

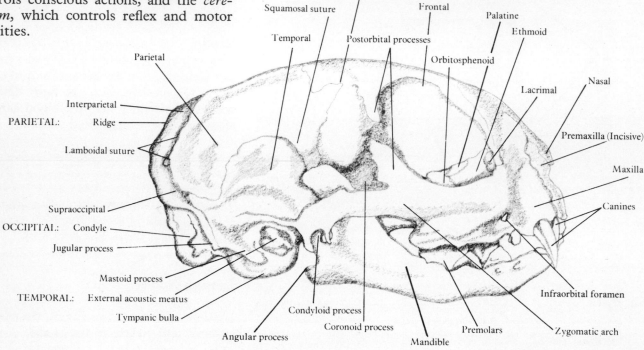

A cross-section of the vertebral column.

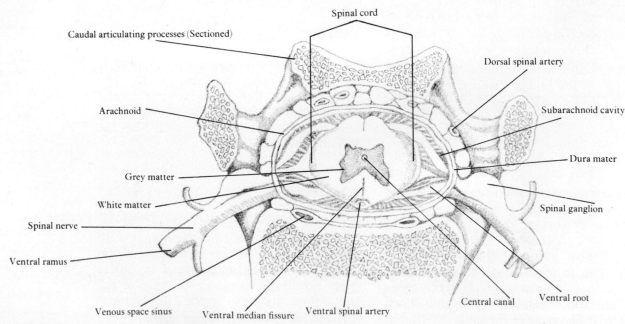

Respiratory System

Like other mammals, cats have a lung on each side of the chest separated by a partition. This separating membrane is very thin, and is easily damaged if the animal sustains a chest injury. If one of the cat's lungs collapses, the other will also.

Respiratory organs of the head.

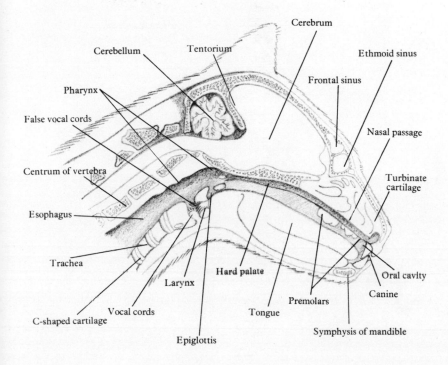

Circulatory System

Cats are warm-blooded and have complex, highly developed circulatory systems.

Heart

The heart is located very near the lungs. It has four chambers, forming two pumps; one side circulates blood in the lungs and the other takes care of circulation in the rest of the body.

Blood

Cat's blood contains *red blood cells* to carry oxygen, *white corpuscles* to fight disease, and *platelets* which help the blood clot, all suspended in a fluid called *plasma*.

Spleen

The spleen is three to four inches long and is located behind the stomach. It acts as a filter and also stores blood.

Lymph Nodes

Lymph nodes are also filters, destroying bacteria and viruses in the blood.

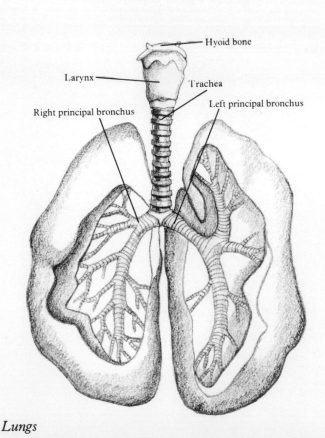

Lungs

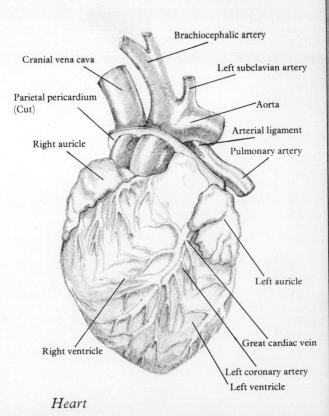

Heart

34

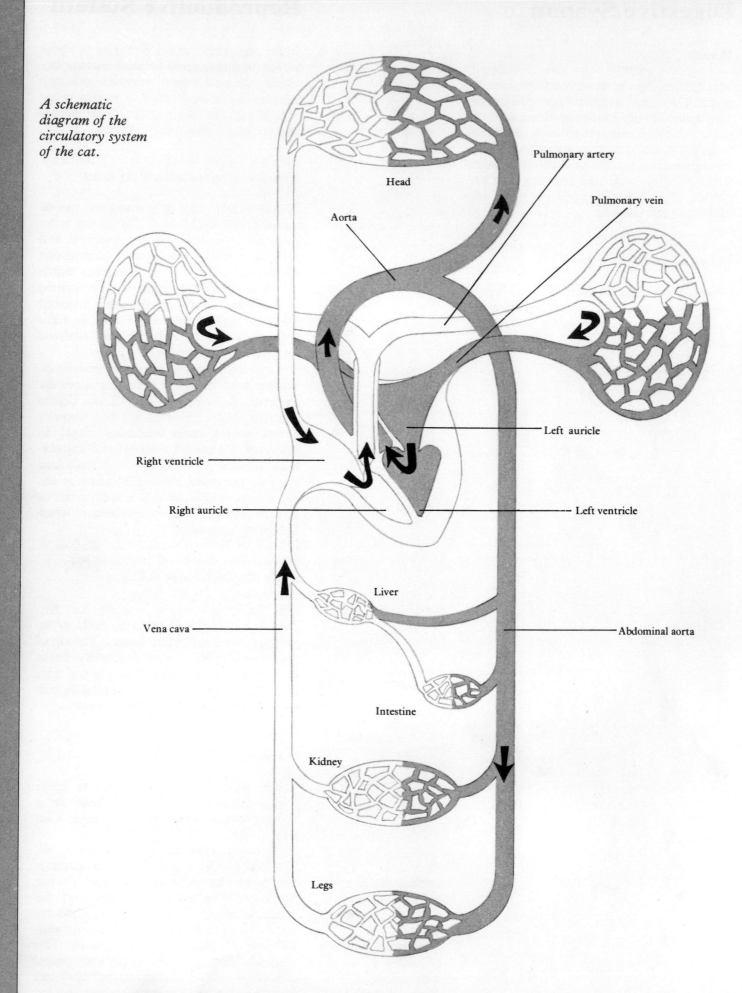

A schematic diagram of the circulatory system of the cat.

Head

Pulmonary artery

Pulmonary vein

Aorta

Right ventricle

Left auricle

Right auricle

Left ventricle

Liver

Vena cava

Abdominal aorta

Intestine

Kidney

Legs

Digestive System

Mouth

The cat has lips to hold food. Inside the mouth there is a rough tongue that can be used to lap up liquids or for cleaning.

Cats develop two sets of teeth; the baby teeth fall out at about five months, and the kitten may lose weight or even run a fever while its adult teeth are growing in. Cats do not often have cavities, but they are prone to gum trouble.

Other Digestive Organs

The cat's esophagus, stomach, intestines, liver, pancreas, and excretory systems function in much the same way as in humans.

Reproductive System

Male cats reach sexual maturity at about eleven months; most females mature between six and twelve months although females have been known to become pregnant as early as four months. Some breeds mature much faster than others.

Female Reproductive System

The *vulva*, or lips of the vagina, can be seen just below the anus. The *vagina* is the passageway connecting the external and internal parts of the system. Internally, the reproductive system functions much as it does in humans; eggs (*ova*) are formed in two ovaries; when the queen is mated the ova travel down two *Fallopian tubes* into the *uterus* where they are fertilized and the kittens develop.

Like humans and other mammals, female cats are only fertile at periodic intervals, during their *estrous cycle*. Unlike humans, however, cats are not sexually active during their *anestrous* stage. In addition cats do not ovulate until copulation is taking place, and a female can become pregnant by several toms at the same time although this is not usual as female cats do show preference when accepting a mate.

Male Reproductive System

The unaltered tomcat usually has two *testicles* suspended outside the body in the *scrotum*, to manufacture sperm. The tip of the *penis* is covered with tiny barbs, but it is not known what part they play, if any, in the mating process. The seminal fluid is manufactured by the *prostate gland*.

What sex is it?

Many people have very definite ideas about whether they want a male or a female kitten (see Choosing your Cat, page 210).

To discover a cat's sex, lift the tail gently. Female cats will have two openings that form what looks like the letter 'i' – the vertical slit below is the vulva and the small round dot above is the anus. Males have two round openings: the anus and, beneath it, the tip of the penis. The testicles, between the anus and penis, cannot be seen on kittens, though they can often be seen and felt on older cats.

 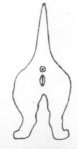

Above
A lilac Siamese
with her kittens.

Left
Determining the sex
of kittens –
Left : male
Right : female.

Catalog

Colors and Patterns

Most show cats must meet very stringent requirements regarding color and pattern. The descriptions below are adapted from the standards prescribed by the Cat Fanciers' Association, Incorporated (CFA), the largest cat registering organization in the world.

Spectrum A

(a) Solid Colors

Black
The coat must be dense and coal-black from the roots to the tip, with no rusty patches or pale undercoat. Nose leather must be black and paw pads should be black or brown. Eyes should be copper.

Blue
Blue is really a shade of gray. Coat color must be level in tone from nose to tip of tail and from roots to tips of hair. Although the lighter shade (lavender gray) is preferred, a sound darker shade is better than an unsound lighter shade. Nose leather and paw pads should be blue. Eyes should be copper.

Cream
The coat must be an even, buff cream without markings, sound to the roots. Lighter shades are preferable. Nose leather and paw pads should be pink and the eyes copper.

Red
The coat must be a clear, rich red without shading, marking, or tipping and should be even from lips and chin to tail. Nose leather and paw pads should be brick-red and eyes should be copper.

White
The coat should be pure white with no yellowish patches. Nose leather and paw pads should be pink. Eyes can be blue, copper, or one of each. In this last case, the depth of color must be of equal intensity.

(b) Shaded

Chinchilla Silver
The undercoat should be pure white with the fur on the head, back, flanks and tail delicately tipped with black giving a silvery appearance. The cat's chin, ear tufts, chest and stomach should be pure white although the legs may be slightly shaded. Eyes, lips and nose are outlined in black. Nose leather should be brick-red and paw pads black. Eyes should be green or blue-green.

Shaded Cameo or *Red Shaded*
The undercoat should be white with red tipping, shading down like a mantle from face, sides and tail, from dark on ridge to white on chin, chest, stomach and under the tail. The legs should be the same tone as the face. The general effect is much redder than the Shell Cameo. Nose leather and paw pads must be rose-colored and eyes should be outlined in rose and copper-colored.

Shaded Silver
The undercoat should be white with black tipping shading down like a mantle from face, sides and tail, from dark on the ridge to white on the chin, chest, stomach and under the tail. The general effect is of pewter rather than the silver of the Chinchilla Cameo. Eyes, lips and nose are rimmed in black. Nose leather should be rich red color and paw pads should be black. Eyes must be green or blue-green.

Shell Cameo or *Red Chinchilla*
The undercoat should be white with the fur on the head, back, flanks and tail lightly tipped with red to give a sparkling appearance. Chin, ear tufts, stomach and chest must be white, but face and legs can be very lightly shaded. Nose leather and paw pads should be rose-colored and the copper eyes should be rose-rimmed.

Top, far left: Abyssinian kitten. Top center: Odd-eyed White Short-hair kitten. One eye is blue and the other is orange. Below left: The Russian Blue is similar to the Blue Burmese and is rapidly gaining in popularity. Below: Shaded Cameo.

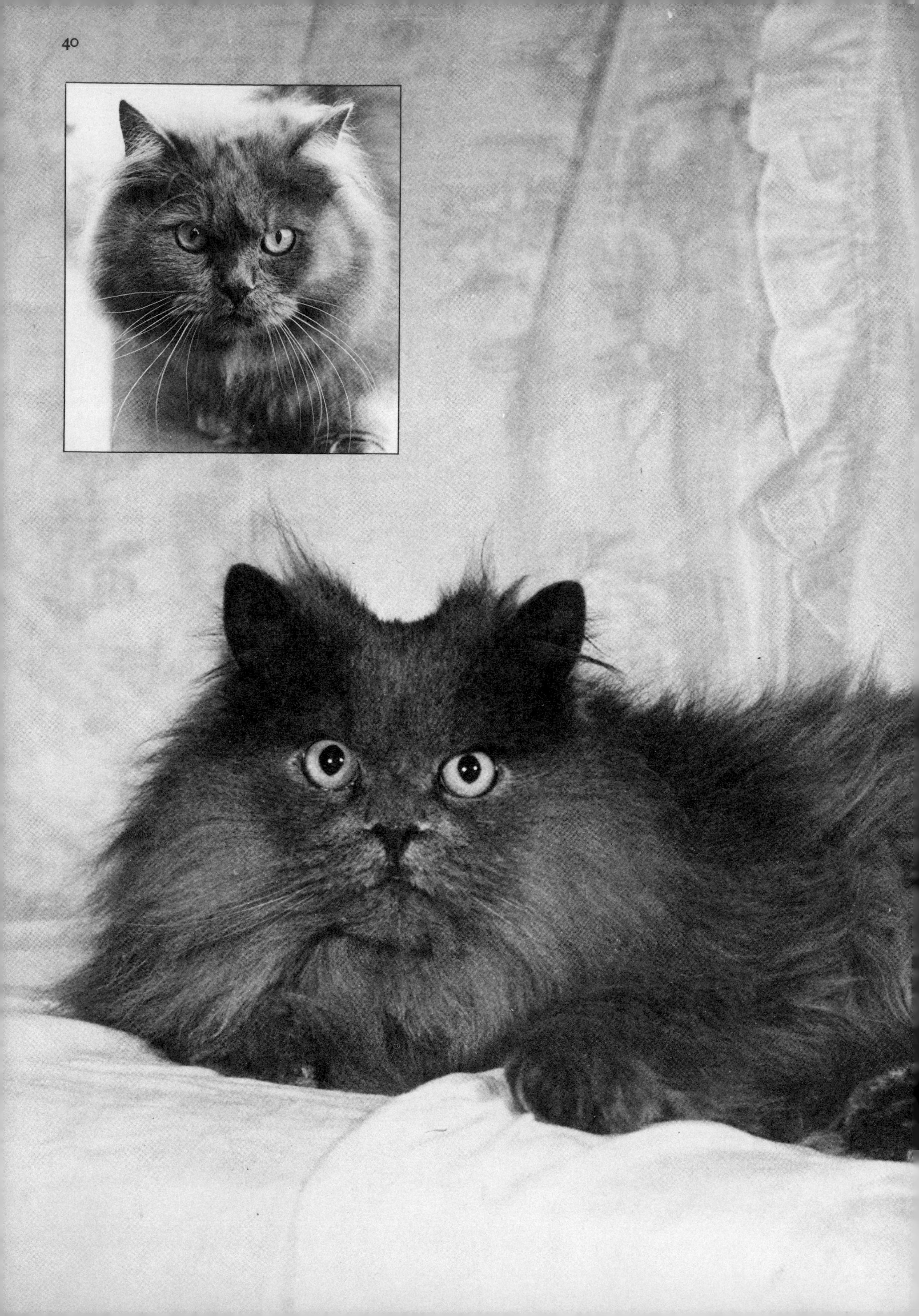

(c) Smoke

Black Smoke

The undercoat should be white with deep black tipping. Motionless, the cat appears solid black, but the white undercoat shows when it moves. Points and mask should be black except for a narrow band of white at the base of each hair which can be seen when the hairs are parted. Ruff and ear tufts should be light silver. Nose leather and paw pads must be black and the eyes, copper.

Blue Smoke

The undercoat must be white with deep blue tipping. Motionless, the cat appears solid blue but the white undercoat shows when it moves. Points and mask are blue except for a narrow band of white at the base of each hair which can be seen when the hairs are parted. The ruff and ear tufts should be white, the nose leather and paw pads should be blue and the eyes, copper.

Red Smoke

The undercoat should be white with deep red tipping. Motionless, the cat appears solid red but the white undercoat shows when it moves. Points and mask are red except for a narrow band of white at the base of each hair which can be seen when the hairs are parted. Eyes are rose-rimmed and golden in color. Nose leather and paw pads are rose.

Far left inset and left : Smokes are among the most beautiful of long-haired cats.

Above : The Silver Spotted Short-hair is not to be mistaken for the Tabby although both are equally prized.
Far right : Silver Tabby Short-hair.
Below : Brown Tabby Long-hair.

(d) Tabbies

The American CFA recognizes two tabby patterns: classical and mackerel. In England, they are treated as one class.

Classic Tabby Pattern
The classic tabby pattern is composed of the following elements in a dense, clearly defined color on a contrasting ground.

The legs must be ringed with 'bracelets' coming up to the body and the tail must have even rings on it as well. Several unbroken 'necklaces' must be visible on the neck and chest (the more the better). Frown marks form an intricate 'M' on the forehead. Swirls must be present on the cheeks and an unbroken line should run back from the outer corner of the eye. Vertical lines on the head should run back to the shoulder markings. Shoulder markings in the shape of a butterfly with both upper and lower wings outlined and with dots on the wings must be clearly visible. A vertical line should run down the spine from the butterfly to the tail with parallel vertical lines on either side (called 'spinals'). The three lines should be well-separated by strips of the ground color. A bulls-eye (a large blotch surrounded by two or more unbroken rings) should

appear on each side. The two bulls-eyes should be identical. A double, vertical line of spots, or 'buttons' should run along the chest and stomach.

Mackerel Tabby Pattern
In many respects the markings are similar to the classic tabby pattern. Although the lines are much narrower, they must still be dense and clearly defined. As in the classic pattern there are 'bracelets' on the legs, rings on the tail, 'necklaces' on the neck and chest and an 'M' on the forehead with unbroken lines running back from the eyes and from the head to the shoulders. However, in the mackerel tabby pattern, the spine lines run together, forming a narrow saddle while narrow pencilings run around the body. The pattern on the body should look like clouds in the sky.

All tabby colors outlined below appear in both classic and mackerel patterns.

Blue Tabby
The pale ivory ground color of the coat has deep blue markings with fawn overtones or 'patina' appearing over the entire coat. Nose leather is dusty rose and paw pads are rose-colored. Eyes are copper.

Brown Tabby
The copper-brown ground color has dense black markings and the lips and chin should be the same color as the rings around the eyes. The back of the leg is black from paw to heel. Nose leather is brick-red and paw pads should be black or brown. Eyes should be copper.

Cameo Tabby
The ground color should be off-white with red markings. Nose leather and paw pads should be rose-red and eyes, copper.

Cream Tabby
The ground color should be very pale cream with buff or cream markings that are dark enough for good contrast. Nose leather and paw pads should be pink and the eyes, copper.

Red Tabby
The ground color should be red with deep red markings. The cat should have brick-red nose leather, pink paw pads and copper eyes.

Silver Tabby
The ground color should be pale, clear silver with dense black markings. The cat should have brick-red nose leather, black paw pads and green or hazel eyes.

(e) Parti-colors

Bi-color
The coat of a Bi-colored cat should be black, blue, cream or red with white feet, legs, underparts, chest and muzzle. White under the tail and around the neck is acceptable and a blaze on the face in the form of an inverted 'V' is desirable. Eyes should be copper.

Blue-Cream
In this case the coat should be blue with clearly defined, well-broken patches of cream on the body, legs, tail and head. Paler shades are preferred. Eyes should be copper. (Note: In Britain and on the Continent, the colors should be softly intermingled with no distinct patches for a shot-silk effect that is especially effective on long-haired cats. This standard is very difficult to attain.)

Calico
Here the coat should be white with well-defined, unbrindled patches of red and black. White predominates on the underparts. Eyes should be copper. (Small red and black spots on white are characteristics of the unrecognized Harlequin.)

Dilute Calico
The coat should be white with well-defined, unbrindled patches of blue and cream; white predominates on the underparts. Eyes should be copper.

Tortoiseshell (Tortie)
The coat must be black with well-defined, unbroken, distinct patches of red and cream on body, head, legs and tail. A red or cream blaze from forehead to nose is desirable. Eyes are copper.

Calico Short-hair (inset) and Persian.

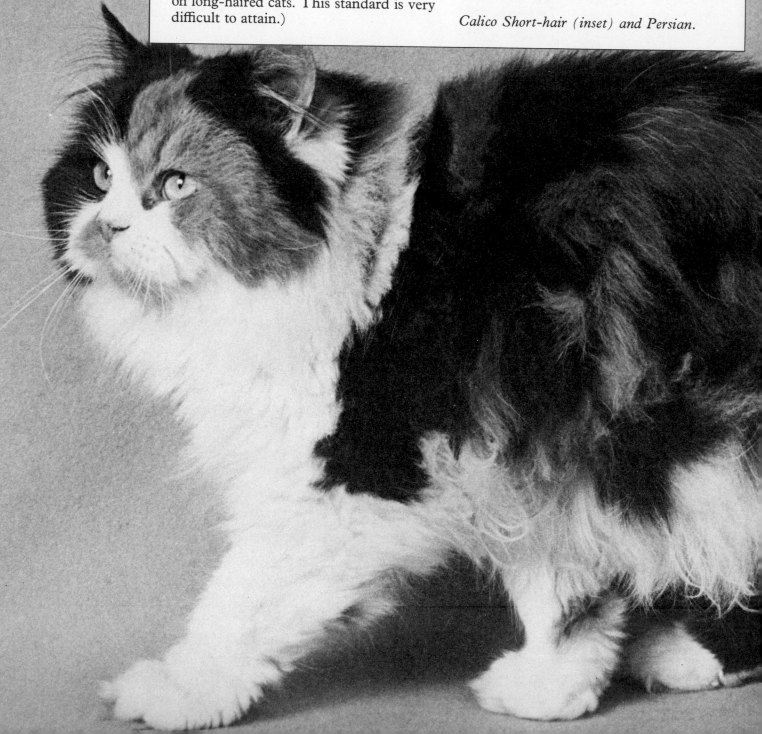

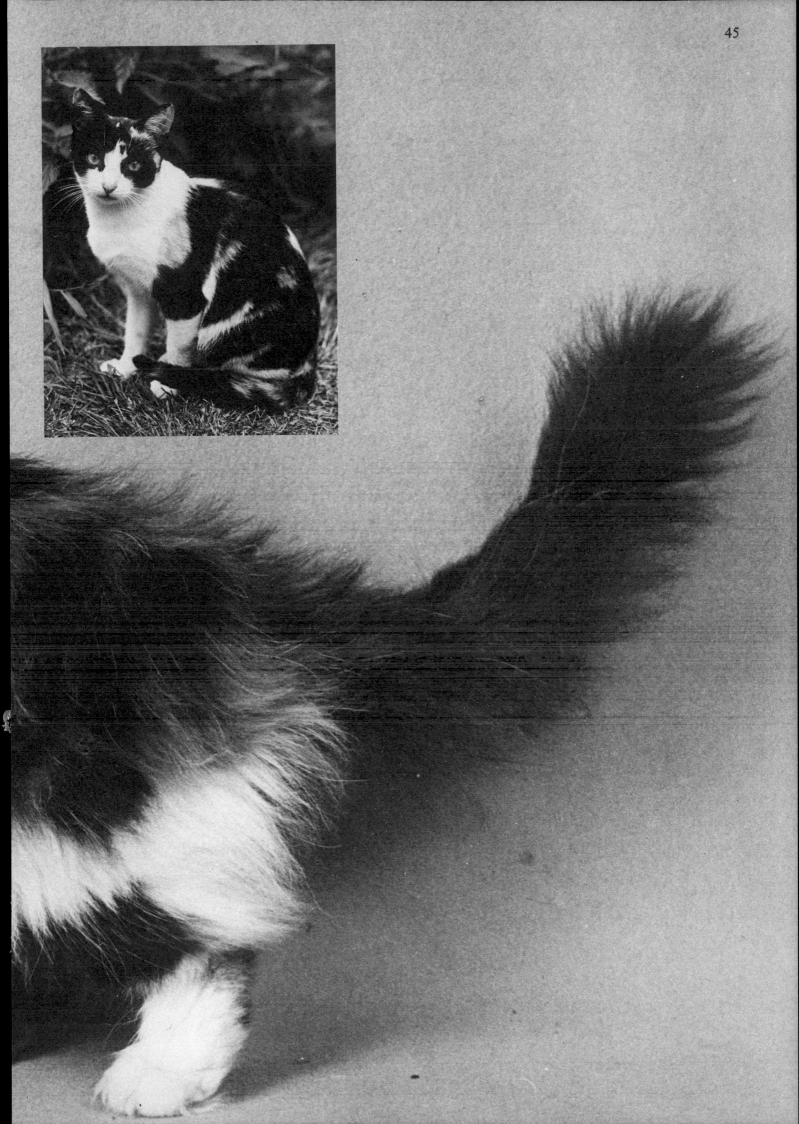

Spectrum B

Spectrum B describes the colorpoint pattern and the four classic point colors. For other colors, see Colorpoint Shorthair.

The colorpoint pattern consists of a basic body color and a contrasting point color. The points appear on the cooler extremities of the cat, and have sometimes been called 'temperature points.'

The points, which must be well-defined, of a contrasting color, and of the same color density, are the mask, ears, feet, tail, and sex organs. There should not be any ticking or white hairs in the points.

The mask should cover the entire face, including the whisker pads, and be connected to the ears by 'tracings'; it should not, however, extend over the top of the head. Eyes are vivid blue for all colors.

Blue Point
Body is a glacial, bluish white, shading to white on the underparts. Points are blue; nose leather and paw pads are slate-blue.

Chocolate Point
Body is ivory, with no shading. Points are warm, even milk-chocolate; nose leather and paw pads are cinnamon.

Lilac Point (Frost Point)
Body is glacial white with no shading. Points are frosty gray with a pink tinge; nose leather is pale lilac and paw pads are cold pink. [Note: In Britain the standard calls for an off-white body with shading to the back that is the color of the points. Points are pinkish gray. Nose leather and paw pads must be faded lilac.]

Seal Point
Body is cream with warm, pale fawn shading to the back. Points are dense, dark, seal-brown; nose leather and paw pads are the same color as the points. Faults include grayness in the coat, a dark smudge on the belly or throat, white toes, or brindling in the points.

Top left, inset : The ever popular Siamese Seal Point.
Bottom left, inset : Tabby Point or Lynx Point Siamese.
Top right, inset : Seal Point Himalayan or Colorpoint.
Left : The Balinese is Foreign or Oriental in type but has long hair. It should not be mistaken for the Himalayan which is Persian in type.

Encyclopedia of Cats

Below : Siamese kitten.
Far right : Portrait of a Cheetah.

Abyssinian

The Abyssinian (or 'Aby') is sometimes called the cat from the Blue Nile (Abyssinia is present-day Ethiopia) and has long been thought to resemble the sacred cats of ancient Egypt. It is believed to have arrived in England in 1868; in 1909 it was brought to America, where it quickly became very popular.

Abyssinians – affectionate, highly intelligent cats with small, melodious voices – make delightful pets. They are happy, busy animals that dislike close confinement and always take a keen interest in their surroundings.

With its medium-sized, well-muscled, short-haired body, the Abyssinian is perhaps the most feral-looking of all the domestic breeds. The shape of its body is Oriental, like that of the Siamese, but not as long. It is slender, lithe, and graceful, with a fairly long tapering tail, slender legs and neat oval feet.

The head is a rounded, medium, well-proportioned wedge with longish ears that are broad at the base and sharp at the tip. Eyes are large, almond-shaped, and very expressive.

Abyssinians have very soft, dense, resiliant coats. Two colors – Ruddy (the most common) and Red – are recognized by cat fanciers; a Cream Abyssinian has been bred but has not yet achieved recognition.

A long-haired Abyssinian, the *Somali*, has been recognized as a breed, but is not accepted for show competition.

Ruddy Abyssinian
The coat of the Ruddy Abyssinian is reddish brown with each hair ticked with two or three shades of black or dark brown. The undercoat next to the skin is ruddy, with the outer tips of the hairs being the darkest shade. Fur on the stomach and the inside of the forelegs is a lighter shade that harmonizes with the overall body color; the back of the hind legs is black and the chin is often white. Eyes are gold or green (sometimes hazel), the nose is red, and paw pads are black or brown.

Red Abyssinian
This breed's coat is a rich, warm, coppery-red, ticked with chocolate brown. Deeper shades of red are preferable.

Acinonyx
See Cheetah

African Lion
See Lion

African Wild Cat
Felis libyca

The African Wild Cat, also known as the Bush Cat, ranges throughout Africa, in the Middle East as far north as Syria, and as far east as India. The species has also been found on Crete, Sardinia, Corsica, and Majorca. It prefers lightly forested terrain, avoiding deserts and jungle.

Usually a nocturnal hunter, it will often venture out on cool, cloudy days in search of birds or small mammals.

There are differing reports about the appearance of the African Wild Cat, which is not surprising when one considers its wide distribution. In general, it is slightly larger than the domestic cat, with mackerel tabby (see Colors and Patterns) markings. These markings are lighter than those of the domestic cat. Ears are reddish at the back and underparts of the body are yellowish. The tail is longer and more tapering than that of the European Wild Cat, but has the same distinctive rings.

American Blue
See American Short-hair; Russian Blue

American Short-hair

Once called simply the domestic short-hair, this all-American cat traveled to the New World on the *Mayflower*, and has been an integral part of American life ever since. It is a working cat – a solid citizen, a good companion, and infinitely adaptable – that now has a full pedigree from the Cat Fanciers' Association (CFA).

Although the American Short-hair developed from the same stock as the British Short-hair and is still very similar, several differences have emerged. The American Short-hair is a well-built cat with the well-developed, rippling muscles and latent power of the trained athlete. It has a powerful medium-to-large body with heavy shoulders and a well-developed chest, firm strong legs of medium length, and a medium-length tail that tapers from a thick base and ends bluntly.

The head is large and well-proportioned, slightly longer than it is wide. The muzzle is square, the chin firm, the cheeks full and the nose medium (snub noses are considered faults). The medium size, wide-set ears are slightly rounded. Eyes are large and round, set well apart, and slant slightly at the outer edge. They should be bright, clear, and alert.

The American Short-hair conformation covers a wide range of breeds, including the Chinchilla and Shaded Silver. It is recognized in all colors and patterns of Spectrum A (see Colors and Patterns).

Andean Cat
See Mountain Cat

Angora

Angora (now called Ankara, the capital of Turkey) is thought to have been the home of the first long-haired cats seen in Europe. Cross-breeding and a preference for the Persian type virtually eliminated the breed in Europe, and only a few Angoras remained in Turkey. There they were deeply appreciated but they were not known elsewhere.

Turkish authorities eventually realized that the breed was in danger of total extinction and began a small breeding program. In 1962 and again in 1966, Colonel Walter Grant of the US Army was able, through his friendship with zoo officials, to bring two unrelated pairs of Angoras to the United States. The imports aroused a new interest among breeders and in 1970 the Cat Fanciers' Association recognized the Turkish Angora as a separate breed, establishing a provisional standard. They have still not been recognized in Britain.

Right : American Short-hair.
Below : Abyssinian kitten. In the past these cats were known as 'Bunny' or 'Rabbit' cats because of their ticked fur.

The Angora is slightly smaller than medium in size with a small head and tapering, upright ears. The eyes are large, almond-shaped, slightly slanted, and wide-set; they can be either blue, amber, or one of each color (some blue-eyed Angoras suffer from deafness). The tail is long, full, and tapering, and should not be kinked. When the cat is relaxed and moving it carries its tail horizontally over its body, almost touching the ears. Paw pads, nose leather, and lips are pink.

The coat should be fine, medium length, and soft with a silky finish. There are tufts of hair between the toes. Only white Angoras are presently eligible for the CFA Championship competition, though they have been bred in other colors from Spectrum A (see Colors and Patterns).

The Turkish Government and the Ankara Zoo deserve great credit for their work in saving this very special cat from extinction.

Archangel

See Maltese; Russian Blue

Balinese

The Balinese is basically a long-haired Siamese. The mutation appeared in America in litters of purebred Siamese and it was found that when the mutations were mated they bred true. In other words, a Balinese can only be produced now by mating one Balinese with another. They

Balinese cat and her kitten.

were recognized as a breed in the United States in 1963 and in the UK in 1974.

Balinese have voices and characters similar to Siamese cats, but are considered by some to be less demanding. Like the Siamese, too, they are highly intelligent and very affectionate animals.

Balinese cats should not be confused with Persians or Himalayans, which have much longer coats. The coat on a Balinese is soft, silky, and about two inches long, requiring much less attention than that of other long-haired cats.

The Balinese body is tight, slim, and elegant, with fine bones and firm muscles. Balinese cats should be medium in size and the same width at the shoulders and hips. Legs are long and slim, with the hind legs longer than the front. The tail is long, thin, and tapers to a point; the tail hair spreads out like a plume.

The head is a long, tapering wedge that starts from the nose and flares out to the ears in straight lines. In profile, the slope from the top of the head to the tip of the nose is a long, straight line. Ears are very large and pointed, and continue the lines of the wedge. Eyes are medium-sized and almond-shaped, of a deep, vivid blue. They should never be crossed. Balinese have fairly long necks.

The Balinese falls under Spectrum B (see Colors and Patterns). Points and mask should be clearly defined without brindling or white hairs. The whole face should be covered by the mask. The coat will probably darken as the cat gets older, but the shading should remain even.

Bay Lynx
See Bobcat

Bengal Tiger
See Tiger

Bi-colored Long-hair
See Bi-colored Persian; Colors and Patterns

Bi-colored Persian
The Bi-colored Persian (often called Particolored Persian) was originally shown only in black and white and entered under the name Magpie. Later it was entered under the 'Any Other Color' classification. It was recognized as a separate breed in the mid-1960s. Bi-colored Persians are important in breeding long-haired Calico Cats.

Conformation should be that of the Persian: big, cobby body with short thick legs, round broad head and short bushy tail (see also Persian).

The coat should be long, flowing, and silky. It must combine white with one other solid color; tabby markings are considered faults. (See also Colors and Patterns)

Bi-colored Persian.

Bi-colored Short-hair
See Colors and Patterns

Birman

According to legend the Birman, also known as the Sacred Cat of Burma, guarded the temples in that country in ancient times. Even today they are treated with reverence in Burma, since many people believe that they are reincarnations of Burmese priests who will, when they die, carry the priests' souls to paradise.

Birmans were introduced into France in 1919, but nearly disappeared during the Second World War. Enough were saved, however, to ensure the preservation of the breed after the war. They were recognized as a separate breed in 1966 in Britain and in 1967 in the United States. They are gaining rapidly in popularity, partly because of their beauty and partly because of their intelligence and affectionate nature.

The Birman has a long body with medium-length, heavy legs; large, round, firm paws; and a medium-length, bushy tail. The head is wide and rounded with full cheeks, and is slightly flat above the eyes. Ears and nose are medium in length. Eyes are almost round, and of a bright china blue.

The golden beige coat is long and silky, with a heavy ruff around the neck, and slightly curly hair on the belly. The coat does not mat, making Birmans extremely easy to care for.

Birman coloring falls under Spectrum B (see Colors and Patterns) except for the feet, which are tipped with white like a glove. On the front paws these gloves should end in an even line at the third joint; on the back they cover the entire paw, ending in a point that goes up the back of the hock like a gauntlet. These points are often called 'the laces.'

Birman adult and kitten (inset).

Black Long-hair

See Black Persian

Black-footed Cat

Felis nigripes

The Black-footed Cat is now very rare even in its habitat in Africa which includes the Kalahari Desert, Botswana, and parts of the Orange Free State and the Transvaal.

It is a nocturnal hunter, preying on birds, lizards, and the like.

Slightly smaller than the domestic cat, it has a pale brown coat with a white underbody and indistinct spots which darken and merge together toward the legs to form three rings. The soles of its feet are black (a characteristic also of domestic tabbies).

The Black-footed Cat has successfully crossbred with domestic cats, but such breeding is not a common occurrence.

Black Panther

See Leopard

Black Persian

Although the Black Persian (or Black Long-hair, as it is known in Britain) is one of the oldest pedigree colors known, the numbers being shown are not increasing because it is so difficult to obtain a perfect, jet-black coat.

Not only are coats often marked by occasional white hairs and bands which show up under lights, but the coats require constant attention and grooming to prevent their being marked by sunshine or rain. The coats do not become dense and shiny until the cat is a year to a year and a half old, and the rusty or gray appearance of the kittens often discourages would-be breeders.

Black Persians are useful for breeding Tortoiseshells, Whites, and Bi-colors. (See also Colors and Patterns; Persian)

Black Short-hair

This is the cat associated with the devil and witchcraft in more superstitious times. Today black cats are still regarded with lingering misgivings in America and Ireland, but in Britain they have come to be thought of as lucky cats.

A pedigree Black conforms to the standards for its body type (see American Short-hair and British Short-hair), with orange or deep copper-colored eyes and shiny, glossy, jet-black fur. As with black long-haired cats, short coats suffer from excessive sun or damp, and constant grooming is necessary to avoid rusty patches. Hand grooming with a chamois leather is an excellent way to remove grease and leaves a beautiful sheen.

A close-up and a full portrait of the Black Short-hair.

Black Smoke Short-hair
See Smoke Short-hair

Blue American Short-hair
See American Short-hair; Russian Blue

Blue Burmese
See Burmese

Blue Chinchilla
See Chinchilla

Blue Cream Burmese
See Burmese

Blue Cream Long-hair
See Blue Cream Persian

Blue Cream Persian

Blue Cream Persians are very attractive cats, produced by mating Blues and Creams. Males are rare and are always sterile. Body should conform to that of the Persian (see Persian); eyes should be large, round, and of a copper or dark orange color. (See also Colors and Patterns)

Blue Cream Point
See Colorpoint Short-hair; Himalayan

Blue Cream Persian.

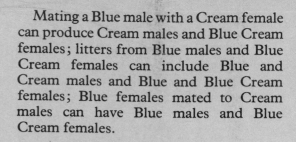

Blue Cream Short-hair

As with the Blue Cream Persian, this variety is almost entirely female; males are always sterile. Again the type is the result of Blue and Cream matings, though it sometimes appears in Tortoiseshell litters if both parents carry blue genes.

Blue Cream Short-hairs should conform to the standards for their body type (see American Short-hair; British Short-hair; Colors and Patterns), except that eyes may only be copper, orange, or yellow.

They are very popular cats, both for their pleasant personalities and the large variety of kittens they can produce.

Blue Long-hair
See Blue Persian

Blue Lynx Point
See Colorpoint Short-hair

Far right : Blue Persian (or Blue Long-hair as it is called in Great Britain).
Below : This Blue Colorpoint kitten is usually called a Blue Point Himalayan although both names are acceptable. (See page 126.)
Overleaf : A hungry Bobcat takes its kill to its lair deep in the forest.

Blue Persian

The Blue Persian has been very important in the improved breeding of nearly all solid-color Persians and in the development of new colors such as Colorpoints. It is one of the most attractive and photogenic breeds.

Lighter shades are preferred, but evenness of color is more important than tone. White hairs in the coat, green eye rims, and kinked tails are considered faults. Kittens are often born with tabby markings, but lose these quickly as they grow up. Although this cat should have a snub nose, one that is too short indicates overbreeding. The head should be broad, the ears small, the eyes round and copper-colored, and the ruff large and well-developed.

Mating a Blue male with a Cream female can produce Cream males and Blue Cream females; litters from Blue males and Blue Cream females can include Blue and Cream males and Blue and Blue Cream females; Blue females mated to Cream males can have Blue males and Blue Cream females.

Blue Point
See Colors and Patterns; Himalayan; Siamese

Blue Russian
See Maltese; Russian Blue

Blue Short-hair

There are several recognized breeds of Blue Short-hairs. Each breed has certain characteristics which set it apart from the others (for example, each has differently colored eyes). If a cat is of poor quality, however, these distinctions become blurred and even experts cannot always be sure of the actual breed.

Recognized breeds of Blue Short-hairs are:

Blue American Short-hair
Blue Burmese
Blue Exotic Short-hair
Blue Japanese Bobtail
Blue Manx 'Longie'
Blue Oriental Short-hair
British Blue
Chartreux
Korat
Maltese
Russian Blue

Blue Smoke Persian
See Smoke Persian; Colors and Patterns

Blue Smoke Short-hair
See Smoke Short-hair

Blue Tabby
See Colors and Patterns; Tabby

Blue Tortie Point
See Colorpoint Short-hair

Blue Tortoiseshell and White
See Colors and Patterns (Dilute Calico); Calico (Dilute Calico).

Bobcat
felis rufa

The Bobcat is also known as the Bay Lynx and is closely related to, but smaller than, the Northern Lynx.

It ranges over a large area in North America from southern Canada to south Mexico, preferring open ground, but is able to adapt to many other habitats. Its diet consists mainly of birds and small mammals but it has been known to kill poultry, sheep, calves, and even deer. Its pelt is of little value, but it is often hunted for sport.

The Bobcat's coat is spotted and colored a rusty brown on the back, graduating to creamy white underneath. This coloring applies to the tail also – an important way to differentiate the Bobcat from the Lynx is by the size of its tail. Bobcats with pale brown fur have also been sighted, and the size and pattern of the spots can vary a great deal.

Size of the animal varies from 32 to 50 inches for males and from 28 to 48 inches for females. Litters contain up to four kittens.

Bobtail
See Japanese Bobtail

Bombay

This shiny black hybrid is a recent addition to the show scene. It was originally produced by mating American Short-

A Bobcat (or Bay Lynx) chases a deermouse in the snow in the mountains of Colorado.
Inset, far right: The Bobcat's coloring allows it to blend into its environment with ease.

hairs and Burmese, and has been called 'the cat with the patent leather coat and copper penny eyes.'

The standards for body type are almost exactly the same as those for the Burmese: a medium-size, muscular body with legs in proportion and a straight, medium-length tail; a round head with a full face and short, well-developed muzzle; alert, wide-set ears that are medium in size, broad at the base, and slightly rounded at the tips; and round, wide-set eyes.

In judging, 55 percent of the Bombay Standard is concerned with coat and color – more than any other breed. The coat must be fine, short, and satiny, and lie very close to produce that 'patent leather' sheen. Fur must be black to the roots. Nose leather and paw pads are black. Eye color ranges from yellow to deep copper (never green).

British Blue

The British Blue is probably one of the most popular short-hairs in the United Kingdom, largely because of its gentle, placid disposition, affectionate nature and high intelligence. The females make excellent mothers.

Blues conform very closely to British Short-hair standards, but their coats are more plush. The color of the coat can vary from light to medium blue, but it must be even, with no white hairs.

The British Blue is essentially the same as the Exotic Short-hair (blue) in America and the Chartreux in Europe. It is recognized as a separate breed in the United States, but is not accepted for CFA show competition.

British Cream
See Cream Short-hair

British Short-hair

The British Short-hair is similar to its American cousin, but has slightly different standards: shorter legs and tail, smaller ears, and rounder head and eyes. The coat should be fine and soft, but not wooly.

British Short-hairs are not currently accepted for show competition by the American CFA.

Right: The white British Short-hair is similar in most respects to the American Short-hair: the British nose is slightly smaller and the coat more plush.

Bronze Mau
See Egyptian Mau

Brown Burmese
See Burmese (Sable)

Brown Tabby
See Colors and Patterns; Tabby

Sable or Brown Burmese.

Burmese

Burmese (called Zibelines in France) were developed in the United States and can be traced back to a single female (probably a Siamese hybrid) named Wong Mau. Wong Mau arrived in New Orleans in 1930 in the company of a sailor. She was eventually given to Dr Joseph C Thompson of San Francisco who decided to try to continue this sable brown breed.

An experimental breeding program was established with the help of cat geneticists and breeders, and despite many problems – lack of a brown male and Wong Mau's own mixed ancestry – the breed we know today was evolved.

Burmese are hardy, sociable cats that make excellent companions and tend to be very possessive about 'their' families.

The Burmese is a medium-size cat with heavier bones and more muscle than its size would indicate; a round, strong chest; and a straight back. Legs are slender and in good proportion to the body; hind legs are longer than front legs. Paws are round. The tail is medium, slender, and straight.

The head is round, with a blunt wedge-shaped muzzle and a full face. There is a strong lower jaw and a distinct nose break. Ears are medium in size, broad at the base and slightly rounded at the tip; they are wide-set and tip slightly forward. The wide-set eyes are a rounded almond shape.

Sable (or 'Brown') Burmese is the only color recognized by the CFA in America, and to the purist a solid-color, satin-sheen, sable brown will probably always be the only proper color for the breed. Because of its hybrid ancestry, however, other colors have emerged; blue, champagne, and platinum are the most common, and have been recognized by other organizations. In England, especially, other colors are very popular and are encouraged.

Right: The ever-popular Blue Burmese.
Below: This Siamese kitten is similar in type to the Burmese but with a less solid body and more pointed face.

The two most popular types of Burmese cats: on the left is a Sable or Brown Burmese and on the right is a Blue Burmese. Depending on the genealogy of the cats involved both colors can occur in the same litter as can any of the other varieties of Burmese cats.

Blue Burmese
This color was achieved by mating the lighter-colored kittens from a Sable Burmese litter, and the required conformation is the same as for the Sable Burmese. The coat should be a bluish-gray with a silvery tinge on face, ears, and feet; the back and tail are slightly darker. Eyes are yellow; they can have a slight greenish tinge, but should never be a distinct green. Paw pads are gray and nose leather is dark gray. Kittens have tabby markings which fade.

Blue Cream Burmese
This is a female-only type, with the standard Burmese conformation. This color is popular in Britain, where the standard for Blue Creams calls for a smooth mixture of the two colors. (See Colors and Patterns.) Nose leather and paw pads are blotched blue and pink.

Brown Burmese
See Sable Burmese

Champagne Burmese
This is a very popular color, called Chocolate in the United Kingdom. The coat should be a warm, even, milk-chocolate color; ears and mask can be slightly darker. Paw pads are slightly redder and nose leather slightly browner than the coat.

Champagne Tortie Burmese
Recognized only in Britain, this variety should be a mixture of chocolate and

Above : Blue Burmese.

cream, without barring. Colors may be mingled or blotched, and solid color feet, legs, and tails are acceptable. Nose leather and paw pads are chocolate and pink, and can also be plain or blotched. Adherence to Burmese conformation is important.

Chocolate Burmese
See Champagne Burmese

Cream Burmese
The Cream Burmese is a rich cream color, paler on the underparts, darker on back and tail, and darker still on the ears. Slight tabby markings on the face are accepted. Nose leather and paw pads are pink.

Lavender Burmese
See Platinum Burmese

Lilac Burmese
See Platinum Burmese

Platinum Burmese
The Platinum (or Lilac) Burmese was only recently recognized in Britain. The coat should be dove gray with a frosted, pinkish sheen, slightly darker on ears and mask. Nose leather and paw pads are a lavender pink. This variety results from mating two Champagne Burmese that carry a blue gene, or a Champagne and a Blue.

Platinum Tortie Burmese
The colors, platinum and cream, should be distributed without barring. Conformation is more important than coloration or markings.

Red Burmese
The coat color should be a golden red, fading to tangerine on the underparts. Eyes are darker and slight tabby markings are acceptable. Nose leather and paw pads are chocolate but pink is acceptable.

Sable Burmese
The Sable Burmese has a close-lying, satin-textured coat of a deep, rich, warm sable brown that gradually becomes slightly lighter on the underparts. Otherwise the color is absolutely even, with no shadings or markings. Kittens are sometimes coffee-colored, with shadow markings and a few white hairs. Nose leather and paw pads are brown. Eyes should range from yellow to gold; green eyes are considered faults and blue eyes disqualify the cat on the show bench – as do kinked tails or white spots in the coat.

Tortoiseshell Burmese
This is a female-only type. Burmese conformation is more important than coat color, which is a mingled or blotched mixture of brown, cream, and red. Legs and tail are often a solid color. Nose leather and paw pads are plain or blotched, chocolate or pink.

Right : The Oriental or Foreign Short-hair is similar in configuration to the Siamese but has the colorpoints eliminated. The cat here is an Oriental or Foreign Smoke, a breed not yet recognized. (See page 158 for further information.)
Below : Oriental Lavender Queen and kittens.

Bush Cat
See African Wild Cat

Caffre Cat
See African Wild Cat

Calico Cat

Calico cats come in both long- and short-haired varieties (called Tortoiseshell and White Long-hair and Short-hair in the United Kingdom). The Calico Short-hair is believed to have originated in Spain, and is one of the earliest known varieties.

The Calico is a difficult cat to reproduce since it is an almost all-female type. A Black or White male makes the best stud, but breeding is a chancy matter at best. Care should be taken to avoid mating cats with white hairs or tabby markings, since these traits will often be reproduced in the kittens.

Conformation and coat quality should be that of the appropriate Persian or Short-hair standard.

Coloration requirements vary from association to association on both sides of the Atlantic. In America the CFA and most other associations call for predominantly white underparts and black and red patches (see Colours and Patterns), but some others ask for black, red, and cream patches. The patches must always be clearly defined and free from brindling. Feet and legs, the whole underside of the body, tail, chest, and most of the neck should be white with splashes on the nose. The white should also come up to cover the lower parts of the sides. Eyes are orange- or copper-colored; hazel eyes are sometimes permitted in short-hairs.

In England the standard calls for well-distributed black, red, and cream patches interspersed with white.

Dilute Calico
Dilute Calicos were the result of mating Calicos and Blue and White Bi-coloreds. They are called Blue Tortoiseshell and White Long-hairs and Short-hairs in the United Kingdom. (See Colors and Patterns)

Right : Calico Cat.

Cameo

Cameos are attractive long-haired cats developed in America during the 1950s and recognized in 1960. They still have not gained recognition in England.

Coloration is more important than conformation which should be the same as for other Persians.

Cameos are found with shaded colors – Shell Cameo and Shaded Cameo – in Smokes, and with tabby markings (see Colors and Patterns). There is also a Tortoiseshell Cameo that is slowly gaining recognition; it has a silvery white undercoat and standard tortoiseshell markings, with ticking of red and cream or black and blue.

Tabby Cameo coats are also recognized in Exotic Short-hairs by some governing bodies.

Left : Smoke Cameo.
Below : Shaded Cameo.

Canadian Hairless
See Sphynx

Caracal Lynx
Felis caracal

This distinctive wild cat once ranged over an enormous area from south Russia and the Ukraine, through the Middle East, to north and central India and much of Africa. Now, however, it is rapidly disappearing. The Caracal likes wide-open country, usually thinly bushed or mountainous. It avoids forested regions, and is quite able to survive in semi-desert country. It hunts by bursting from cover and hurling itself upon its prey which can be as small as a hare or as large as an impala. It can also leap into the air and snatch birds as they take flight; Caracals have even been known to kill eagles. They can be trained to hunt, and have on occasion been used in packs by sportsmen in Asia.

A small (35–40 inches total length), elegant cat, the Caracal gives an impression of great strength. The coat is an even reddish-yellow on an adult; many Caracals have silver hairs, giving them a yellowish-gray appearance. The chin and underparts are white, and there are dark patches above the eyes which look almost oriental, and at the base of the whiskers. Kittens are reddish brown.

The Caracal's ears are its most distinctive feature; they are large, long, and pointed, with long black tufts. The tail is short, like that of the lynx.

Caspian Tiger
See Tiger

Central American Jaguar
See Jaguar

Champagne Burmese
See Burmese

Champagne Tortie Burmese
See Burmese

A Caracal Lynx.

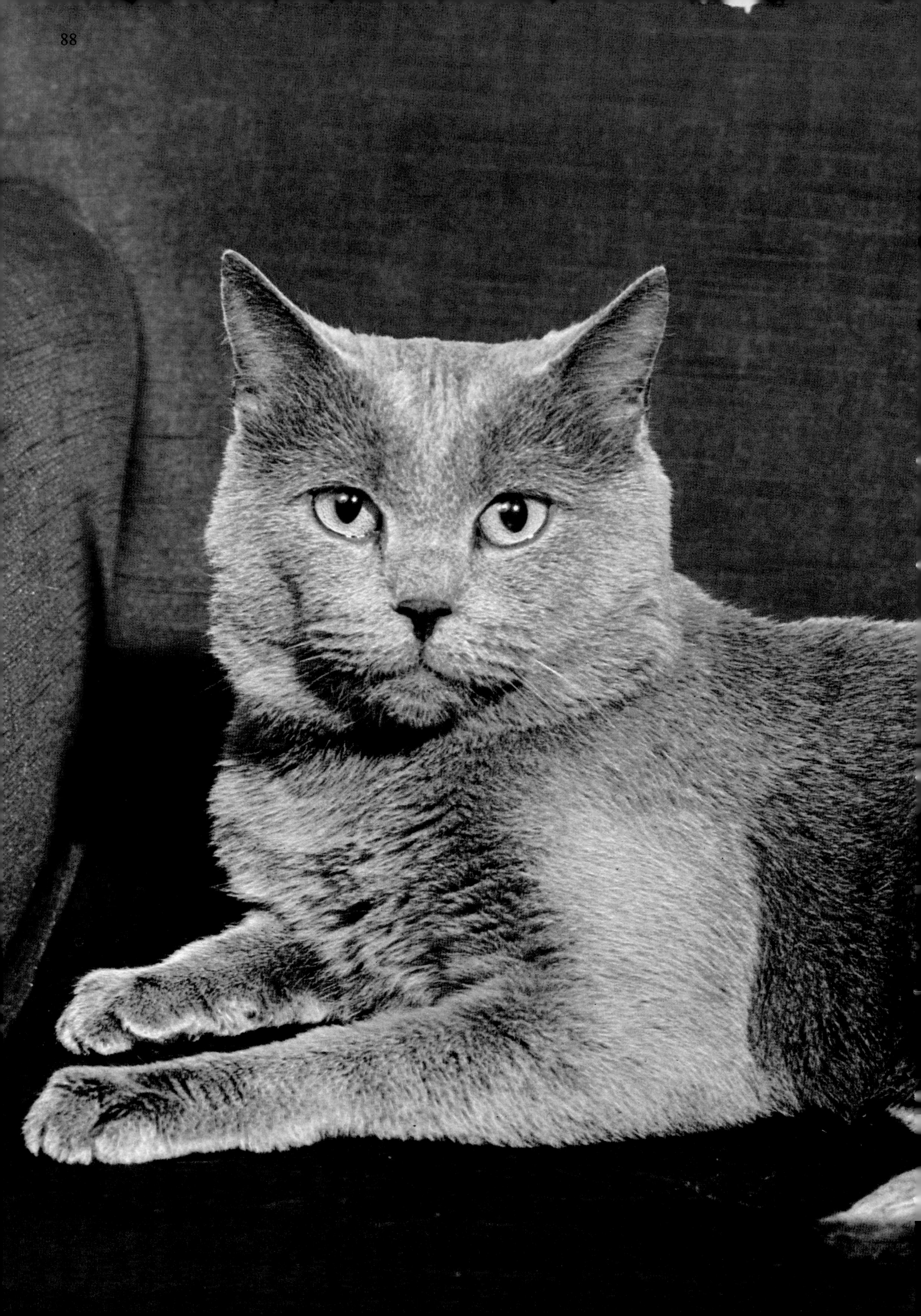

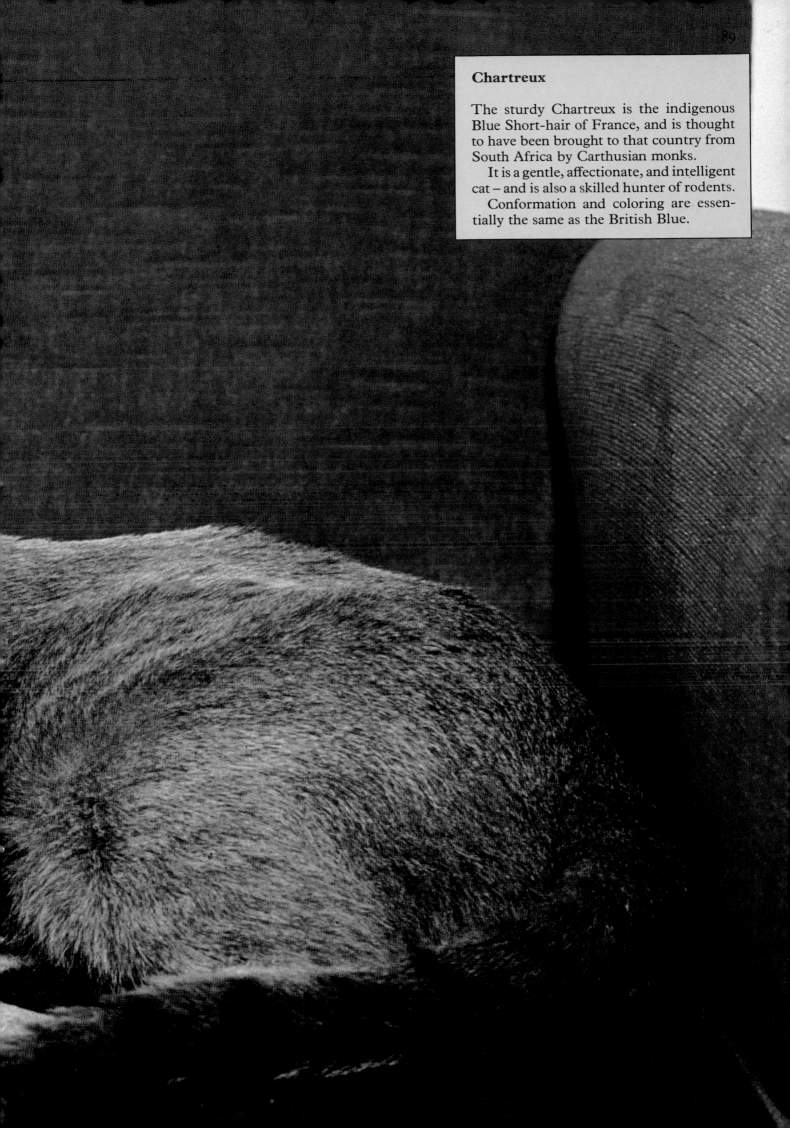

Chartreux

The sturdy Chartreux is the indigenous Blue Short-hair of France, and is thought to have been brought to that country from South Africa by Carthusian monks.

It is a gentle, affectionate, and intelligent cat – and is also a skilled hunter of rodents.

Conformation and coloring are essentially the same as the British Blue.

Chat Sans Poils
See Sphynx

Cheetah

There are still two types of Cheetah: the African (*Acinonyx jubatus jubatus*) and the Asian (*A jubatus venaticus*).

At one time they were found throughout Africa and the Middle East and in large areas of Asia as far east as India. Today, however, they are rarely seen outside South Africa and a very few places in Asia. Protective legislation has been passed in North Africa, but the species is in danger of extinction there unless the laws take effect immediately. Cheetahs have not been seen on the eastern Mediterranean coast for over 100 years, and none have been reported in India for more than 20 years.

Cheetahs are the fastest animals on earth; their maximum speed (which they can only maintain for a very short time) is over 60 mph; in a sudden burst from cover they can attain 45 mph in as little as two seconds.

They inhabit open country with just enough cover to assist their hunting and enough grass to feed their prey (gazelles, other deer, hares, etc.), tending to avoid heavily forested and mountainous regions. Cheetahs hunt by both day and night. Although they are not easily trained, they adapt very well to domestication and can be used as hunting animals, often becoming very attached to their owners.

Cheetahs are long, slim, elegant animals, with bodies about 4.5 feet long and tails of

about 2.5 feet. They stand about three feet high. The head is small in relation to the body, with jaws that lack the strength of other big cats. The claws are permanently extended from the age of about ten weeks, and the paws are ridged for better traction. This, along with extraordinarily powerful hind legs and a supple back accounts for the very high speeds.

Kittens are born with smoky gray fur and a silver mane. When they are about ten weeks old the coat turns tawny; the coloring is completed with the addition of small black spots. Two heavy black stripes run from the corner of the eyes to the edge of the mouth, outlining the face and giving the animal a sad but noble expression.

The long-legged and graceful Cheetah.

Chestnut Brown Foreign
See Havana Brown

Chinchilla

This small, long-haired cat was created almost a century ago in Britain from a cross between a Silver Tabby and a Smoke; in America it is often called Silver Persian. Many consider it to be the most beautiful of the long-haired cats.

Conformation should basically be that of other long-haired varieties, except for its lighter bone structure which gives it a dainty appearance. Unfortunately this often counts against it in America, where it is expected to meet the same standard as the heavier breeds.

The head is round and broad; the snub nose has a brick-red tip; and the ears are wide-set and well-tufted. The eyes should be large, emerald or blue-green in color. The tail should be short and bushy.

The coat should be thick, long, and silky, pure white on the underparts, chin and ear tufts. All the other hairs are delicately tipped with black, giving the animal a shimmering, silvery appearance. Heavy tipping, yellow patches, or brown, cream, or tabby markings are considered faults. Kittens are born with darker fur and tabby markings which eventually disappear. (See also Colors and Patterns.)

Blue Chinchilla
This cat, the result of mating a Chinchilla with a Blue Persian, is being developed in England, but has not yet been recognized as a separate variety. The adult cat has a pure white undercoat, tipped on the back, tail, flanks, head, and ears with blue-gray. Legs may have ticking. Eyes can be orange or amber. In the UK this variety can be entered in the 'Any Other Color' class.

Chinchillas – right, below and overleaf!

Chinese Desert Cat
Felis bieti

The Chinese Desert Cat was only discovered during the 1880s, and even today very little is known about its habits.

It inhabits Mongolia, the outer provinces of China, and the Tibetan Steppes, in areas that are generally either dry grassland or semi-desert. Its diet probably consists of small mammals, reptiles, and birds.

In size it is only slightly larger than the domestic cat. Its color is grayish yellow, with white underparts and a dark-ringed tail.

Chinese Tiger
See Tiger

Chocolate Burmese
See Burmese

Chocolate Cream Point
See Colorpoint Short-hair

Chocolate Lynx Point
See Colorpoint Short-hair

Left and below : Chinchilla kittens.

Chocolate Point
See Colors and Patterns; Siamese

Chocolate Self Long-hair
See Himalayan

Chocolate Tortie Point Burmese
See Burmese

Clouded Leopard

This expert tree-climber can be found in the forests of Java, Taiwan, the Malay Peninsula, and parts of mainland China. Not much is known about its habits; it is

Above : Clouded Leopard.

said to hunt at night and its diet is assumed to include small mammals but not birds.

Males can be as large as 3.5 feet plus a one-foot tail, and weigh up to 50 pounds. Females are a foot shorter and weigh about 35 pounds. They are slender cats, with coats that vary from grayish yellow to brown. Brown blotches with clouded centers run vertically, covering the body, tail, flanks, and legs (where they give way to spots). The head and face are also spotted, and the underparts are white.

Colorpoint Long-hair
See Himalayan

Colorpoint Short-hair

The Colorpoint Short-hair is the result of the desire of breeders in America to extend the basic colorpoint pattern (see Colors and Patterns) beyond the four classic colors (Seal Point, Chocolate Point, Blue Point, and Lilac Point) to include other colors and patterns.

This was accomplished by mating Siamese and American Short-hairs, to produce a cat that retained the Siamese conformation and colorpoint factor, but acquired additional colors and patterns from the American Short-hair.

Their success is an outstanding example of the art of breeding. In addition, the Colorpoint Short-hair is a warm, friendly cat that makes an excellent pet.

The Colorpoint Short-hair should be identical to the Siamese in every respect save color (see Siamese). The cats are divided into three categories: Solid Color Point, Lynx (or Tabby) Point, and Parti-Color Point. Eyes in all cases should be deep blue.

Solid Color Point

(a) *Red Point :* Experimental breeding between Seal Point Siamese females and Red Tabby Short-hair males began during the Second World War; Red Points were recognized in America in 1956 and in England in 1966. The body should be clear white with any shading the same color as the points which are deep reddish brown. Nose leather and paw pads are flesh or coral.

(b) *Cream Point :* As above, except that the points are apricot.

Lynx Point

Also known as Silver Point Siamese, Shadow Point, and Tabby Colorpoint Short-hair. Lynx Points tend to have gentler natures than other Siamese.

In all of the colors described below, the body color may be lightly shaded. The points contain distinct, darker shaded bars separated by a lighter background color. The ears are the basic point color with a paler, thumbprint-shaped mark in the center.

(a) *Blue Lynx Point :* Cold, bluish white to platinum-gray body, shading to a lighter color on stomach and chest, with deep blue-gray points on the lighter ground. Nose leather is slate or pink, edged in slate; paw pads are slate-colored.

(b) *Chocolate Lynx Point :* Ivory body with warm mild chocolate points on lighter ground. Nose leather is cinnamon or pink, edged in cinnamon; paw pads are cinnamon.

(c) *Lilac Lynx Point :* Glacial white body and frosty gray points with a pinkish tone on a lighter ground. Nose leather is lavender pink or pink, edged in lavender pink; paw pads are lavender pink.

(d) *Red Lynx Point :* White body with deep red points on a lighter ground. Nose leather and paw pads are flesh-color or coral.

(e) *Seal Lynx Point :* Cream or pale fawn body color, with seal brown points on a lighter ground. Nose leather is seal brown or pink, edged in seal brown; paw pads are seal brown.

Parti-color Point

In all colors the points are a basic solid color mottled with patches of one or more contrasting colors. A blaze on the mask is desirable; when such a blaze is present the nose leather may be mottled.

(a) *Blue Cream Point :* Cold bluish white to platinum-gray body, lighter on chest and stomach; deep blue-gray points uniformly mottled with cream. Nose is slate-colored although flesh or coral mottling is permitted with a blaze. Paw pads are slate but flesh or coral mottling is permitted where the point color extends into the pads.

Right : Lynx Point – an excellent example of one type of Colorpoint Short-hair.
Below : This picture of a Long-haired Colorpoint or Himalayan (page 126) shows the difference in the length of fur between the Long-hair and the Short-hair.

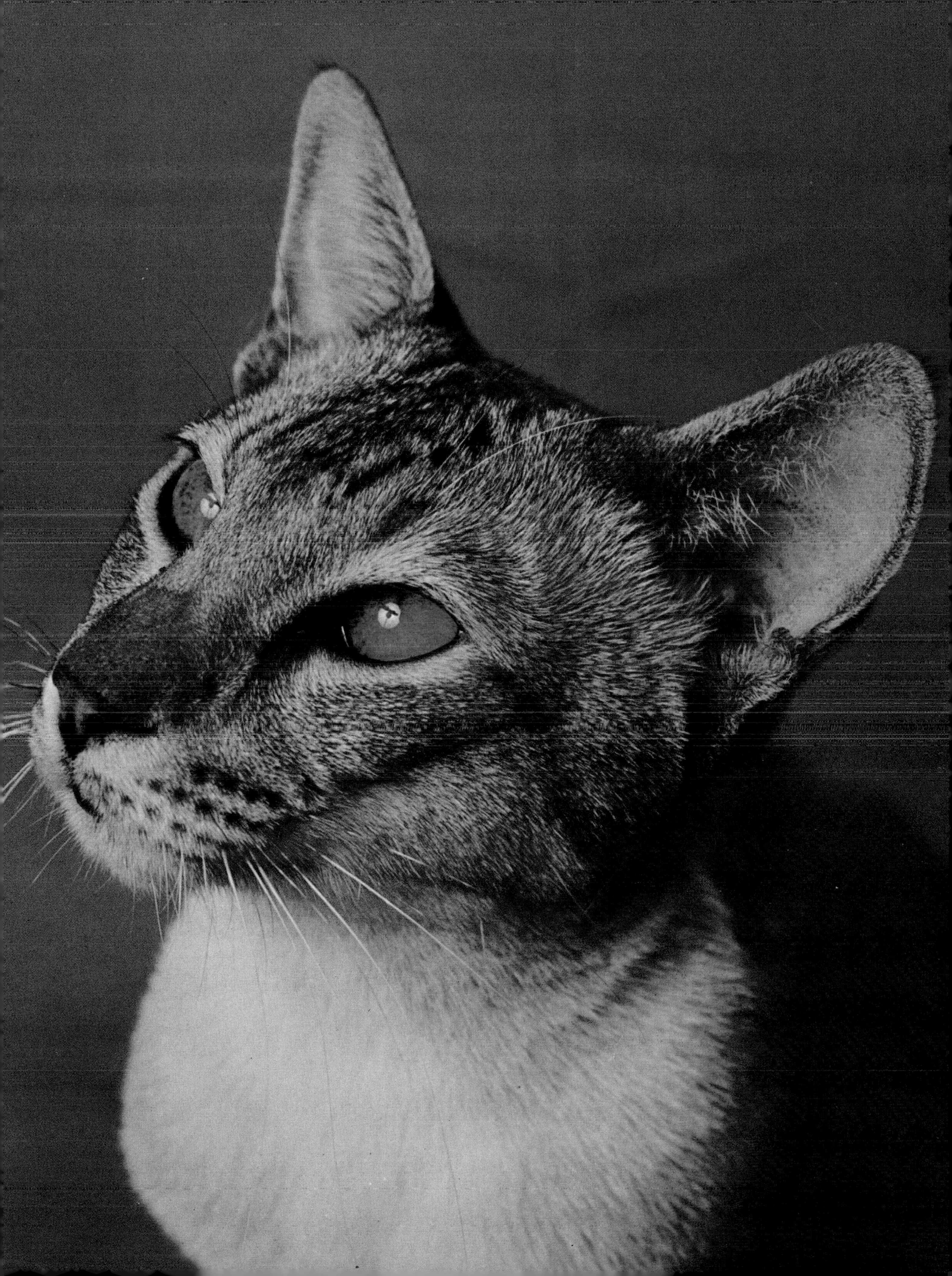

(b) *Chocolate Cream Point:* Ivory body; warm milk chocolate points uniformly mottled with cream. Nose leather is cinnamon but flesh or coral mottling is permitted with a blaze. Paw pads are cinnamon but flesh or coral mottling is permitted where the point color mottling extends into the pads.

(c) *Lilac Cream Point:* Glacial white body; frosty gray points with a pinkish tone uniformly mottled with pale cream. Nose leather is lavender pink although flesh or coral mottling is permitted with a blaze. Paw pads are lavender pink but flesh or coral mottling is permitted where the point color extends into the pads.

(d) *Seal Tortie Point:* Pale fawn to cream body, shading to a lighter color on chest and stomach; seal points uniformly mottled with red and cream. Nose leather is seal brown, and flesh or coral mottling is permitted with a blaze. Paw pads are seal brown, and flesh or coral mottling is permitted where the point color mottling extends into the pads.

Colors and Patterns
See pages 39–47

Copper
See Supilak

Cornish Rex

This unusual cat with its short curly coat originated from an accidental mutation in a litter of ordinary short-haired kittens produced by a farm cat in Cornwall, England in 1950. The breed was developed during the 1950s and achieved recognition in the United Kingdom in 1967.

The body of the Cornish Rex is Oriental – medium in length, slender, and strong – resembling that of the Siamese. Legs are long and straight with oval paws and the tail is long and tapering.

The head is medium in size, wedge-shaped, and narrowing to a strong chin. In profile the head is flat, with a sharp angle at the forehead and a straight line from forehead to nose. The large ears are set high and are wide at the base with rounded tips; eyes are medium and oval.

The coat is short and curly, and can be any color in Spectrum A and some

The Cornish Si-Rex is the result of the mating of a Cornish Rex and a Siamese.

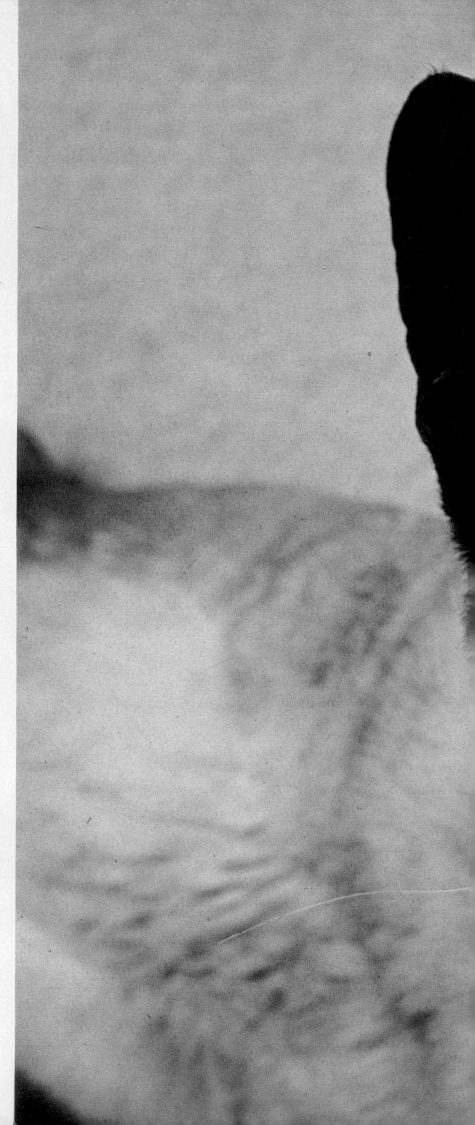

variations from Spectrum B (see Colors and Patterns). It is especially thick on the back and tail, giving the animal a plushy appearance. The curliness is due to the absence of guard hairs. Any white markings must be symmetrical except in the Calico. See also Rex.

Cougar
See Puma

Cream Abyssinian
See Abyssinian

Cream Burmese
See Burmese

Cream Persian

This popular variety originated from mating Blues and Reds.

The body should be solid and conform to Persian standards (see Persian). The tail should be short, but flowing.

The coat is long and dense, without white hairs, and should not be too red (see Colors and Patterns) or too harsh in texture. When the cat is molting the coat tends to darken, and regular brushing is required to maintain its cream color.

In mating, the occasional introduction of a Blue may help keep the pale cream color and avoid the 'hot' red tinge mentioned above. When a Cream is mated with a Blue male, the litter can contain Cream males and Blue Cream females. A Cream male mated with a Blue female may produce Blue male kittens and Blue Cream females. Female Creams are usually obtained by mating a Cream male with a Cream or Blue Cream female.

Left : Cream Persian or Long-hair.
Below : Cream Short-hair.

Cream Point
See Colorpoint Short-hair

Cream Short-hair

Cream Short-hairs are beautiful and much-admired cats, but are very difficult to breed to standard.

Body conformation should be that of the Short-hair (see American Short-hair and British Short-hair). Kittens are often born with barred markings which they may or may not lose as they mature; bars, stripes, and especially ringed tails are the most common faults in adult show animals.

Cream Tabby
See Colors and Patterns; Tabby

Cymric

The Cymric is a recognized breed and has been developed in America since 1960, but the CFA has not yet accepted it for show.

It is a hybrid, probably produced by mating a short-haired Manx with a Persian (though some consider it to be a mutation).

Except for its long coat, the Cymric should conform to the Manx standard (see Manx). Its most notable feature is its rounded rump, created by its short back, high hindquarters, and taillessness. The head is long and round with prominent cheeks; the nose is long; the ears are wide tapering to a point at the tip.

All colors and patterns of Spectrum A are possible (see Colors and Patterns).

Below: Cream Short-hair kitten.

Desert Cat, Chinese
See Chinese Desert Cat

Desert Cat, Indian
See Indian Desert Cat

Devon Rex

The Devon Rex originated from a mutation in Devon, England in 1960, and at first was thought to be similar to the Cornish Rex. Subsequent events showed, however, that an entirely different gene was involved, and the Devon Rex was recognized as a separate breed in Britain in 1967. It has not yet been accepted by many American organizations.

Good-tempered and quiet, the Devon Rex makes an excellent pet for apartment dwellers.

The Devon Rex is of medium length with long slim legs, a wide chest and slender neck, and a long, thin, tapering tail.

The head is wedge-shaped with a flat skull, full cheeks, and a strong chin. There is a definite nose break. Whiskers and eyebrows are crinkled, and of medium length. Ears are large. The large eyes are oval and wide-set and should match the coat in color.

The coat is thinner than that of the Cornish Rex. It should be short, without guard hairs, fine, wavy, and soft. The Devon Rex is bred in most colors and patterns of Spectrum A and some of B (see Colors and Patterns). See also Rex.

Right : Devon Rex.
Overleaf: Two attractive Devon Rex kittens.
Overleaf, inset : An adult Devon Rex.

Dilute Calico
See Calico; Colors and Patterns

Egyptian Cat
See African Wild Cat

Egyptian Mau

Visitors to the ancient tombs at Thebes in Egypt can see a frieze showing a hunting scene in which a spotted cat is stalking ducks for an Egyptian hunter. Almost 3500 years later that cat's modern-day counterparts are living in many countries other than Egypt.

The Egyptian Mau – the only domesticated (natural breed) spotted cat – was developed during the 1950s from cats imported from Cairo, Egypt. It is still relatively rare, and has been only provisionally accepted for CFA shows.

The Mau's body should strike a nice balance between the compact Burmese and the lithe, elegant Siamese. It is graceful and medium in size and length with well-developed muscles. The hind legs are longer than the front legs; paws are small and almost round. The tail is medium in length, thick at the base and tapering slightly. Bodies that are too cobby or Oriental and tails that are short or 'whip' are considered faults.

The head is a modified, slightly rounded wedge without any flat planes. There is a slight rise from the bridge of the nose to the forehead which in turn flows into the arched neck without a break. The muzzle is rounded, and allowances are made for broad heads or stud jowls in males.

Ears are large, broad at the base, moderately pointed and alert. Hair on the ears should be short and close-lying, and the ears can be tufted. The inner ear is a delicate, translucent shell-pink.

The eyes should be neither round nor Oriental, but large, almond-shaped, and slightly slanted. All colors of Egyptian Mau have light, gooseberry-green eyes; a slight amber cast is permissible.

The coat of an Egyptian Mau should be medium but long enough for two bands of ticking separated by lighter bands of color to be visible. It is fine, silky, shiny, and resiliant.

There are some similarities between the Egyptian Mau and the Tabby pattern, and in fact in Britain the Mackerel Tabby pattern is allowed in show animals. The forehead carries the distinctive 'M' (or 'scarab') and frown marks which form lines between the ears. These lines run down the back of the neck, breaking into elongated 'spots' along the spine and coming together again at the rear haunches to become a dorsal stripe that continues to the tip of the tail.

Right and below: Egyptian Maus. These cats are still fairly rare and are not yet recognized in Great Britain. Below is a Bronze Egyptian Mau and on the right is a Silver.

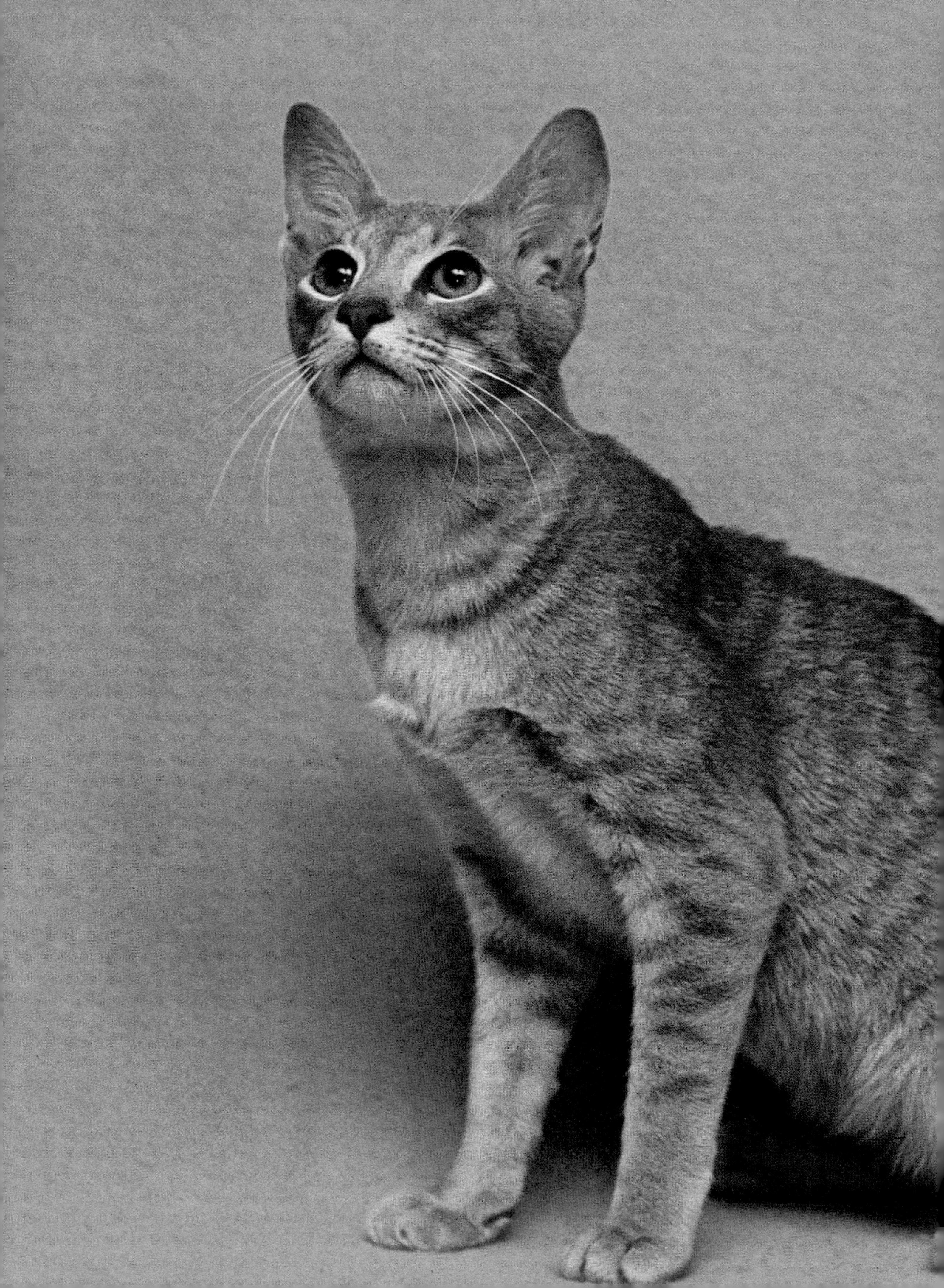

There are two 'mascara' lines on the cheeks. One starts at the corner of each eye and runs along the contour of the cheek; the other starts at the center of the cheek and curves up to almost meet the first.

The tail is heavily ringed (banded); there are one or more necklaces (preferably broken at the center) on the upper chest; and the upper forelegs are heavily barred. On the body random spots of varying size and shape should be evenly distributed, though the pattern need not be the same on both sides. The spots should be distinct, and may not run together to form a mackerel tabby pattern. There are 'vest pocket' spots on the underside of the body.

Transitional spots and stripes on the haunches and upper hind legs break into bars on the thighs and spots on the lower hind legs.

The Egyptian Mau is recognized in three colors: Bronze, Silver, and Smoke.

Bronze Mau

The ground color of the Bronze Mau's coat is light bronze becoming darkest over the shoulders and shading to tawny buff on the sides and creamy ivory on the underparts; markings are dark brown. Backs of the ears are tawny pink and tips are dark brown. Nose, lips, and eyes are outlined in dark brown; bridge of nose is ocher. The upper throat, chin, and the area around the nostrils should be creamy white. Nose leather is brick-red; paw pads are black or dark brown. There is black or dark brown hair between the toes and the same color extends slightly beyond the paws on the hind feet.

Silver Mau

The coat of the Silver Mau has a pale silver ground color with charcoal markings. Backs of the ears are grayish pink, and tips are black. The upper throat, chin, and area around the nostrils should be almost white. Nose leather is brick-red and paw pads are black. There is black hair between the toes, and black extends slightly beyond the paws on the hind feet.

Smoke Mau

The ground color of the Smoke Mau's coat is charcoal gray with a silver undercoat; markings are jet-black. Nose, lips, and eyes are outlined in black. The upper throat, chin, and the area around the nostrils should be the lightest charcoal gray color. Nose leather and paw pads are black. There is black hair between the toes, and black extends slightly beyond the paws on the hind feet.

Left: Egyptian Mau.

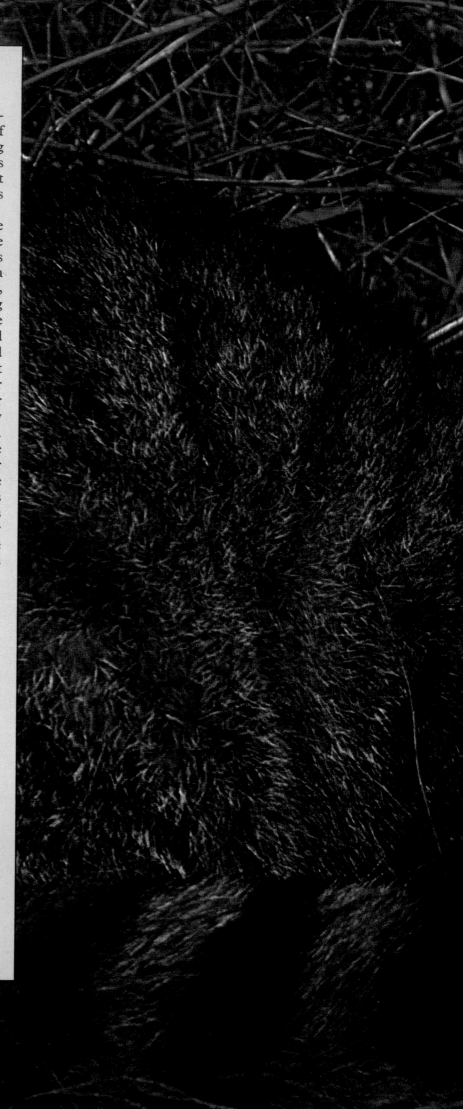

European Wild Cat
Felis silvestris silvestris

The European Wild Cat ranges from Scotland and the more remote regions of Wales, throughout Europe (excluding Scandinavia) and into Western Asia. It is a protected species in Germany and recent surveys indicate that its population is increasing in Scotland.

These animals are virtually impossible to tame at any age, although some have been known to form loose, wary alliances with people. The European Wild Cat is a diurnal hunter, preying mainly on rabbits, rodents, and small birds. However young lambs, fawns, poultry, and beetles have been known to have been on the menu, and reports from the west coast of Scotland have it that some have also learned the art of fishing. The cats can be traced by their black droppings, which they do not cover up as domestic cats do, and by their paw prints which are usually in a straight line.

The European Wild Cat is about the size of a large domestic cat, but has longer leg bones and a shorter intestine. The skull and teeth are larger and the head is flat. The tail is of medium length and is very blunt; it is full, bushy, and is heavily ringed. The coat markings resemble the mackerel tabby pattern with black stripes on a gray ground. The underparts are buff.

Exotic Short-hair

The Exotic Short-hair was deliberately created by American breeders to fulfill a desire for a cat with the beauty of the Persian but without the problems associated with the Persian's long flowing coat.

The breed was produced through careful matings of American Short-hairs and Persians and is the only hybrid cross allowed today in the United States.

The Exotic Short-hair is identical to the Persian in conformation, with large round eyes, small ears, snub nose, cobby body, and short thick legs and tail (see also Persian).

The coat should be medium in length, dense, soft, and glossy. The Exotic Short-hair can occur in all the colors and patterns of Spectrum A (see Colors and Patterns).

Right : Scottish Wild Cat.

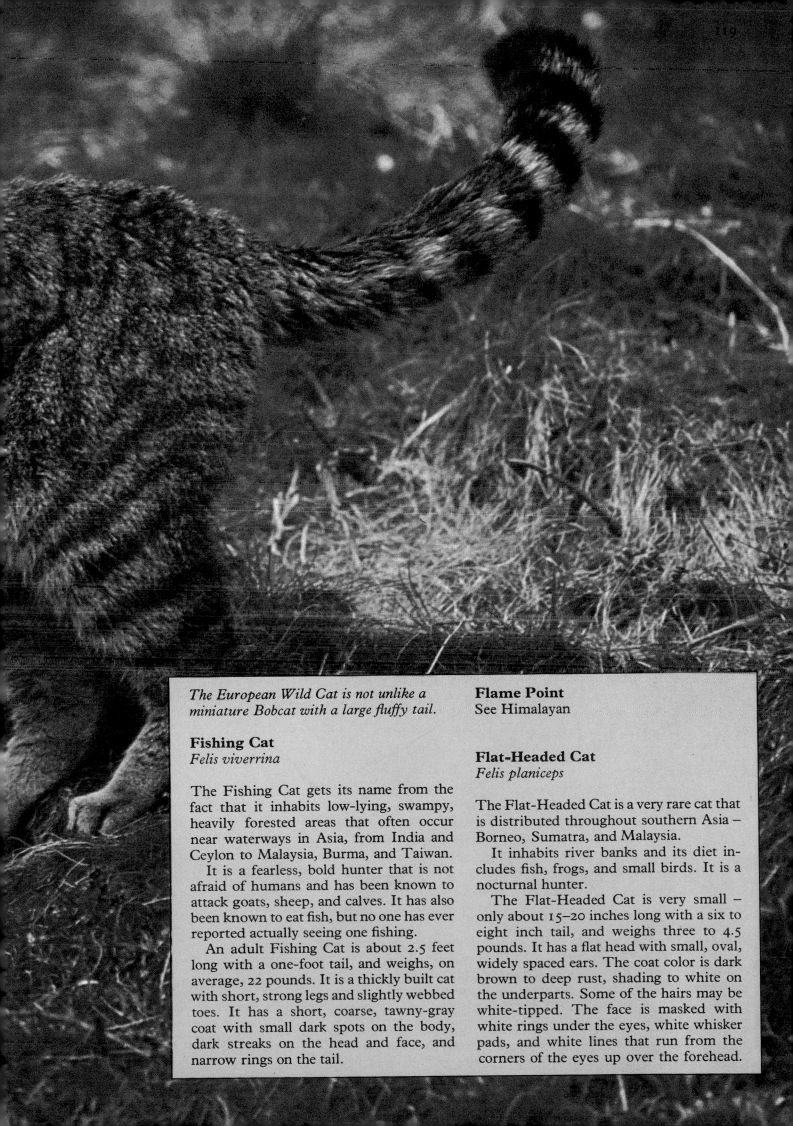

The European Wild Cat is not unlike a miniature Bobcat with a large fluffy tail.

Fishing Cat
Felis viverrina

The Fishing Cat gets its name from the fact that it inhabits low-lying, swampy, heavily forested areas that often occur near waterways in Asia, from India and Ceylon to Malaysia, Burma, and Taiwan.

It is a fearless, bold hunter that is not afraid of humans and has been known to attack goats, sheep, and calves. It has also been known to eat fish, but no one has ever reported actually seeing one fishing.

An adult Fishing Cat is about 2.5 feet long with a one-foot tail, and weighs, on average, 22 pounds. It is a thickly built cat with short, strong legs and slightly webbed toes. It has a short, coarse, tawny-gray coat with small dark spots on the body, dark streaks on the head and face, and narrow rings on the tail.

Flame Point
See Himalayan

Flat-Headed Cat
Felis planiceps

The Flat-Headed Cat is a very rare cat that is distributed throughout southern Asia – Borneo, Sumatra, and Malaysia.

It inhabits river banks and its diet includes fish, frogs, and small birds. It is a nocturnal hunter.

The Flat-Headed Cat is very small – only about 15–20 inches long with a six to eight inch tail, and weighs three to 4.5 pounds. It has a flat head with small, oval, widely spaced ears. The coat color is dark brown to deep rust, shading to white on the underparts. Some of the hairs may be white-tipped. The face is masked with white rings under the eyes, white whisker pads, and white lines that run from the corners of the eyes up over the forehead.

Above: A close-up of an Oriental or Foreign white Short-hair. (See also page 159.)
Far right: Cinnamon Oriental or Foreign, an unusual type of Oriental Short-hair.
Below: Geoffroy's Cat.

Foreign Black
See Oriental Black

Foreign Lilac
See Oriental Lavender

Foreign Short-hair

This term is used in the United Kingdom to refer to the conformation generally called 'Oriental' in the United States. Although Siamese come under this category, it generally is understood to cover Abyssinians, Burmese, Cornish and Devon Rex, Havanas, Korats, and Russian Blues, as well as the cats known in America as 'Oriental Short-hairs.' (See also Oriental Black, Oriental Lavender, Oriental Short-hair and Oriental White.)

Foreign White
See Oriental White

Frost Point
See Colors and Patterns; Siamese

Geoffroy's Cat
Felis Geoffroyi

Geoffroy's Cat is a South American native, found from Brazil to Patagonia and sometimes in parts of southern Bolivia.

It avoids areas inhabited by humans preferring mountainous regions and foothills. It is an excellent climber and, like the Jaguar, rests on the lower branches of trees and lies in wait for its prey. Its diet consists mainly of birds and small mammals, but it occasionally has been known to raid remote ranches.

The average size of this strongly built cat is two feet, with a one-foot tail. Its head is large in proportion to the rest of its body. The coat can be either gray or brown with dark spots. The ears are black with a brown patch.

122

Above : Rex kitten. Right : Known as the Havana Foreign or Chestnut Brown Foreign in the United Kingdom the Havana Brown makes an affectionate and intelligent pet.

German Rex

A cousin of the Cornish Rex, the German Rex was bred in Germany after the Second World War. During the 1950s it was used in developing the Rex breed in the United States.

Like the Cornish and Devon Rex, the coat is curly and without guard hairs.

See also Rex.

Golden Cat, Temminck's
See Temminck's Golden Cat

Hairless Cat
See Mexican Hairless; Sphynx

Havana Brown

The Havana Brown, an attractive, solid-color, mahogany-brown short-hair, was developed in England, where it is known as the Havana Foreign or Chestnut Brown Foreign. Solid brown short-hairs had occasionally appeared in cat shows for many years. The earliest example on record is a cat that was exhibited in 1894 as a 'Swiss Mountain Cat.' Again in 1930 a solid brown entry appeared in the category 'Brown Cat.'

After some years English breeders, working with Siamese, Russian Blues, and other short-hairs of mixed ancestry, were able to produce a solid brown short-hair that bred true (in other words, that produced solid brown kittens). Today the Havana Brown is an established breed, and only Havana-to-Havana matings are acceptable. The name derives from the rich, warm color, which is close to that of Havana cigars.

These affectionate, soft-voiced cats make admirable pets. They often have the unusual habit of using their paws to investigate strange objects by touch, instead of relying on their sense of smell as do most other breeds. They are generally healthy animals, but do suffer in very cold or damp weather.

Havana Brown kittens enjoy their evening meal.

The Havana's body is medium in length; firm and muscular with fine bones and graceful proportions. The legs are long and slim, with the hind legs slightly longer than the forelegs, and oval paws. The tail is also of medium length and should be in proportion to the body, with no sign of a kink.

The head is longer than it is wide with a distinct profile stop at the eyes, a fine rounded muzzle, and a definite break behind the whiskers. Ears are large and wide-set with slightly rounded tips; there is very little hair on either the outside or the inside. A Siamese head shape, a receding chin, and the lack of a profile stop at the eyes are all considered faults. Eyes are almond-shaped, slanting, and colored chartreuse green.

The coat is medium-length, smooth, and glossy; in color it is a rich, warm, chestnut or mahogany brown, as opposed to the shorter, darker, sable brown of the Burmese. The color must be even from nose to tail and from tip to root. White spots are considered faults. Whiskers should be brown; nose leather and paw pads are a rose color that harmonizes with the coat.

Havana Foreign
See Havana Brown

Himalayan

The Himalayan (called Colorpoint Longhair in Britain) is the fastest growing breed in the world today. It is a magnificent hybrid that combines Persian conformation and coat quality with Siamese colors and patterns. In the comparatively short time since 1950, when the 25-year experimental breeding program first began to show results, the Himalayan has become the third most popular breed, surpassed only by the two breeds from which it was mainly developed – the Siamese and the Persian.

The enormous amount of genetic research in the United States, Britain, and Scandinavia to produce the Himalayan was necessary in large part because both the desired characteristics – long hair and colorpoint pattern – are carried by recessive genes (see the section on Genetics and Breeding, p. 236). In the United States breeders used Siamese and Persians, but in the United Kingdom experimenters used other short-hair colors as well, including the Havana Brown. In the United States today Persian-Siamese crosses can be registered as Himalayans, but in the near future only Persians will be permitted

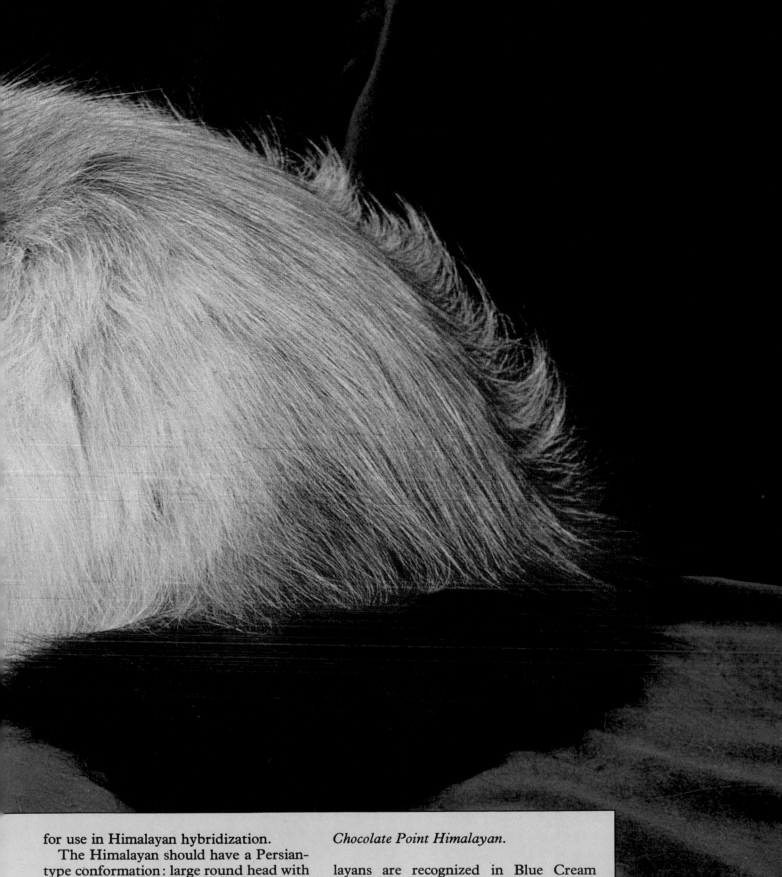

for use in Himalayan hybridization.

The Himalayan should have a Persian-type conformation: large round head with small ears, large round eyes, and deep nose break; cobby body; short, thick neck and legs; and large round paws (see also Persian). Any similarity to either the Siamese or the Peke-Face Persian is considered a fault. All Himalayans have deep blue eyes.

The coat should be long, thick, and soft, with a full frill. The four classic colors and patterns of Spectrum B (Blue Point, Chocolate Point, Lilac Point, and Seal Point) are recognized. In addition, Hima-

Chocolate Point Himalayan.

layans are recognized in Blue Cream Point, Flame Point, and Tortie Point.

Other colors of Himalayans are also being produced, but have not yet been admitted to the show bench. The three most popular are the Lynx Point (see Colorpoint Short-hair), solid Chocolate, and solid Lilac (called Chocolate Self Long-hair and Lilac Self Long-hair in Britain).

The development of these varieties has led in turn to the production of other rare and exotic colors.

Blue Cream Point Himalayan
The body color of this breed is bluish or creamy white, shading to white on chest and stomach; points are blue with patches of cream. Nose leather and paw pads are slate-blue, pink, or both.

Flame Point Himalayan
The body color of this breed is creamy white, with orange flame points. Nose leather and paw pads are flesh or coral pink.

Tortie Point Himalayan
The body color of this breed is creamy white or pale fawn; points are seal brown with unbrindled patches of red and cream. A red or cream blaze on the face is desirable. Nose leather and paw pads are seal brown with flesh or coral mottling.

Himbur

The Himbur is a hybrid produced in America by crossing the Himalayan with the Burmese. The Himbur is recognized as a separate breed, but has not yet been accepted for show competition.

Indian Desert Cat
Felis ornata

The Indian Desert Cat is so closely related to the other wild cats that some zoologists maintain that it ought not to be classified as a separate species at all.

This small cat (about the size of the European Wild Cat) inhabits the drier regions of northwest India, feeding on the usual small rodents and birds.

Indian Lion
See Lion

Indian Tiger
See Tiger

Indo-Chinese Tiger
See Tiger

Right: A pair of Indian or Asiatic lionesses in the Gir Forest, India. Below: An Ocelot hunts for insects in a rotting tree trunk. (See also page 154.)

Jaguar
Panthera onca

Along with Pumas (Cougars or Mountain Lions) Jaguars are the only big cats left in the New World, and unfortunately their numbers are decreasing due to disturbance of their habitat and human exploitation for their skins. Distribution ranges from southern California through Central America into South America as far south as Patagonia.

The Jaguar prefers thick cover – jungle and swampland – but in California and at the southern edge of its range it will roam in plains and deserts in search of food. It has been found in mountainous regions in Colombia as well. An expert climber and a good swimmer, the Jaguar hunts mam-

mals such as deer and tapirs, wild turkeys, other birds, fish, and even small alligators and crocodiles. Jaguars have been known to attack cattle, but rarely humans.

Both the Jaguar and the Central American Jaguar (*Panthera onca centralis*) resemble the Leopard, with rosettes on a coat that varies from almost white to tawny. The rosettes, however, are larger than the Leopard's and therefore fewer in number; they become solid on legs and flanks, and form into rings near the end of the black-tipped tail. The average Jaguar is about 7.5 feet long (including a two-foot tail) and weighs about 250 pounds. Central American Jaguars are somewhat smaller.

A pair of Jaguars romp beside a desert waterhole in mid-summer.

132

Jaguarondi
Felis yagouaroundi

The Jaguarondi is a wild cat that ranges from southern Texas through Mexico to the Argentine.

A solitary animal that is as active by day as by night, the Jaguarondi lives on small mammals and reptiles, birds, and fish – and fruit, which is very unusual in a carnivorous animal. It is able to travel long distances by moving from tree to tree, and is also very fast on the ground.

Despite its name, the Jaguarondi bears no resemblance to the Jaguar, but has a head shaped amazingly like an otter's. Its long, graceful, short-legged body is either dark gray or brown (both colors can appear in the same litter). An adult is 4 to 4.5 feet long (including a 1.5-foot tail) and can weigh up to 20 pounds.

Japanese Bobtail

This is the indigenous cat of Japan, that originally came from China and Korea. It was imported into the US in 1969.

The Japanese Bobtail is a familiar figure in traditional Japanese art, and is believed to bring good luck; even today, Japanese Bobtails sit beside doorways or in shop windows with paws raised in greeting.

A slender but muscular, medium-sized cat, the Japanese Bobtail has hind legs that are longer than its forelegs. They are angled, however, so that the body is nearly level when the cat is standing. The legs are long and slender but strong.

The Japanese Bobtail's distinctive tail is usually about 4 inches long and can be straight or curved. The hair on the tail is longer and thicker than the rest of the coat, and looks like a pom-pom.

The head is an equilateral triangle, with high cheek bones and a broad muzzle that curves into a distinct whisker break. Ears are large and wide-set at right angles to the head. Eyes are also large, oval, and slanted.

The coat is medium in length, soft, and silky. Preference is given to the traditional good-luck color, *mi-ke* (mee'-kay): black and brilliant reddish-orange spots or shapes on a white ground. Other popular colors include black, white, red, black-and-white, red-and-white, tortoiseshell, and tortoiseshell-and-white; a variety of other colors is now accepted as well. Dramatic, contrasting colors are preferable. Colors of eyes, nose leather, and paw pads should harmonize with the coat as described in Spectrum A (see Colors and Patterns).

The solitary Jarguarondi, despite its name, is not at all like the Jaguar. It is able to move through the trees as quickly as it can on the ground and is one of the few carnivores which will pick and eat fruit from a tree.

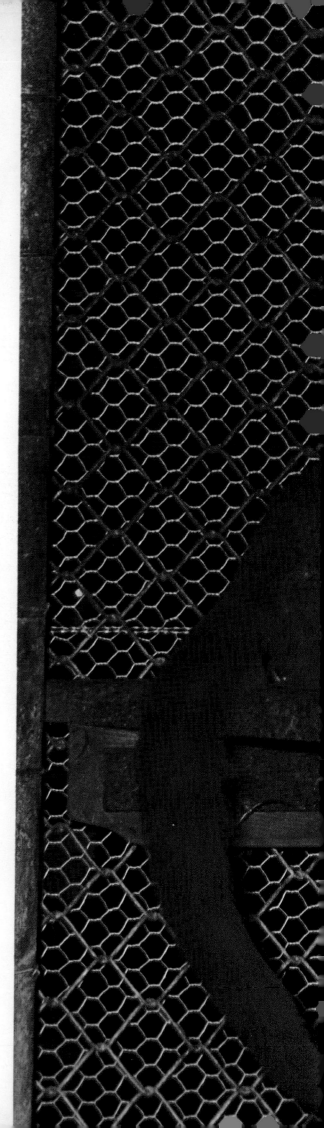

Javan Tiger
See Tiger

Jungle Cat
Felis chaus

The Jungle Cat, also known as the Swamp Cat, inhabits a large area from Egypt and the Middle East to Southeast Asia.

Jungle Cats like scrub and dry grassland, and often are found near small villages where they can obtain an occasional chicken to supplement their basic diet of other birds and small mammals. They have been tamed, but have never come to trust humans completely.

The Jungle Cat weighs about 20 pounds and is up to 3.5 feet long, making it slightly larger than a large domestic cat. The body is usually grayish brown with white underparts and chin. There are faint, broken stripes on the body and dark rings on the tail, which also has a dark tip.

Kaffir Cat
See African Wild Cat

Kodkod
Felis guigna

The Kodkod inhabits the foothills of the Andes in South America. It is becoming very rare and has not been studied in detail.

Kodkods live mainly on rodents and other small mammals, and occasionally raid farmyards for chickens. They may hunt in packs.

This small cat is only 1.5 feet long with another nine inches of tail. The coat is grayish brown with small black spots on the back and sides. Black lines run up the face and over the head, and the tail is ringed in black.

Korat

The Korat, the good-luck cat of Thailand, has a long and well-documented history, dating from a Thai manuscript that may have been written as early as 1350 AD. Korats come from the northeastern province of the same name, and are called *Si-Sawat* in Thailand (a reference to a fruit plant whose seed is the same silver blue color as the Korat).

The breed was exhibited in Britain as early as 1896 and a few were brought to the United States during the 1930s, but there were no serious attempts at breeding until the late 1950s. The Korat Cat Fanciers' Association was founded in 1965 to protect the purity of Korat bloodlines and ensure that only those cats with Thai ancestry are registered.

Korats are rare even in Thailand, and have been highly valued there for many years; originally they could not be purchased, but had to be given as a gift. They are quiet, intelligent cats who take an active part in family life. They dislike sudden noises, however, and are apt to be nervous at shows.

The Korat is a hard, muscular, medium-sized cat that is surprizingly heavy for its size. Its lines are all curves; it has a rounded back, well-proportioned legs (the hind legs are slightly longer than the front), and a medium-length tail that tapers to a rounded tip. A *non-visible* kink is permitted in show animals.

The head is heart-shaped, from the eyebrow ridges to the strong, well-developed chin. There is a slight stop between the nose and the forehead, and the nose curves slightly downward just before the nose leather. Ears are very large, with rounded tips and a wide flare at the base. Eyes are also large; they are rounded when fully open but have an Oriental slant when partly or completely closed. Eyes should be a luminous green but an amber cast is acceptable. (The green color usually appears in mature cats; kittens often have yellow, amber, or golden-green eyes.)

The coat is close-lying and is silver blue in color tipped with silver. The tipping appears all over the coat especially where the hairs are shortest. The coat should be free of shading, tabby markings, and white spots. Nose leather and lips are dark blue or lavender. Paw pads range from dark blue to lavender with a pinkish tinge.

Far left: The Jungle or Swamp cat roams throughout the Middle East and Southeast Asia. Below: A color portrait of the Oriental Lavender, discussed in detail on page 157.

Leopard
Panthera pardus

Leopards can be found from Africa to southern Asia, though they are almost extinct in parts of north and south Africa. A sub-species, *P pardus japonensis*, inhabits northern China. As one of the world's most beautiful cats, the Leopard has long been hunted for its hide, and is now on the list of endangered species.

The Leopard is a solitary, secretive cat that prefers thick cover. It is a good climber and will often lie in wait on the lower branches of trees, dropping down on its prey and killing it with a deep bite that severs the jugular vein or crushes the neck vertebrae. After dining on the more succulent parts it will often carry the rest of the carcass up a tree, safe from other predators such as hyenas. Prey consists of many animals including antelopes, baboons and other monkeys, and large rodents. Leopards have also been known to attack domestic cattle and children, but do not often bother adults.

These beautiful cats (third largest in the world) average 7.5 feet in length and weigh from 100 to 180 pounds. The ground color of the coat is tawny brown, lighter on the underparts and chin, with small rosettes (clusters of spots) all over the body. These become spots on the head and legs. There is also a dark brown melanistic form called the Panther or Black Panther; both color variations may be found in the same litter. (See also Clouded Leopard.)

Above and overleaf: Leopards.

Leopard Cat
Felis bengalensis

The Leopard Cat is the most common small wild cat in Southeast Asia; it is also found in Tibet and northern India, China, and eastern Siberia.

Hunted both for its hide and for exploitation as an exotic pet, the Leopard Cat faces extinction if measures to preserve it are not taken soon. Its popularity as a pet is hard to fathom, since it is as ferocious and hard to tame as the European Wild Cat – and as unhappy in captivity.

It lives in hilly areas and on the outskirts of jungles, but avoids the denser forests. It is a good climber and often drops on its prey like a leopard; its diet includes large birds, small mammals, and even the occasional small deer. Leopard Cats are nocturnal hunters.

The Leopard Cat is only about 2.5 feet long, and looks something like a small leopard. Its coat is yellowish or grayish, with dark brown spots (not rosettes). The spots on the tail form into bands at the tip. Streaks extend from the forehead down the back of the head, and from the corners of the eyes, under the ears and down the neck. Ears are black with a white spot.

Leopard, Clouded
See Clouded Leopard

Leopard, Snow
See Snow Leopard

Lilac Burmese
See Burmese

Lilac Cream Point
See Colorpoint Short-hair

Lilac Lynx Point
See Colorpoint Short-hair

Lilac Point
See Colors and Patterns; Siamese; Himalayan

Lilac Self Long-hair
See Himalayan

Lilac Tortie Burmese
See Burmese

Far left: A Leopard Cat kitten. Below: An adult Leopard Cat perched on a tree. Leopard Cats are slightly larger than the European Wild Cat (page 116) but are equally difficult to tame.

Lion
Panthera leo

Lions once ranged from Europe and the Middle East throughout Africa and India. Man has sadly decimated the Lion population however, and today the 'King of Beasts' survives in only a few small areas in Africa and in the Gir Forest in India.

One reason Lions are such easy victims is that they prefer open country. Their diet includes both large animals (antelopes, zebras, and goats) and small animals (rats), and they also eat carrion. Lions are the only social cats, living in prides of up

to thirty comprised of an older male, several females and adolescent males, and as many as ten cubs. Lions usually hunt by executing a carefully planned campaign; a small party will chase a herd of herbivores into an ambush formed by the rest of the party. Females often make the kill; cubs do not join the hunt until they are two.

Both African and Indian males average about 9 feet in length and weigh from 300 to 400 pounds; females are smaller and lighter. The body is long and muscular, with short powerful legs and a thin, medium-length, tufted tail. Some experts claim that the Indian Lion is slightly stockier than the African. The head is long with a straight profile and small, very rounded ears. The African male has very thick hair on its mane (which covers the head and shoulders), elbows, and tail. The Indian sub-species has a smaller mane, but more hair on chest, elbows, and tail. Females do not have manes.

Cubs are born with spots which all but disappear as they mature. Coat color of the adult varies from pale fawn to tawny blue, and the mane is tawny brown to black.

Below : A pride of Lions rests on the Serengeti Plains.

Lions occasionally find peace by climbing trees.

Lion, Mountain
See Puma

Little Spotted Cat
See Tiger Cat

Long-hair
See Persian

Lynx, Bay
See Bobcat

Lynx, Caracal
See Caracal Lynx

Lynx, Northern
See Northern Lynx

Lynx Point
See Colorpoint Short-hair

Magpie
See Bi-colored Persian; Colors and Patterns

Maine Coon

Maine Coon Cats, according to New England experts, are the biggest, smartest, most beautiful cats in the world. Its name comes from an early legend that these king-size (thirty pounds) cats are part raccoon.

Although this is obviously impossible, the Maine Coon's actual origins are as obscure as those of the American Short-hair. Some experts believe that it is the result of uncontrolled matings between the short-haired cats brought to America in the seventeenth century and Angoras or Persians imported by sailors in the 1800s.

Justifiably proud cat lovers in Maine have kept pedigree information on Maine Coon Cats for many years; the Maine Coon Cat Club was established in 1953, and every year since then a Maine State Champion Coon Cat has been selected in Skowhegan, Maine.

The body of a Maine Coon is large, muscular, broad-chested, and long, so that it has a rectangular shape. Legs should be medium in length, in good proportion to the body, and substantial. Paws are large, round, and well-tufted; the tufts make it easy for the cat to 'snowshoe' across the frozen Maine countryside in winter. The

Left: Tabby patterned Manx Cat. Overleaf: A white Manx cat.

tail is long and tapering.

The head is medium, with a square muzzle, high cheekbones, firm chin, and a medium-length nose. The ears, which are set high and well apart, are large, tapered, and tufted; 'Lynxline tips' (tufts on the tips of the ears) are especially desirable. Eyes are large and wide-set, slanting slightly upwards toward the ears.

Maine Coon Cats are penalized if they have a delicate bone structure, and are disqualified for having a receding chin, crossed eyes, a kinked tail, or an incorrect number of toes.

The coat is heavy and shaggy, shorter on the shoulders than on the stomach and haunches. The shagginess is most noticeable on the underparts and on the long-haired tail. There is a 'muttonchops' frill on the chest. Texture of the coat is silky and smooth. An even coat is a fault.

The Maine Coon Cat is bred and recognized in every color of Spectrum A (See Colors and Patterns); in addition, any color or combination of colors except those in Spectrum B is accepted. Eyes may be green, gold, or copper; in whites, eyes may also be blue or odd-eyed.

Maltese

The Maltese, which was very popular in America at the turn of the century, is no longer a recognized breed. It is a short-haired Blue that has now been superceded by the Russian Blue.

Manchurian Tiger
See Tiger

Manx

There are many myths about the tailless Manx: one, for example, tells how the Manx was very late for the Ark and had its tail cut off by an over-anxious Noah as he slammed the door shut. Attempts have also been made to establish a relationship between the Manx and the bobtailed cats of the Orient.

In fact, the taillessness of this unique breed undoubtedly arose from a mutation within the small confines of the Isle of Man – a 221-square-mile island in the Irish Sea off the west coast of England. Recent research has shown that the Manx has a different phenotype and is not genetically related to the Far Eastern cats.

The Manx makes a delightful pet – healthy, intelligent, and fond of people.

It is also reputed to be an excellent ratter. Breeding Manx cats can be tricky, however. The mutation which causes the taillessness affects the vertebral column; if vertebrae are missing anywhere other than at the end, kittens will be born dead. Thus breeding is best left to experts.

There are three variations found in Manx cats. *Rumpies* have no tail at all, and a hollow is found where the tail usually begins. Only Rumpies are accepted for show. *Stumpies* have one- to five-inch tails, and *Full-tails* or *Longies* have complete tails. All three tail lengths are often found in the same litter.

Over all, the Manx should give the impression of roundness. The body should be solid, compact, and well-balanced, with a round, broad chest, substantial round short front legs, and a round rump ('as round as an orange,' to quote the British Standard) created in part by the short back and high hindquarters.

The hind legs are much longer than the forelegs, with a heavy, muscular thigh and a strong lower leg. In America Manx cats are disqualified for having a visible tail joint, polydactylism (wrong number of toes), or the inability to stand or walk properly (the high, deep flanks can cause a rabbit-like gait).

The head is round, with prominent full cheeks and a rounded muzzle. Ears are wide-based, tapering, and rather long, but should be in proportion to the head.

The beautiful, plush coat is something like a rabbit's, with a short, thick, cottony undercoat and harder, glossier guard hairs.

The Manx is recognized in all the colors and patterns of Spectrum A (see Colors and Patterns), and in combination of colors and patterns which includes white. Eyes, nose leather, and paw pads should correspond with the coat color.

There is considerable variation in the number of points allocated to the Manx characteristics in the United States and Britain as is shown in the following chart.

	USA	Britain-Europe
Taillessness	10	15
Hindquarters (height)	–	15
Body	25	–
Back (shortness)	5	15
Rump (roundness)	–	10
Legs/Feet	15	–
Flank (depth)	5	10
Coat (not color)	15	10
Head Ears	10	10
Color Pattern	5	5
Eyes	5	5
Condition	5	5

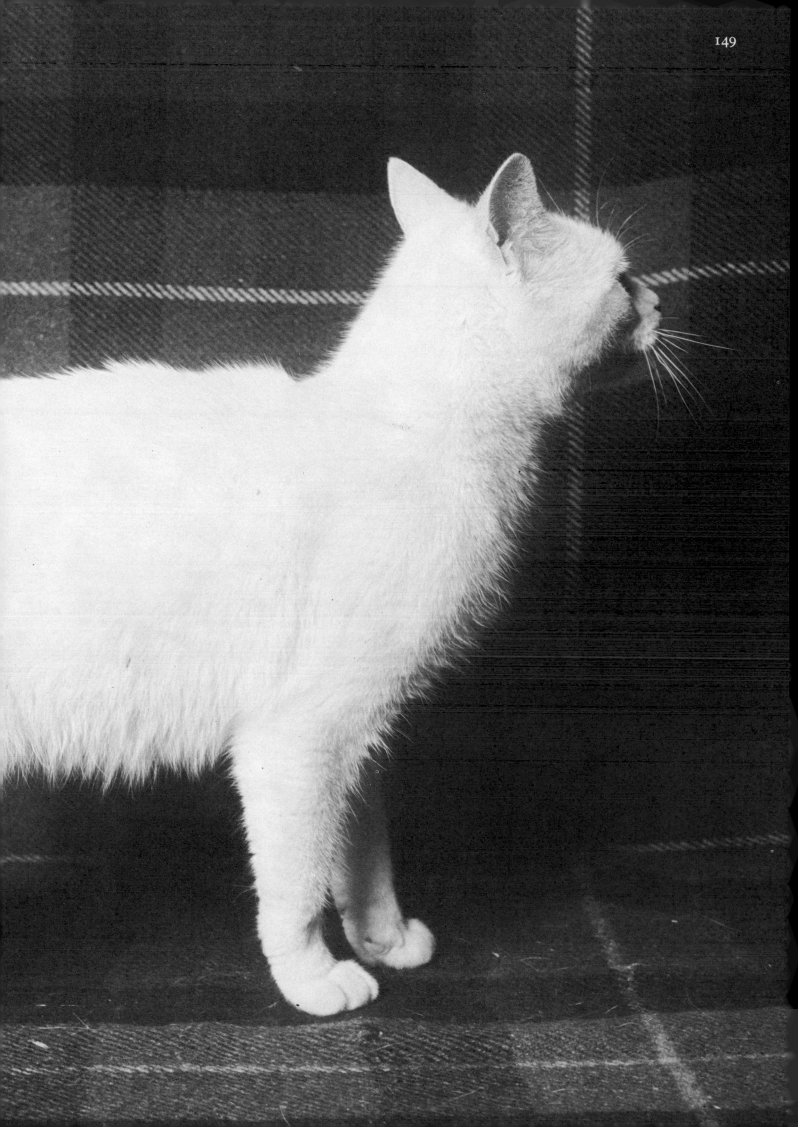

Manxamese

The Manxamese is a short-haired hybrid obtained by crossing Manx with Siamese to produce a cat with the colorpoint pattern of Spectrum B (see Colors and Patterns).

Marbled Cat
Felis marmorata

The Marbled Cat is another beautiful, but extremely fierce wild cat about which very little is known.

It is found on the slopes of the Himalayas, throughout Burma and the Malay Peninsula, to Borneo and Sumatra. It hunts along riverbanks and in small clearings, and is known to be a good climber. Thus it is reasonable to assume that fish and birds form some part of its diet, along with small rodents and other mammals.

The Marbled Cat is only a little larger than a domestic cat, and very much resembles the Clouded Leopard. It has a soft, heavy coat with body markings that are large on the back, gradually decreasing into spots on the legs and head, and forming rings on the tail. Lines on the head run from the eyes to the ears. The muzzle of the Marbled Cat is finer, its ears longer, and its tail longer and thicker than those of the Clouded Leopard.

Margay Cat
Felis weidi

The Margay Cat inhabits Central and South America. Not much is known about its habits, but it is reported to spend a lot of time in trees. Like the Ocelot it is in

Below: The Margay Cat.

demand as an 'exotic pet,' but since even kittens raised in captivity can be unpredictable and dangerous when they mature, most zoologists discourage the practice. (See also Ocelot, page 154.)

The Margay is closely related to the Ocelot and is similar in appearance. It averages three feet in length, including a one-foot tail, and weighs about 12–15 pounds. Ground color ranges from tawny to gray with clearly defined black spots that often have a center corresponding to the ground color. There are horizontal lines on the neck and chest, spots on the paws, and rings on the tail. Underparts are usually white with a yellowish tinge, and there is a white streak on either side of the nose and under the eyes. The ears are longer than the Ocelot's and are dark-rimmed on the inside.

Mau
See Egyptian Mau

Mexican Hairless

This is an extinct breed; the last known pair, said to have been purchased from Indians who claimed they were the last of an Aztec breed known only in New Mexico, died early in this century.

They are said to have had very short fur on their backs and tails which fell off in warm weather. They had long bodies, long thin tails, and wedge-shaped heads with big ears, long whiskers, and amber eyes. Both cats were flesh-colored with a mousey gray shade along the back.

Moon Cat
See Sphynx

Mountain Cat
Felis jacobita

Little is known about the Mountain Cat (sometimes called the Andean Cat). It lives in the mountainous regions of Chile, Peru, Argentina, and Bolivia, and its diet consists mainly of small rodents.

Though small (less than 2.5 feet total length) it is strongly built. Its coat is light brown with darker brown bars. The tail is about a foot long, very bushy, and has a dark brown tip.

Mountain Lion
See Puma

Northern Lynx
Felis lynx

The Northern Lynx once roamed throughout the temperate forests of the Northern Hemisphere but civilization – the disappearance of much of its habitat and exploitation for its long, soft fur – has driven it into remote regions where dwindling numbers of the animals are still persistently hunted.

Most of the Northern Lynx population is found today in Alaska, where it is still relatively common. Other small pockets exist in northern New England, the Adirondacks, and the Great Lakes region of North America and in parts of Scandinavia, the Balkans, and the Iberian Peninsula.

The Northern Lynx inhabits thick bush and forest doing most of its hunting at night. It is an agile climber and a good hunter; its diet is varied, including birds, rodents, and other small mammals such as foxes, roe deer and skunks.

Bigger and more beautiful than a Bobcat, the average Northern Lynx is just under four feet long and weighs between 36 and 40 pounds. Its long soft fur can be almost white, but usually it is a mixture of tawny and yellow hairs with some longer silvery guard hairs and a few indistinct spots, giving it a shadowy, etherial appearance. A ruff of long hair on the cheeks outlines the face. The ears are long and light brown in color with a long slender black tuft; the tail has a black tip.

Far right: A close-up of the face and head of an Egyptian Mau (page 112). Below: Northern Lynx.

Ocelot
Felis pardalis

Paradoxically the Ocelot is in grave danger of extinction on one hand, because of the high commercial value of its beautifully marked coat, while on the other hand, it is becoming increasingly popular as an 'exotic' pet. Unfortunately it is very difficult to breed ocelots in captivity.

It inhabits dense, tropical areas from Central America to Equador and Northern Argentina. It could once have been found in southwestern United States, where it is now nearly extinct.

Ocelots spend much of their time relaxing in trees, but hunt on the ground, often in pairs. They generally remain in their own clearly defined territory. Their diet includes almost any animal they can overpower – deer, fawns, domestic lambs and calves, rodents, frogs, monkeys, birds, and even snakes. Since they are good swimmers, fish may be included as well.

Many experts believe that the Ocelot has two breeding seasons (June and December). Litters usually consist of two kittens, born in a nest of grass or other soft material built in a hollow log or under a bush.

The average male Ocelot is four feet long (including a one-foot tail) and weighs about 35 pounds. Females are somewhat smaller. It has a small head and rounded ears, a long neck, a relatively short body, and long thick legs.

The coat varies from pale grayish yellow to cinnamon; the ground color is darkest on the back gradually becoming lighter on the sides. The underparts, chin, and whisker pads are a creamy white. Markings consist of dark brown spots and blotches, bordered in black. The blotches on the tail tend to be darker and more solid. Two stripes run from either side of the nose up over the forehead, two more cross the cheeks, and there are four or five stripes on the neck.

The Ocelot (or Margay) as a Pet:
Ocelots and margays are the most popular wild cats now being kept as pets. Both are reasonably docile, but do require a lot more patience, knowledge, dedication, and work than ordinary house cats. Before you acquire an ocelot then, you will have to be sure that you have the time, energy, and facilities necessary for the success of the enterprise. Check too to see if there are any local ordinances in your community which prohibit keeping a wild animal as a pet.

Right: A young Ocelot.

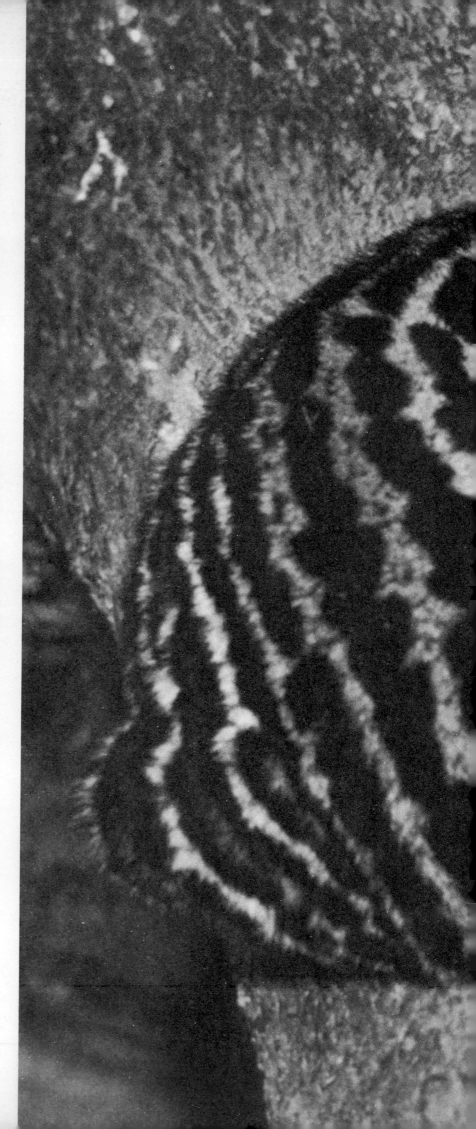

Decide if you want an ocelot or a margay. Ocelots are much larger, and therefore margays are usually considered more suitable for homes with children. Ocelots love water and will be especially happy if there is a swimming pool – though they will also enjoy playing in the bathtub or under the garden hose. Decide too whether you want a male or a female. Males are usually more docile and survive surgery (neutering) better than females.

If you cannot find an older pet that someone wishes to part with, you will have to order one from an importer. Be sure to check the organization's reputation carefully. Be prepared to spend a lot of money and wait some time for delivery. You may also have to spend some time nursing the animal back to health; many arrive at their new homes with nutritional deficiencies and parasites.

Both ocelots and margays are very playful. The ocelot loves to leap at you from ambush and wrap itself around your legs. The margay prefers to jump down on you from heights. Teaching them to play games ('fetch' for example) can often provide an acceptable substitute.

Ocicat

The Ocicat is a hybrid breed produced in America by mating a Siamese Chocolate Point male and an Abyssinian-Siamese crossbred female. It is now produced by

crossing the Abyssinian with the American Short-hair, or either of these with the Ocicat itself. Although it is a recognized breed, it has not yet been accepted for championship competition.

The Ocicat has an Oriental conformation, with a head like the Abyssinian and golden oval eyes. The coat pattern is spots on a pale cream ground color, with tabby markings on the throat, legs, and tail. The markings are dark chestnut brown for the Dark Chestnut Ocicat or milk chocolate color for the Light Chestnut. The fur is short and silky.

Odd-eyed White
See White Persian; White Short-hair

Orange-eyed White
See White Persian; White Short-hair

Oriental Black
See Oriental Short-hair

Oriental Lavender

The Oriental Lavender (called Foreign Lilac in Britain) is only produced when both parents carry genes for Blue and Chocolate. The coat should be frost-gray with a pinkish tone; eyes should be a rich green (see also Oriental Short-hair).

Below: Oriental Short-hair kittens.

158

Oriental Short-hair

The Oriental Short-hair is a hybrid produced by crossing Siamese, American Short-hairs, Colorpoint Short-hairs, and other Oriental Short-hairs. It has the conformation of the Siamese (called 'Foreign' in Britain), but the colorpoint pattern has been eliminated. It has provisional acceptance from the American CFA.

Just as many breeders spent years trying to transfer the colorpoint pattern to Persian-type cats (see Himalayan), others are working to transfer the more exotic colors and patterns of Spectrum A (see Colors and Patterns) to the Siamese-type.

158

There are only a few minor differences between the Oriental Short-hair and Siamese standards. Males may be a bit larger than females; the tail is thin at the base; and cats are penalized for having crossed eyes. Oriental Short-hairs may have green or amber eyes in addition to bright blue (see also Siamese).

Oriental Short-hairs are recognized in White, Ebony (black), Blue, Chestnut (Self-Chocolate), Lavender (Lilac), Red, Cream, Silver, Cameo, Ebony (or Black) Smoke, Blue Smoke, Chestnut (or Chocolate) Smoke, Lavender Smoke, and Cameo (Red) Smoke and in Classic, Mackerel, and Spotted Tabby patterns.

Oriental White

Oriental Whites can be difficult, delicate cats, very prone to diseases.

The Oriental White should have a completely white coat with no trace of a colorpoint pattern. Eyes can be green or bright blue; gold-eyed cats are not accepted for the show bench. Paw pads and nose leather are pink.

Ounce
See Snow Leopard

Below : Oriental Short-hair.

Pallas's Cat
Felis mamul

Pallas's Cat inhabits wooded and mountainous areas in Asia from Persia to Tibet and Mongolia; it is also found in the deserts of China. Its diet consists mainly of rodents and other small mammals.

This unusual looking animal is about the size and weight of a domestic cat. It has an exceptionally low forehead and low, wide-set ears. Some experts argue that these features enable the cat to hunt by sight instead of by sound, crouching behind large rocks and watching its prey unobserved.

Two coat colors have been reported: dark orange and silvery gray. The face markings include black stripes on the sides, black and white rings around the eyes, and spots on the forehead. There is a 'beard' of long fur around the cheeks. The tail is very bushy, with dark rings and a black tip.

Pampas Cat
Felis colocolo

The Pampas Cat is another wild cat about which very little is known. Once it could be found throughout the swamps and grasslands of Argentina and Uruguay, but today it has become very rare, facing extinction as its habitat is swallowed up by civilization.

It does most of its hunting at night; its prey consists primarily of birds and small mammals.

The Pampas Cat has silvery gray fur that becomes lighter on the sides and light gray on the underparts. It has a dark, reddish brown line down its back. Other, lighter lines run across the back and sides and from the eyes to the ears.

Panther
See Leopard

*Right : Pallas's Cat.
Below : Oriental
Lavender.*

Panther, Black
See Leopard

Parti-colored Persian
See Bi-colored Persian; Calico; Persian;
Tortoiseshell Persian; Colors and Patterns

Peke-Face Persian

The Peke-Face Persian was developed in
the United States during the 1930s from
Standard Red and Red Tabby Persians. It
is not recognized in England.

As the name suggests, the face should

Above: Peke-Face Persian.
Left: White Persian.

bear as close a resemblance as possible to
that of the Pekinese dog, with a very short
depressed nose, high forehead, large round
eyes, and prominent ears. Peke-Face
Persians often have deformed teeth and
lower jaws, leading to difficulties in
breathing.

In all other respects, conformation
should be that of the Persian (see Persian).

Peke-Face Persians are only recognized
in two colors: Red and Red Tabby (see
Colors and Patterns).

Persian

The Persian is the aristocrat of domestic cats – the paragon of pedigreed breeds. The origin of the breed is obscure, but many experts believe that it first appeared in Persia and Turkey, and is a descendant of some Asian wild cat. During the nineteenth century, long-haired cats were known to exist in Afghanistan, Burma, China, Russia, and Turkey.

Persians are usually sedate, dignified cats, very conscious of their beauty and their position in life. Their coats must be groomed daily to keep them free of loose hair, knots, tangles, and grease – and to keep the rugs and furniture relatively hairless. Show cats are usually groomed twice a day.

The Persian is a medium to large cat, but quality is more important than size. It has a cobby body: low-lying, long, and thick-set with a deep chest, massive shoulders and rump, and a short, well-rounded middle. The back is level and the legs short, thick, round and firm. Like all pedigree cats, the Persian has five toes on its front paws and four on its hind paws; polydactylism (an incorrect number of toes) is a fault. The tail is short and bushy, and should be in good proportion to the body. It is carried at an angle lower than the body, without curves.

The head, set on a short, thick neck, is round and massive, with full cheeks, powerful jaws, and a well-developed chin. The ears, which are small, wide-set, and tilted slightly forward, have long tufts of hair. The eyes are large, round, and set far apart. The nose is broad and short – almost snubby – and there should be a definite stop, or break, in the profile.

The Persian coat should be thick and soft, fine textured, with a glossy lively appearance. It should be long all over, including the shoulders; the ruff (longer hair around the head) should be immense, and continue down in a deep frill between the front legs. The condition and coloring of the coat is more important than body type. Persians are recognized in every color and pattern of Spectrum A (see Colors and Patterns), and Persian-type cats are also recognized in the colorpoint pattern of Spectrum B (see Himalayan).

Persian Tiger
See Tiger

Platinum Burmese
See Burmese

White Persian (or White Long-hair).

Platinum Tortie Burmese
See Burmese

Puma
Felis concolor

The Puma, also known as the Cougar and the Mountain Lion, originally ranged throughout the deserts, forests, jungles, and mountains of the Americas. The destruction of its habitat and relentless hunting have, however, considerably reduced its range.

Pumas are strong, athletic animals, capable of jumping about fifteen feet in the air, covering more than 35 feet in one forward leap, and dropping over fifty feet to the ground. Males will travel up to fifty miles when hunting. The average life span is about eighteen years.

Pumas breed all year round, producing litters of between one and four cubs. Kittens remain with their mother for up to two years, but adult Pumas are solitary animals. They are avid hunters and will eat almost anything from mice to domestic cattle. Pumas rarely attack humans.

There are about thirty sub-species, which vary greatly. The smaller Pumas of the tropics can have a total length of only four feet and weigh as little as 46 pounds, while the larger cats living in cooler climates may measure up to eight feet in

length and weigh up to 260 pounds. Generally, females are smaller and more slender. In appearance the Puma rather resembles the lioness but its head is rounder.

Coat color can vary from light fawn to dark brown or black, but short reddish brown fur with white underparts is most common. Body markings consist of a black ridge running down the back to the end of the black-tipped tail. Whisker pads are black, and black lines run from the pads up the sides of the nose to the eyes. Kittens are born with spots and rings on the tail which disappear as they mature.

Below : Puma.

Ragdolls

Ragdolls are a unique breed that derive their name from their limpness; when picked up they relax completely and flop over like a ragdoll. They are very placid creatures and completely fearless. This is, in fact, their weakness, for it puts them in great danger of injury, especially from other animals and children. They should never be allowed to wander or make contact with other animals, and require a great amount of care and attention.

Ragdolls are similar to Birmans, but are larger and have thicker fur. Markings are either Seal Point or Lilac Point with the Birmans' white boots and mittens.

Red Abyssinian
See Abyssinian

Red Burmese
See Burmese

Red Lynx Point
See Colorpoint Short-hair

Red Persian
See Solid Red

Red Point
See Colorpoint Short-hair; Himalayan

Red Self
See Colors and Patterns; Solid Red

Red Tabby
See Colors and Patterns; Tabby

Solid Red (US) or Red Self (UK).

Rex

The Rex is a spontaneous mutation of the domestic cat. Its short, tightly curled coat gives it an exotic appearance that appeals to many. Moreover, many people who are allergic to cat hairs find the Rex, because of its special coat, the perfect pet.

The first Rex was discovered in 1950 on a farm in Bodmin Moor, Cornwall, England; his mother was a short-hair with a normal coat and his father unknown. He was named Kallibunker. His owner, Mrs Nina Ennismore, contacted professional breeders and a program to preserve the mutation was established. Kallibunker was first bred back to his dam, resulting in several curly-coated kittens. A careful combination of inbreeding and outcrossing to normal-coated cats established the Kallibunker bloodline (see Cornish Rex).

The second spontaneous Rex mutation was discovered in Germany by Dr Scheur-Karpin. This Rex was a female named Lammchen, and her breeding was also carefully planned to preserve the bloodline (see also German Rex).

The next important mutation was Kirklee, a kitten discovered in Devon, England in 1960. Genetic research resulted in the discovery that a different gene was involved in this mutation: Cat Gene 1 was therefore assigned to the Kallibunker (Cornish Rex) bloodline and Cat Gene 2 to the Kirklee bloodline (see also Devon Rex).

A long-haired version of the Rex was found in an animal shelter in San Bernadino, California a few years later. This variety was named the Marcel. This cat was successfully used in several short-coated Rex breeding programs, but there was not much interest in preserving the long-haired variety and it has since died out.

The Rex's arched back and muscular hind legs make it capable of attaining very high speeds as well as helping it make quick starts, changes of direction and high jumps. Its overall conformation is discussed in more detail in the entries for Cornish Rex and Devon Rex.

The coat, which is very important, is short, very soft and silky, and tightly curled due to the complete absence of guard hairs. This unique coat makes the Rex very warm to the touch.

Show cats are disqualified for having a kinked or abnormal tail, an incorrect number of toes, or any coarse guard hairs.

Most Rex colors are those described in Spectrum A (see Colors and Patterns), but Other Rex Colors (ORC) are also accepted for show.

Rex.

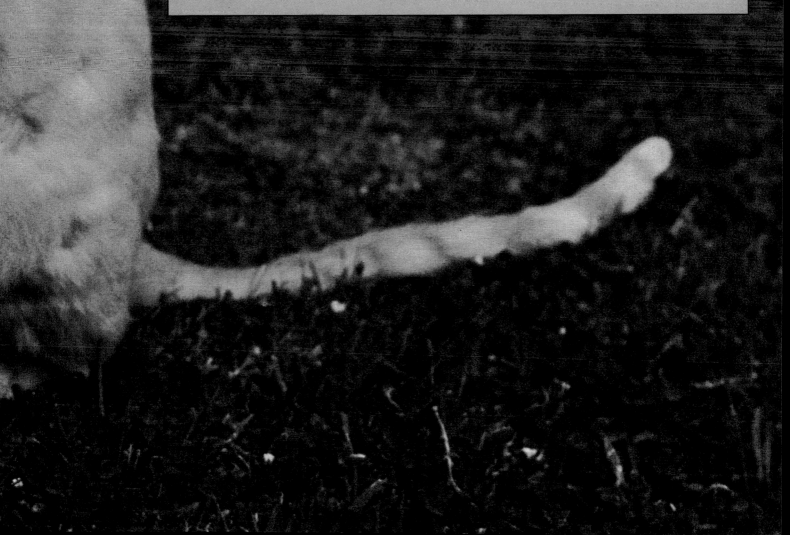

172

Ruddy Abyssinian
See Abyssinian

Rumpie
See Manx

Russian Blue

The origin of the Russian Blue is not known. It is thought that sailors brought the breed from Archangel, Russia to England, and in fact, it was called the Archangel Cat for many years. It is said to have also been the treasured pet of the czars.

Besides being beautiful, Russian Blues are quiet, shy, gentle animals that become firmly attached to their owners. They make lovely pets, especially in smaller houses or apartments.

The Russian Blue has fine bones and a long, lithe, sinuous body. Legs are long and the tail tapering. The neck is long and slender, though it appears short because of the thick fur on the neck and the animal's very high shoulder blades (ideally, the shoulder blades should almost touch behind the neck).

The head, which is short, should be wedge-shaped with a narrow, flat skull and a straight, receding forehead.

Below and inset : Russian Blue.

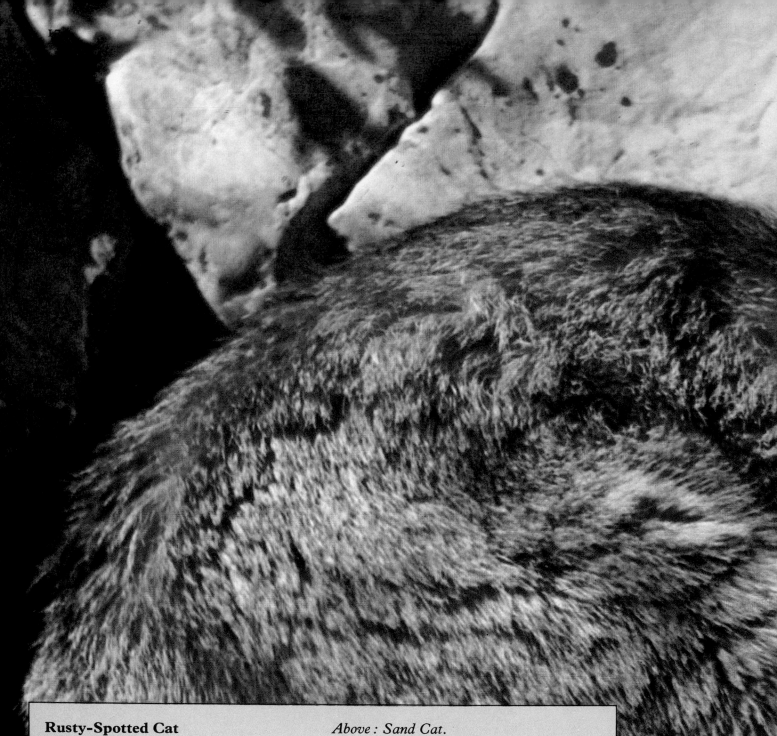

Rusty-Spotted Cat
Felis rubiginosa

The Rusty-Spotted Cat is a small, elegant, wild cat that inhabits tall grass and brush areas in southern India and Sri Lanka. Although it is not hunted it is extremely rare. Its diet includes small birds and mammals.

Unlike most other wild cats, Rusty-Spotted kittens are quite easily tamed.

The average Rusty-Spotted Cat weighs just over three pounds and is about two feet long (including a nine-inch tail). Coat color varies from reddish brown to fawn, with white underparts. The spotted markings, which tend to be elongated, are very pronounced on the back, fade on the sides and become darker and more dense on the legs. There are only a few faint markings on the tail, but the tip is almost black. There are streaks on the forehead and

Above : Sand Cat.

from the corners of the eyes to just under the ears, similar to the Leopard Cat.

Sable Burmese
See Burmese

Sand Cat
Felis margarita

The Sand Cat inhabits semi-desert areas and rocky wastes in North Africa and parts of the Middle East as far north as southern Russia.

Very little is known of its life and habits, but it is thought to be a nocturnal hunter preying chiefly on rabbits and small rodents. It is also reported to dig shallow burrows in the sand where it hides during

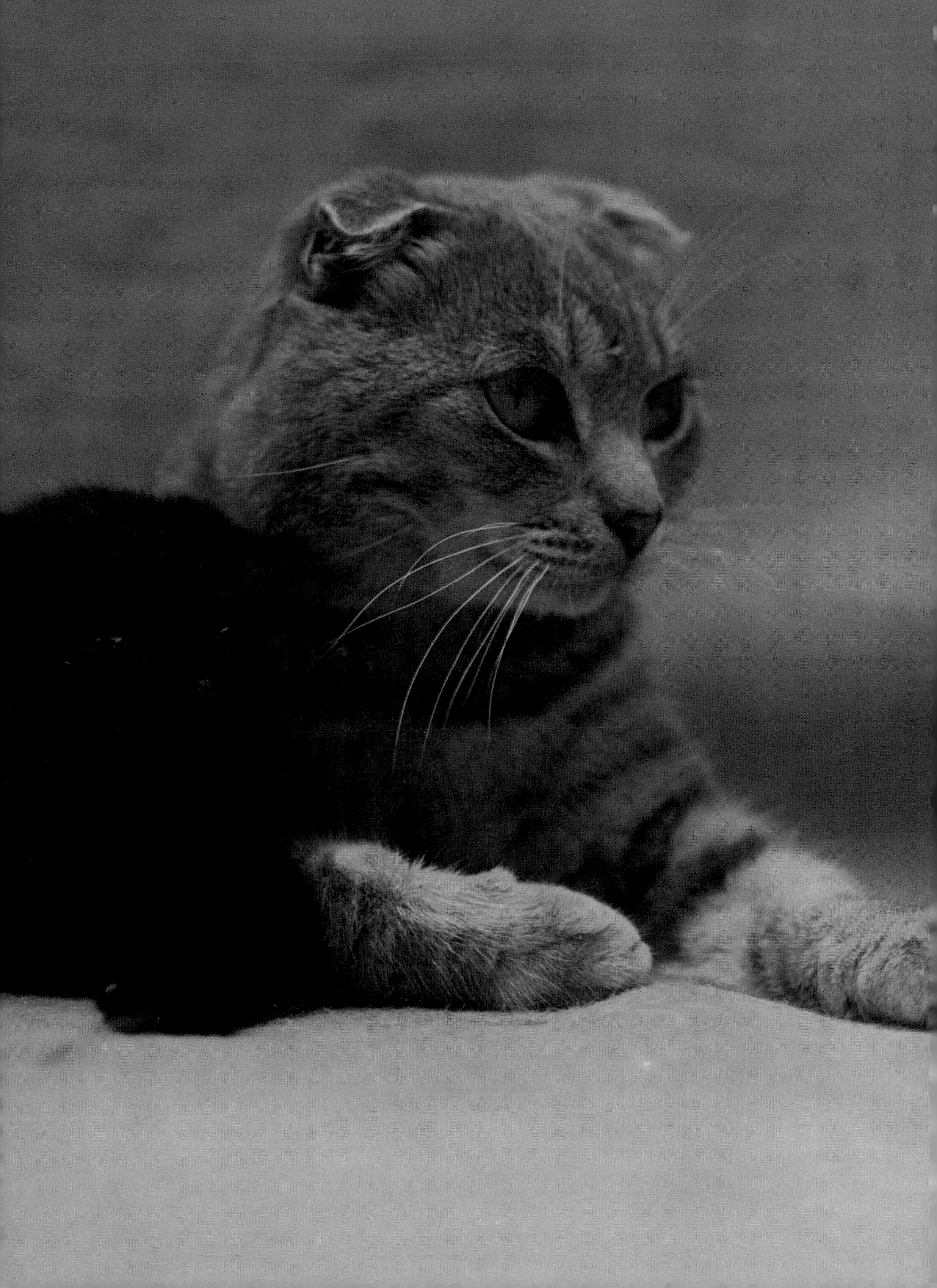

Left and above : Scottish Fold.

the daytime and where it bears its young.

The Sand Cat is about the size of a domestic cat with a very short muzzle and large, expressive eyes. Its ears are set far apart – almost at the sides of the head; they are wide at the base with a black patch on the back. The paws are heavily furred, which is probably a great help in the sandy areas where the animal lives.

Coat color varies from yellowish to grayish brown. The only markings are a few stripes on the legs and tail which also has a black tip.

Scottish Fold

Mutations of cats with dropped ears have undoubtedly appeared at intervals throughout history, but the Scottish Fold, first discovered on a farm in Perthshire, Scotland in 1961, represents the first attempt to preserve the mutation.

It is a very appealing cat that is growing in popularity, but is also meeting with some opposition; it is recognized as a breed but is not accepted for show competition.

The Scottish Fold has a round, short, muscular body with a short, thick coat. The head is large with large round eyes and the ears have a distinctive fold.

Scottish Wild Cat
See European Wild Cat

Seal Lynx Point
See Colorpoint Short-hair

Seal Point
See Colors and Patterns

Seal Tortie Point
See Colorpoint Short-hair

Serval
Felis serval

Servals range across Africa south of the Sahara inhabiting open savannahs and never straying far from a water supply.

They are nocturnal hunters that prey on mole rats and other rodents and small mammals, lizards, and birds. Since they are good climbers as well as strong swimmers, Servals have been known to capture nesting birds. Litters usually consist of three kittens; the female Serval population is much larger than the male.

A distinctive, strikingly beautiful cat, the average Serval is about twenty inches high and measures about three feet in length with a very short (nine- to ten-inch) tail. It is a light, slender animal that weighs less than twenty pounds. The legs are long and powerful; the head is comparatively small with large, slightly rounded ears that are set high and very close together.

The smooth, short coat is reddish yellow (although a black form has been reported), with underparts that are almost white. Markings are a mixture of spots and stripes. Black stripes run from the forehead, down the neck, and over the shoulders. There are large black spots on the back and flanks, becoming smaller on the lower sides and legs and very small on paws and cheeks. A row of spots runs up from the sides of the nose to the forehead. The tail is ringed and ends in a black tip. Ears are black on the outside with a distinct white spot in the middle.

A Serval spits at the cameraman.

Shaded Cameo
See Cameo; Colors and Patterns

Shaded Silver Long-hair

Still recognized as Shaded Silver Persian
in North America and other parts of the
world, this breed was dropped in Britain
in 1902 because of the difficulties involved
in differentiating between darker-than-
average Chinchillas and lighter-than-aver-
age Shaded Silvers. See also Colors and
Patterns.

Shaded Silver Persian
See Colors and Patterns; Shaded Silver
Long-hair

Shadow Point
See Colorpoint Short-hair (Lynx Point)

Shell Cameo
See Cameo; Colors and Patterns

Short-hair
See American Short-hair; British Short-
hair

Left: Shaded Silver Persian.

Siamese

The Siamese, most popular of all the breeds, almost certainly originated in Siam (Thailand). Legend has it that they were bred by the Kings of Siam and used as palace guards, pacing the walls and leaping on the backs of intruders. This story is speculative to say the least, but we do know that pictures of Seal Points were published in Siam some 400 years ago.

In 1885 the first Siamese cat was exhibited at Crystal Palace in London. It was one of a pair that had been presented to the then British Consul-General in Bangkok, Owen Gould. Siamese cats appeared in America around 1890 and were first exhibited in the early 1900s; the first Standard was published in Britain in 1892.

The original standard called for a stocky, round-headed cat that was often sickly, cross-eyed, and kinked-tailed – quite different from the sleek, elegant animal seen on today's show bench. The revised standard was issued in 1902 and was an immediate success.

Much of the Siamese's popularity lies in its personality. They are intelligent, playful, individualistic animals, prone to demanding a lot of attention and becoming very jealous if it is not forthcoming. They show much more open affection than other breeds and take easily to a lead. Most have a harsh, often imitative voice; the queen's call when she is in heat can be loud, penetrating, and very disturbing.

Siamese have large litters (often as many as five kittens). Kittens are born white, with the points developing as the fur grows. Both females and males mature at a very early age, and care must be taken if females are to be kept from mating before they are really ready for childbearing.

Siamese have been used in producing a surprising number of modern breeds including the Balinese, Bombay, Colorpoint Short-hair, Havana Brown, Himalayan, Lilac Foreign Short-hair, Manxamese, Oriental Short-hair, and Tonkinese.

Today's Siamese is a medium-sized cat with a long, slender, but muscular body and long slender legs. The body must be neither flabby nor bony; the tail is long, thin, and tapering; the paws oval and rather small.

The head should be a long, tapering wedge, medium-sized and in good proportion to the body. It narrows in straight lines to the muzzle and strong chin; there should be no whisker break. Allowances are made for jowls, however, in stud cats. The skull is flat; in profile there is a long

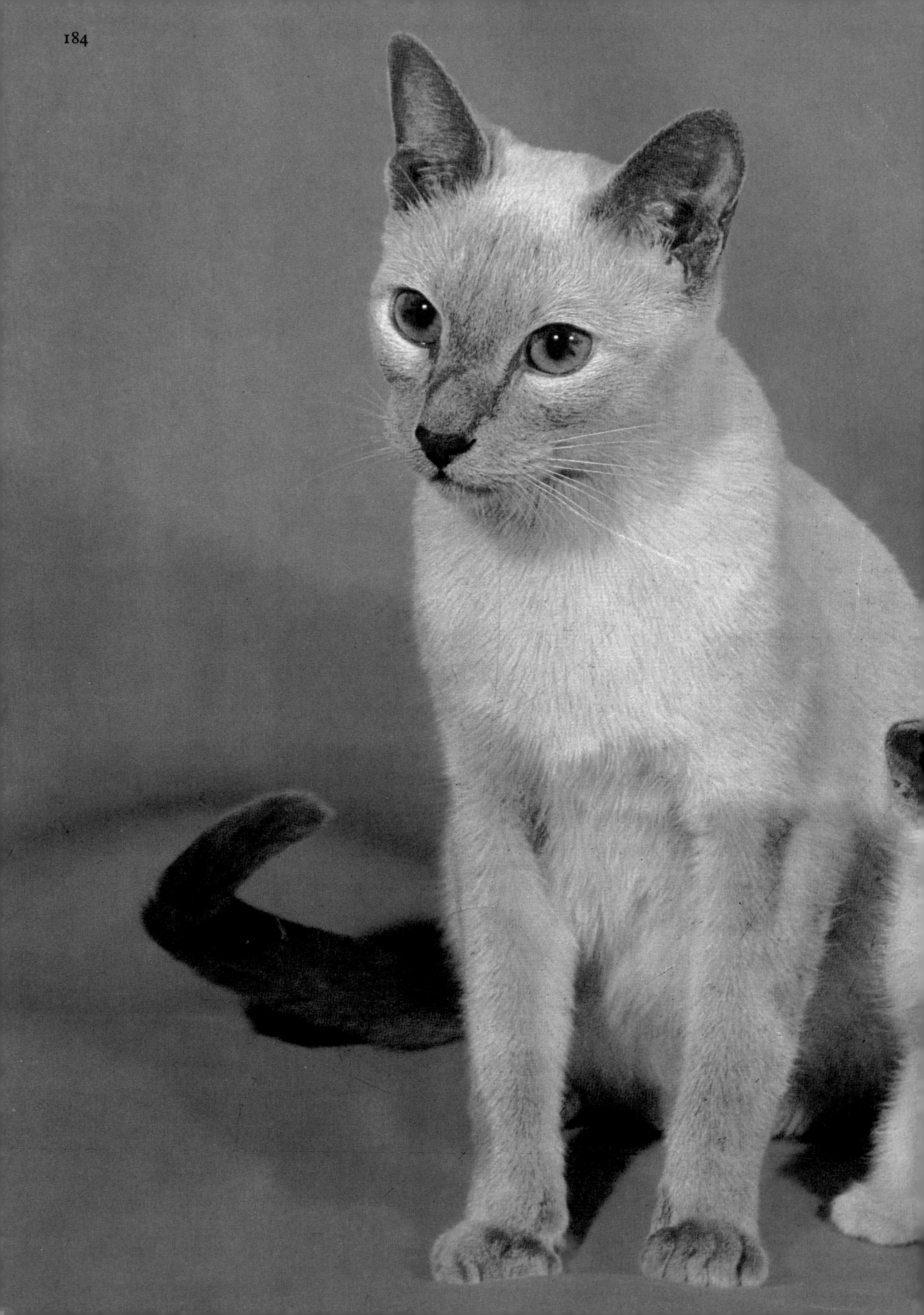

straight line from the top of the head to the top of the nose.

The ears continue the lines of the wedge. They are very large, wide at the base, pointed, and pricked. Eyes are medium sized and almond-shaped, slanting toward the nose in lines that correspond with the shape of the wedge. Show cats cannot have crossed eyes.

Other grounds for disqualification in show cats besides crossed eyes are: any evidence of ill-health; weak hind legs; mouth breathing due to nasal obstruction or a malformed jaw; emaciation; a visible tail kink (though a slight kink is acceptable in Britain), white toes and/or feet; and eyes that are any color but blue. Cats are penalized for having off-color or spotted paw pads or nose leather.

The coat is short, sleek, and close-lying. Siamese are recognized in the colorpoint pattern described in Colors and Patterns, but some notes of general interest about the various colors are appended below.

Blue Point Siamese

The Blue Point was the second variety of Siamese to gain recognition. There are early reports of its being seriously bred in England and America by the 1920s. The Blue Point is possibly more gentle than the other varieties, and loves to be hand-groomed. When grooming, take care not to brush too hard or too much; this will not only leave brush marks in the fur, but will also take out the undercoat.

Chocolate Point Siamese

The Chocolate Point is one of the earliest known varieties, but was only recognized in 1950. This was because the continual occurrence of blue in the points produced a much colder tone, leading people to believe that they were just Seal Points with poor coloration. The development of the colorpoints usually takes longer for Chocolate Point kittens than for other varieties, and the coat tends to grow far darker with age. Chocolate Point coats also react more to climatic conditions, making them difficult to breed and maintain in good condition.

Lilac (or Frost) Point Siamese

Lilac (or Frost) Points were first bred in America from parents who carried recessive genes for Blue and Chocolate. Coloration standards vary between Britain and America (see Colors and Patterns).

Preceding page : Seal Point Siamese.
Left : Lilac Point Siamese and her kitten.

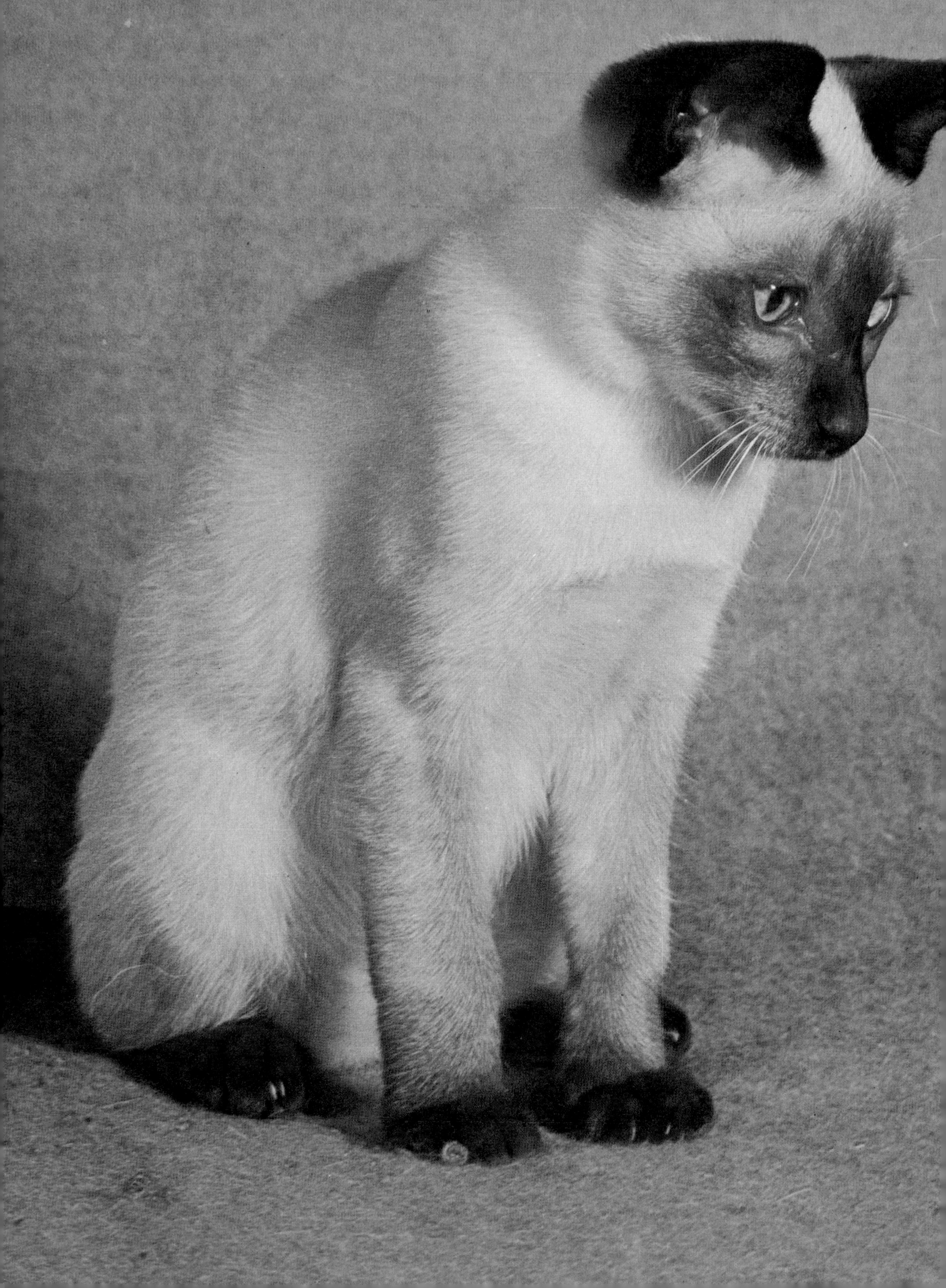

Seal Point Siamese

The Seal Point was the first Siamese variety to be recognized, and is still the most popular. The points begin to form on kittens as a smudge around the nose which becomes more definite as they grow; the line between mask and ears is not clearly defined until the cat is fully adult. The coat darkens with age on most cats and points are apt to develop brindling.

Siberian Tiger
See Tiger

Silver Mau
See Egyptian Mau

Silver Persian
See Chinchilla

Silver Point Siamese
See Colorpoint Short-hair

Silver Tabby
See Colors and Patterns; Tabby Persian; Tabby Short-hair

Left : A four-month old Seal Point Siamese kitten.
Below : Smoke Persian (or Long-hair).

Si-Rex
See Cornish Rex; Devon Rex; Rex

Si-Sawat
See Korat

Smoke Cameo
See Cameo; Colors and Patterns

Smoke Long-hair
See Smoke Persian

Smoke Mau
See Egyptian Mau

Smoke Persian

The Smoke Persian (in Britain, the Smoke Long-hair) is probably the result of uncontrolled matings between White, Black, and Blue Persians around the turn of the century.

The dense, silky coat requires frequent grooming to remove loose hairs and keep it looking its best; the coat should be brushed away from the body.

Most Smoke Persians today are produced by mating Smoke to Smoke, though the type is sometimes improved by outcrossing to a Black. Kittens are born black.

Conformation should be that of the Persian (see Persian); patterning is described in Colors and Patterns.

Blue Smoke Persians
These cats are recognized as a separate variety and result from mating Smoke and Blue Persians.

Smoke Short-hair

Black Smoke and Blue Smoke Short-hairs are recognized in the United States, but not in Britain; several European countries have provisional standards. The fur is short and white with black or blue tipping (see also Colors and Patterns). Conformation should be that of the American Short-hair.

Snow Leopard
Panthera uncia

The Snow Leopard, also known as the Ounce, is one of the five big roaring cats (the others are the Jaguar, Leopard, Lion, and Tiger). It is extremely rare – there are probably only about 400 left – as its beautiful thick coat makes it a prime target for hunters. Both the United States and United Kingdom have banned the import of skins, but the remedy may have come too late.

Snow Leopards range through mountainous regions of southern Russia, Afghanistan, Tibet, Mongolia, and western China. They generally spend the summer in the rocky grasslands between the tree line and the snow line (12,000–18,000 feet) moving down into the upper valleys for the winter. Prey consists of sheep, deer, wild goats, smaller mammals, and birds, depending on the habitat.

Cubs are born in the spring in litters of two to four and remain with their mother until the following spring.

The Snow Leopard is similar in size and weight to the Leopard: about two feet high at the shoulders, averaging 4.5 feet long with another three feet of tail, and weighing from 100 to 200 pounds. It has a long, luxuriant, pale gray coat, with yellowish shading and white underparts. There are black rosettes which are like the Leopard's but bigger; as on the Leopard they shrink to spots on the legs and head. The small ears are outlined in black with a small white spot in the middle. The long, bushy tail is also marked with rosettes which turn into rings near the tip which is black.

Solid Red

The Solid Red, also known as the Red Self or Red Persian, is rare because reproducing the coat color is very difficult; it is often more orange than deep red. Eliminating tabby markings, especially on the face, is also a major problem.

Somali

Somalis are long-haired Abyssinians that are rapidly becoming popular in America. They are slightly larger than short-haired Abyssinians and can be either red or ruddy. The coat is dense and requires comparatively little grooming; there should be a full ruff, with shorter hair on the shoulders. Somalis are quiet, affectionate cats with alert dispositions.

Above : Smoke Persian.
Right : An exceptionally rare photograph of an exceptionally rare animal – the Snow Leopard or Ounce is bordering on extinction as its beautiful coat has made it a prime target for the hunter's gun. The most optimistic estimates put its numbers at 500.

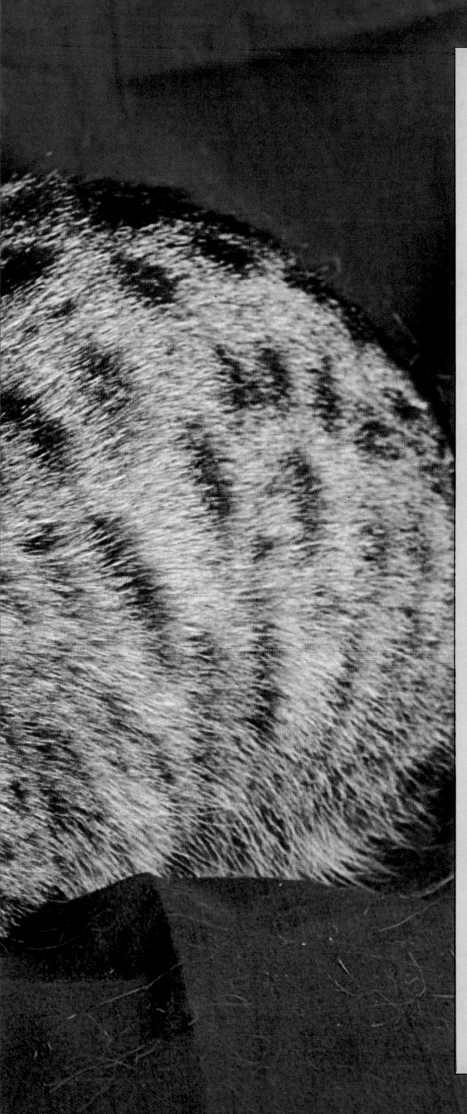

Sphynx

The Sphynx, also known as the Canadian Hairless, *Chat Sans Poils* (cat without hair) and Moon Cat, closely resembles the now-extinct Mexican Hairless.

This mutation was first recorded in 1966, born to a domestic Black and White in Ontario, Canada. The breed was developed from this specimen.

The Sphynx looks something like a sad, wrinkled Pug dog, and is very warm and smooth to the touch. Although they have been produced in the United States and Britain as well as in Canada, there does not appear to be much interest in the breed. It has been recognized by a few associations, but is not generally accepted for show competition.

The body of the Sphynx is slender, with good muscles and a longish tail. The head is a rounded wedge shape with a short nose; ears are very wide at the base and slightly rounded at the tip; the eyes are golden and slightly slanted. The cat has no whiskers.

It may be any color, but solid colors must be even and parti-colors symmetrical. The face, ears, paws, and feet are covered with a fine short down, and there are hairs on the last inch of the tail.

Spotted Cat

Spotted Cats are a British short-haired breed. They are believed by some to have been the original domestic cat in that country, and appeared in the earliest cat shows. The breed died out, however, and it was not until 1960 that serious efforts (involving Silver Tabbies and Black Short-hairs) were made to recreate it. 'Spotties' were given their own standard in 1966.

The body of a show Spotted Cat should be of medium length, powerfully built, and thick set, with a full chest, and short, strong legs. The tail is rather short, and thick at the base, tapering slightly at the tip.

The head should be broad with well-developed cheeks, small slightly rounded ears, and large round eyes that compliment the coat color.

The coat is short and fine. The markings must be distinct spots that contrast well with the ground color; they may be round or oblong, but bars or even broken stripes are considered faults. The spots should cover the entire body. Tabby markings on the face and head are acceptable.

Spotted Cats can be any color in Spec-

Left: Silver Spotted Cat.

trum A (see Colors and Patterns) as long as there is good contrast between ground color and markings. Brown, Red, and Silver are the most popular colors.

Spotted Cat, Little
See Tiger Cat

Stumpy
See Manx

Sumatran Tiger
See Tiger

Supilak

The Supilak, or Copper, is a copper-colored cat from Thailand. It has been recognized as a breed in America, but is not eligible for show competition.

Swamp Cat
See Jungle Cat

Swimming Cat
See Turkish Van Cat

Right: Brown Tabby Short-hair (Classic Pattern). Below: Brown Tabby Persian (Long-hair) kitten. Note the copper eyes and classic markings. Overleaf: An adult Brown Tabby Short-hair on show.

Swiss Mountain Cat
See European Wild Cat

Tabby

The term 'Tabby' is usually applied to any cat with stripes and bars, although the standard for show cats is quite specific about the desired patterning (see Colors and Patterns). It has been claimed that if all the domestic cats in the world were to interbreed, eventually all cats would be tabbies. The 'M' on the forehead is said to be the mark of Mohammed.

The standard for markings applies to both Tabby Persians and Tabby Short-hairs. The two patterns, Classic and Mackerel, are classed together in Britain and separately in the United States. Conformation should be that of either the Persian or the appropriate short-hair (see Persian; American Short-hair; British Short-hair). The most common Tabby varieties are Brown, Red, and Silver; in America, Tabbies are also recognized in Blue, Cameo and Cream.

Brown Tabby Persian
Once very popular, Brown Tabby Persians have become difficult to breed and today few are shown. If like-to-like mating is impossible, the best results will be achieved by mating a Brown Tabby with a Black or a dark Blue and then back to a Brown Tabby. Silver Tabbies lighten the ground color and discolor the eyes; Red Tabbies tend to weaken the conformation. Brindling is becoming a common fault in Brown Tabby Persians.

Red Tabby Persian
Some people believe that this is a male only cat; however, Red to Red mating will produce both sexes.

Silver Tabby Persian
This breed is no longer popular since it is extremely difficult to perfect. Often the markings are smudged and unclear, and brown or bronze tinges tend to creep into the coloring. There is also a problem in finding a mate that will improve the conformation without damaging the markings. Kittens are born nearly all black, and the silver appears after about four months. Kittens *born* with tabby markings often prove to be badly patterned adults.

Blue Tabby Persian
This breed was officially recognized in America in 1962 and first appeared in Brown Tabby litters.

192

Brown Tabby Short-hair

One of the oldest known breeds, this cat's appearance as a pedigreed cat is relatively rare. It is rather difficult to find the right stud; like-to-like matings are likely to lead to deterioration of conformation.

Red Tabby Short-hair

These cats are often marmalade, ginger, or sandy cats. Red Tabby males are often mated with Tortoiseshells or Calicos (both virtually all-female varieties), though it sometimes is difficult to eliminate the tabby markings once they have been introduced.

Silver Tabby Short-hair

The Silver Tabby Short-hair is the most popular of the Tabby Short-hairs. Kittens are born with clear markings that fade and then re-establish themselves at about three months. Silver Tabby conformation is usually better than that of the other types, and Blacks are often introduced to maintain the standard.

Tabby Colorpoint Short-hair

See Colorpoint Short-hair (Lynx Point)

Tabby Point

See Colorpoint Short-hair

Temminck's Golden Cat
Felis temmincki

Temminck's Golden Cat is widely distributed throughout north India, Tibet, southwest China, and Southeast Asia. It is believed to exist in three varieties which seems reasonable considering the large area it covers.

It prefers lightly forested areas and is known to be a good climber, but little else is known of its habits; its prey is believed to include mammals up to the size of small deer and some have been shot while attempting to kill domestic stock. It is said to be easily tamed as a kitten and there are some reports of it being trained to obey and do tricks, like a dog.

An adult Temminck's Golden Cat is about 4.5 feet long (including a 1.5-foot tail) with a thick build, powerful legs, and large feet. The tail is not tapered.

The thick, soft coat is usually a deep golden red that lightens slightly on the neck, chest, and underparts. (Color can vary from location to location, however.) There are distinctive black streaks mingled with white on the face and head.

Tiger
Panthera tigris

The Tiger originated in Siberia, but with the coming of the Ice Age it was forced to move southward, adapting itself to new habitats. At its peak it could be found in a vast area from the Caspian Sea to the Manchurian coast, throughout China, India, and Southeast Asia.

Today, however, its range and numbers have been greatly reduced and the entire species is in grave danger of extinction: there were some 30,000 tigers in 1939, while today there are less than 2000.

There are several reasons for this destruction. The many wars in Asia over the last thirty years wrecked havoc on both the tigers and their habitat – especially in Vietnam, where defoliating chemicals decimated the tigers along with their habitat and food supply. The encroachment of civilization with its land reclamation projects, hydro-electric plants, and so on, has taken its toll. And exploitation for their skins, despite efforts by several governments to curb it, continues to be a major threat.

Bengal or Indian Tiger.

There are eight species of Tiger:

Bali Tiger
Panthera tigris balica
This, the smallest and darkest of Tigers, is now extinct.

Bengal Tiger or *Indian Tiger*
Pt tigris
Although the most numerous species today, the Bengal Tiger is still in need of protection.

Caspian Tiger or *Persian Tiger*
Pt virgata
Very rare and verging on extinction.

Chinese Tiger
Pt amoyensis
The Chinese Tiger is in all likelihood extinct.

Indo-Chinese Tiger or *Manchurian Tiger*
Pt corbetti
This Tiger is the largest and most powerful species but its numbers are decreasing rapidly.

Javan Tiger
Pt sondiaca
This small Tiger with a dark coat is bordering on total extinction.

Siberian Tiger
Pt altaica
The Siberian Tiger is paler than the others, with a long, thick, shaggy coat.

Sumatran Tiger
Pt sumatrae
The Sumatran Tiger is also very rare.

It is sometimes possible to distinguish between these species, though individual Tigers vary so much in size and markings that it is often very difficult. In general,

northern Tigers are bigger and paler than their southern cousins.

Tigers prefer thick cover and dislike excessive heat; during the hottest part of the day they will retire to a cove or a shallow pool. Their hearing is exceptional but their sight is poor, and if a victim is camouflaged and stays very still it will often go undetected. Their diet is varied and is dictated largely by the region; it can include monkeys, deer, domestic stock, and other animals. Tigers have even been known to attack elephants.

They are very solitary animals; males and females only come together for short periods during the mating season. During this time, however, the male will be extremely possessive and will not allow another male near. The female usually has her first litter at about three years of age, and every three years after that. Usual litters are from two to four cubs, who are born complete with markings and weighing two to four pounds. They are born blind and helpless, and remain with their mother until they are about two years old.

The largest tigers can be twelve feet long from head to tail and weigh about 500 pounds; the smallest are about half that size. Tigresses are usually much smaller than the males.

Color varies from buff or pale fawn to rich brown, with dark brown stripes. The number and width of these stripes varies considerably among individuals, not regions. They run vertically on the body, from the center of the back down the sides, and horizontally on the legs. There are more stripes on the rump than on the shoulders. The tail is ringed and ends in a dark brown tip. There are no markings on the nose, but the rest of the head is evenly striped.

A dilute form called the White Tiger has occasionally appeared in India; it is almost white with light brown stripes, blue eyes, and a pink nose.

Tiger Cat
Felis tigrina

The Tiger Cat, also known as the Little Spotted Cat, is another endangered species, in part because it is extensively hunted for its skin.

It inhabits forests and woodlands from Costa Rica in Central America to northern South America. It is an excellent climber, and hunts birds and small mammals.

Tiger Cats do not make good pets – in fact, several people have died trying to tame them. They are quite fierce as kittens and become even more vicious as they grow older.

The Tiger Cat is easily confused with the Margay, though the average size is a bit smaller – perhaps three feet including tail. Markings on the Tiger Cat, moreover, are not as distinct as those on the Ocelot and Margay. A row of dark spots runs down the back, enlarging and forming rosettes on the flanks and sides. The center of the rosettes is darker than the ground color, which is fawn with a grayish tinge. The rosettes become spots again on the legs, gradually becoming smaller until they fade out entirely on the paws. The tail is ringed with large dark blotches. There are dark streaks and white bars on the cheeks and around the eyes, and the whisker pads are spotted.

Tonkinese

The Tonkinese was produced in the United States by crossing a Siamese and a Burmese. It is now being bred on both sides of the Atlantic, in Australia and New Zealand, but has not been recognized.

Tortie

The word 'Tortie' is a commonly used abbreviation for Tortoiseshell.

Tortie Point
See Colorpoint Short-hair; Himalayan

Tortoiseshell and White Long-hair and Short-hair
See Calico

Tortoiseshell Burmese
See Burmese

Tortoiseshell Cameo
See Cameo

Below: Tiger Cat.
Left: Tortoiseshell and White Short-hair.

Tortoiseshell Persian

The coat of this striking cat should be long and patterned with distinct patches of deep rich black, red, and cream. Black should not be predominant. (See also Colors and Patterns.)

Tri-colored cats are one of the oldest known varieties, but they were usually products of random matings. However, cats with tabby markings, stray white hairs, and blurred, indistinct patches, are usually unacceptable as show cats.

The Tortoiseshell Persian is very difficult to reproduce to the high standard required of show cats. It is virtually an all female breed (the few males born are al-

Right :
Tortoiseshell
Persian (or Long-hair).
Below :
Tortoiseshell Short-hair.

ways sterile), so like-to-like breeding is impossible. Instead, breeders must use a Black or Cream male and a Tortie female, with completely unpredictable results.

Conformation should be that of the Persian.

Tortoiseshell Short-hair

Tortoiseshell Short-hairs should conform to the short-hair standard (see American Short-hair or British Short-hair), with the markings described in Colors and Patterns. Breeding these attractive, playful cats is subject to the same difficulties and uncertainties described for the Tortoiseshell Persian.

Turkish Angora
See Angora

Turkish Van Cat

The Turkish Van Cat comes from the Lake Van area of Turkey where it has been kept as a domestic pet for centuries. It is also known as the Van Cat or Swimming Cat. This cat loves nothing more than a swim or a bath in warm (about body temperature) water although care must be taken to see that the animal is thoroughly dried after its dip to prevent colds.

Litters usually consist of only two kittens which are, more often than not, males. Kittens are born with markings that are usually more pronounced than in adults.

A few of these attractive and affectionate pets have been imported to England, where they were recognized in 1969, but they are still comparatively rare outside Turkey.

The conformation of the Turkish Van Cat is similar to the Angora. It should have a long, sturdy body on medium-length legs; a thick, muscular neck and shoulders; a blunt, medium-length tail; round paws with tufted toes; and a small wedge-shaped head. The ears are large and rounded and are set upright, quite close together. The eyes are round and the nose rather long.

The coat consists of a wooly undercoat and long, silky hairs. The color should be chalk white without any yellowish traces. There are auburn splotches on the head and auburn rings on the tail. The background color on the tail is a lighter shade of auburn. Ears are white with a slight pinkish tinge on the inside. Nose leather and paw pads are shell pink.

Van Cat
See Turkish Van Cat

White Persian

This beautiful and popular variety owes much of its development to the Angora. Thus, its conformation differs a bit from the Persian standards (see Persian): its body is slightly longer, the face not quite so round, the ears slightly larger and the nose longer.

The long, silky coat should be pure white; any yellow staining is a fault.

Whites are usually bred by mating Whites with Blacks, Blues, or Creams. Like-to-like mating is difficult and must be carefully planned.

Although they are a fastidious variety they do require frequent grooming. Grease will stain the fur, and a warm bath a few days before a show will vastly improve their appearance. There are three recognized types of White Persian, based solely on eye color.

Blue-Eyed White
This type of White Persian was the first

Left : Turkish Van Cat.
Above : White Blue-eyed Persian kitten.

to be bred. Unfortunately they are almost always deaf. Until recently, this type was rapidly declining in numbers, but breeders are now making a determined effort to re-establish it by introducing Blue Persians and the other two White varieties into their breeding programs. Cats born with a small dark smudge on the underparts usually have good hearing, and there is also the possibility that the smudge will fade as they mature making them suitable for showing. The blue eye color is difficult to reproduce; green eyes are a fault.

Odd-Eyed White
This breed appears in litters of both Blue-Eyed and Orange-Eyed Whites. They were recognized in Britain in 1968. They are not deaf, though many claim that they are hard of hearing on the side that has the blue eye. Conformation is generally better than in Blue-Eyed Whites.

Orange-Eyed White
This breed resulted from a chance mating between a Blue-Eyed White and another

Persian with orange eyes. They were
recognized during the 1930s. Their breeding is much more predictable than for the
Blue-Eyed; they usually have a better
conformation; they are not deaf.

White Short-hair

Conformation should be that of the short-
hair standard (see American Short-hair;
British Short-hair). The coat should be
fine and soft, pure white with no trace of
colored hairs and no tinge of yellow. Like
the White Persian, the White Short-hair
is recognized in three varieties based on
eye color.

Blue-Eyed White
This popular, but rather rare cat is hard
to breed with outstanding conformation.
Most Blue-Eyed Whites are deaf; those
with a dark smudge on their heads between the ears usually have good hearing.

Odd-Eyed White
This breed with one blue eye and one
orange, is not deaf, and plays a useful role
in breeding both other varieties. They can
be found in both Blue-Eyed and Orange-
Eyed litters.

Orange-Eyed White
Like the other White Short-hairs, Orange-
Eyed Whites are born with blue eyes which
then, however, turn slowly to orange as the
cat matures. The orange deepens with age
and often turns to a coppery color in adult-
hood. This variety has good hearing.

White Tiger
See Tiger

Wild Cat, African
See African Wild Cat

Wild Cat, European
See European Wild Cat

Wild Cat, Scottish
See European Wild Cat

Zibeline
See Burmese

*Right : Lynx with her kitten. The kitten
was partially tamed by the photographer
before this picture was taken.*

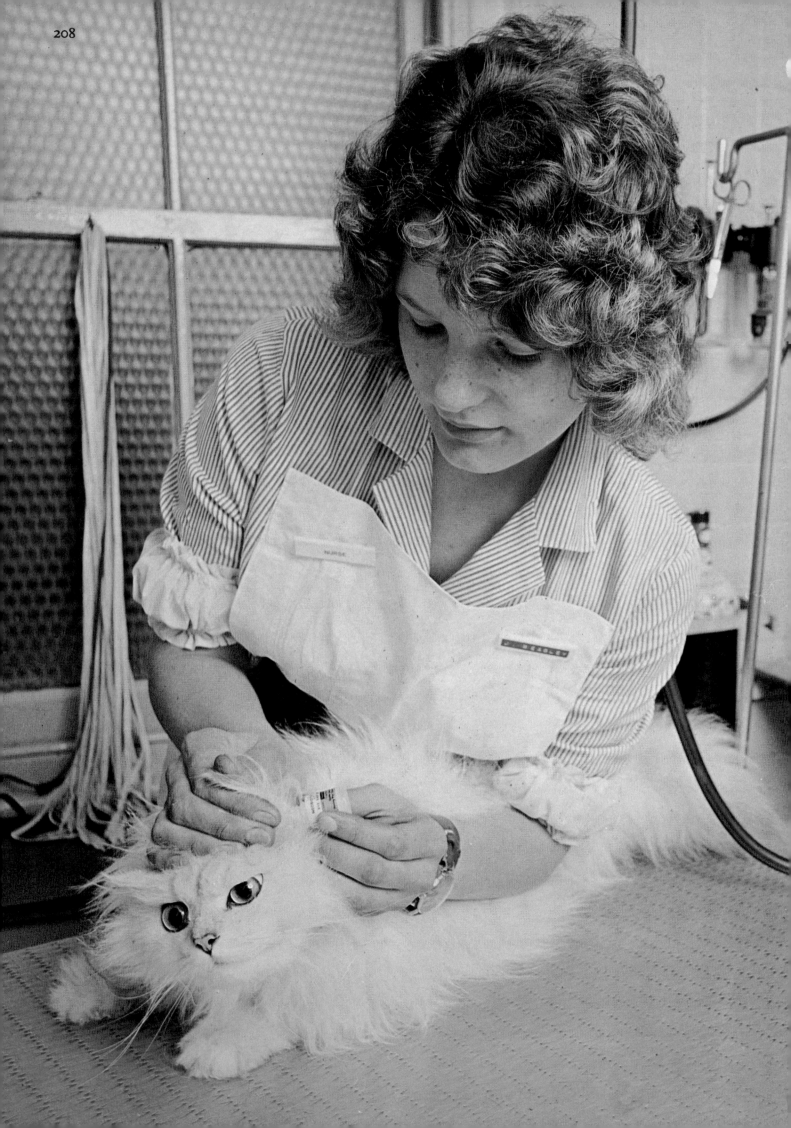

Cat Care

Choosing Your Cat

There are as many reasons for getting a cat as there are people. Some want a companion, others a mouser. Some are concerned with teaching their children about the facts of life and giving them responsibility. For others, cats are a fascinating (and sometimes expensive) hobby.

One of the first decisions that must be made after you have decided to acquire a cat is whether you want a pedigree animal or an ordinary one (if there is any such thing as an 'ordinary' cat!).

If you are shopping for a pedigree cat, you can obtain lists of breeders by contacting your local cat club, checking various cat magazines, or by attending a cat show. Do not be afraid to shop around; prices of both purebred pets and show animals vary widely. If you are not familiar with a breed it is a good idea to go to several shows and/or get expert advice before committing yourself to a large expenditure.

If you are not concerned about your cat's family tree, the list of sources is almost inexhaustible. Friends, the newspapers, open-air markets, and even the street itself are all places to find free cats. Humane societies have more cats than they can handle, and you can adopt one for a minimum fee that covers vaccinations, etc. Pet stores often have kittens for sale.

Check your potential pet carefully. The cat's eyes should be clear and no white should show at the corners. The nostrils should be clear too – mucus is a sure sign of health problems. Ears should be clean, the fur should contain no fleas or flea eggs, and the skin should be free of sores and scabs.

Pet stores and breeders should provide a written list of any shots that have already been given, and most reputable establishments will also give you a health guarantee.

No matter how you obtain your cat, it should be taken to a veterinarian within the first two or three days so that any problems it may have can be spotted early, and it can receive any necessary vaccinations and inoculations.

The sex of the new pet is also worth thinking about ahead of time, even if you have no strong prejudices one way or the other. (To distinguish the sex of a cat refer to page 35.)

Unaltered male cats have an uncontrollable urge to roam in search of females, to fight for them if they find them, and to spray the house if they do not. Your knowledge of first aid will be severely tested if you have an unaltered male, and the smell of his urine, attractive though it might be to his lady friends, will certainly be repellant to you. Castrating or neutering your tom will remove his wanderlust and stop the spraying, but will probably not keep him from fighting.

In addition to the problem of disposing of unwanted litters, unspayed females can be a nuisance when they are in heat, as can their beaux.

It is difficult to put the case in favor of spaying or neutering too strongly. Hundreds of thousands of unwanted kittens are born each year, and to add to their number is simply madness.

Spaying should be done at as early an age as possible, preferably before the cat first comes into heat. Toms are usually neutered between the ages of six and eight months.

Preceding Page: A vet administers eardrops.
It is possible to choose from many cat types: British Blue (above), a Chinchilla (below) and a Rex (bottom) are but a few.

Daily Care of the Healthy Cat

Grooming

Although cats keep themselves reasonably clean, they sometimes need help – especially long-haired cats.

Bathing

There are times when cats get so dirty that a bath is the only solution. Whether it turns out to be a relatively painless experience for everyone or a battle royal depends on how well things are organized in advance.

The best place to bathe a cat is in a laundry tub or in the kitchen or bathroom sink. The bathtub is too low and too large to be convenient for you or comfortable for the cat. Place a rough towel or a rubber mat on the bottom of the sink to give the cat a foothold. Also needed are a large towel for drying the cat, shampoo (human baby shampoo is as good as the special cat shampoos), and vaseline.

Next, banish the children. Bathing is an unpleasant experience for the average cat under the best of circumstances, and a large noisy audience will not improve matters.

Fill the sink with warm water (80–90°F) to a depth of three to four inches. Smear vaseline around the cat's eyes for protection and stand it in the sink, holding it by the back of the neck. Hold it there for a few minutes, talking reassuringly. Then, working slowly and gently, pour water over it, followed by the shampoo. After a few minutes to allow the shampoo to loosen the dirt and grease, rinse the cat thoroughly. One soaping and rinsing is usually sufficient.

It is important to dry the cat well; use a rough towel vigorously and make sure the hair next to the skin is dry. Wipe the vaseline from the eyes and brush and comb out any loose hair. The cat should be kept indoors for five to six hours after a bath. For this reason it is probably best to bathe it at night and keep it indoors till morning. Kittens should only be bathed when absolutely necessary.

Brushing and Combing

Regular brushing and combing, on the order of two or three times a week, will vastly improve a cat's appearance and make it feel better as well.

A cat will enjoy the brushing session if it has grown accustomed to them as a kitten. Older cats may put up a struggle.

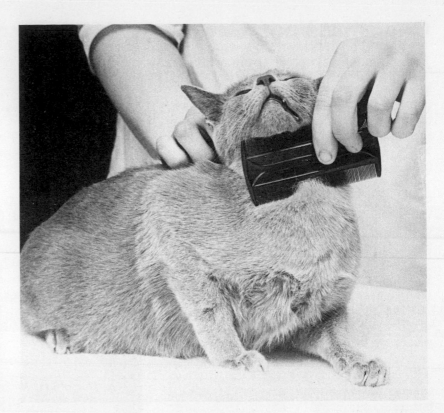

It is not necessary to spend a lot of money on grooming equipment for most cats; small combs and stiff brushes or grooming mits are available at pet stores at reasonable prices. Tweezers and blunt-edged scissors are also useful for dealing with mats and snarls.

Starting at the head, brush in one direction. Work quietly and gently, remembering that too heavy a hand will only irritate the cat and make it less willing to be brushed next time.

Claws

Provided that a cat receives the proper amount of exercise and is provided with a scratching post, its nails should not require trimming whether the cat is an outdoor cat or an indoor cat.

Should a cat's nails become too long for some reason, it is advisable to take it to a veterinarian to have its claws clipped. However, if this is impractical then special clippers are available from pet stores – scissors should be avoided except in an emergency.

To clip a cat's claws place your thumb just above the cat's toe and your index finger on the pad beneath. When finger and thumb are pressed together the claw will extend; clip it just where it begins to curve. *Never* clip the pink area of the claw; it is better to clip too little than too much. If you do happen to clip into the quick and the claw starts to bleed, use an antiseptic powder or spray, apply a compress or clean handkerchief, and hold the paw up for a few minutes until the bleeding stops.

Above: Almost every cat loves to be pampered and grooming with a wide-toothed comb is one of the best ways to do it.

A scratching post is a must, and it is probably better to try a homemade one first. A four-foot post with rough bark (or covered with carpet) on a heavy wooden base will do. It should be placed in a corner where the cat can get at it easily. A toy mouse on a spring attached to the top will give the cat more exercise.

Declawing is the subject of a major controversy; veterinarians and cat owners alike disagree about the relative advantages and disadvantages of the procedure. It is not our intention here to make a stand one way or the other. Plenty of literature is available in cat magazines and from veterinarians, and each cat owner must make the ultimate decision about what is best for his or her pet.

Eyes

Cats' eyes usually do not require much care beyond an occasional trim if the hair around the eyes is getting into them. This should be done very carefully if not by a veterinarian.

Ears

Cats' ears should be examined regularly. Wax can accumulate in the ears but it is fairly easy to remove with a cotton swab after softening with warm mineral oil. Go gently and carefully, since a cat's ears are very sensitive. Ear mites and other ear ailments should be referred to a veterinarian.

Teeth and Gums

While it is not necessary to brush a cat's teeth regularly, brushing does help reduce the build-up of tartar. Massaging the gums with salt water will slow down the growth of bacteria and also help stop bad breath. If a lot of tartar has built up, it is best to let a veterinarian remove it.

Hazards

There is a certain amount of danger associated with the very act of living and functioning in the outside world. For cats, as for small children, however, many potential hazards can be eliminated or their likelihood decreased by simply giving some thought in advance to their environment.

Heights

Cats can, and often do, fall from high places – and their famed ability to land on their feet cannot always save them from serious injury. It should be a standard household rule not to play with the cat near an un-

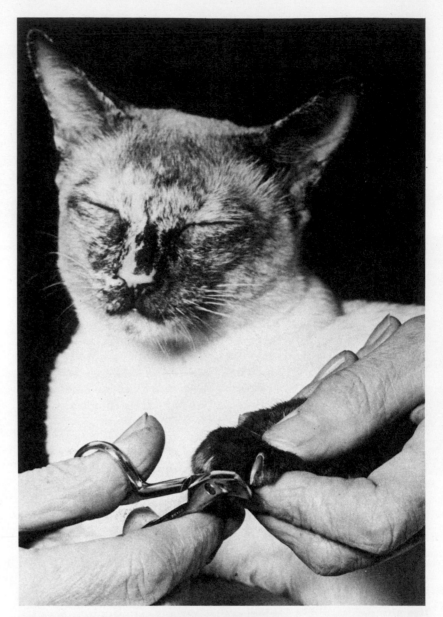

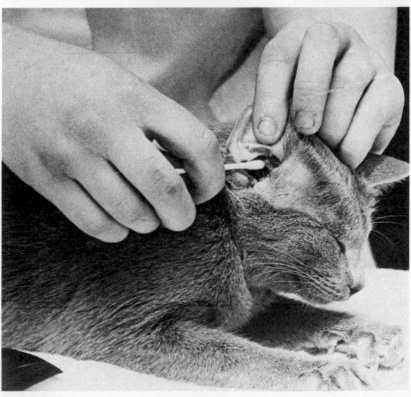

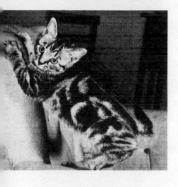

Top left and left: A veterinarian clips the claws of a cat and cleans its ears. These jobs are best performed by a vet and should only be undertaken oneself if no other course of action is available. Above: Behavior – the top photo shows how easy it is for a cat to climb out between window slats, a situation which could be very dangerous. The other two pictures show cats sharpening their claws (a) on the preferable tree trunk and (b) on the living room furniture.

protected window or on roofs, fire escapes, or balconies. Screens on all windows are a good idea; they are good safety devices for children and everyone else in the family, as well as making the windowsill a safe place from which the cat can watch the world go by.

Cats 'stuck' in trees generally manage to get down by themselves sooner or later – sooner if they are left alone to figure out how to do it themselves. People making a scene under the tree usually only convince the cat that it is better off staying put. On those rare occasions when the cat really needs help, the fire department or humane society is probably better qualified to give it than you are.

Electricity
Electrical wires and telephone cords can be irresistible – and very dangerous – playthings. Lamp cords should be run along the walls or under rugs whenever possible. Powdered alum or bitter aloes can be used to coat electrical cords if a cat persists in chewing on them.

Collars
It is possible to find a safe collar, but it sometimes takes some looking. Fit is all-important: if the collar is too loose it can catch on bushes or fences; if too tight it can choke the cat. Flea collars are sometimes useful.

Enclosed Places
The list of places that cats can be shut into when one is not paying attention is virtually endless – drawers, cupboards, closets, refrigerators, trunks, and boxes are only a few. If your cat is missing, start by checking the refrigerator (as the most dangerous spot), and continue around the house from there.

Poisons
All household cleaning agents, paints, insecticides, and of course all drugs and medicines should be kept up high behind closed doors for the safety of both cats and children. (See First Aid – Poisoning, page 233.)

People
Cats who are allowed outdoors always run some risk of meeting one of those unfortunate people who enjoy hurting small animals and there is nothing much anyone can do to prevent it. But cats also run some risk from people in their own home – usually when their owner is carrying something large and heavy and inadvertently trips over them. The best way to avoid this

is to make sure the animal is in another part of the house, or outside, when there is carrying to be done – and to feed it first, since hungry cats are much more likely to be under foot.

Children can often be hazards – usually through ignorance, but occasionally when they vent aggressions on the family pet that they cannot safely take out on their parents or siblings. Children should be taught respect for animals firmly and at an early age – for their own sake as well as for the animal's.

Feeding
See also Nutrition.

Most adult domestic cats prefer to eat once or twice a day, like their larger cousins. But unlike wild cats who must take their meals as they find them house pets soon become creatures of habit and prefer to be fed at the same time in the same place.

The cat's food dish should be placed somewhere out of the way, where the animal can eat in peace without being tripped over or harassed by small children. Cats like to drag their food out of the bowl, so put newspaper or a rubber mat under the feeding dish if you care about your floors.

Cool, clean water should be available at all times.

Food should be served at room temperature. Cats like to take their time over their meal; leave the food for about an hour, then remove whatever has not been eaten.

If a cat misses more than two or three meals in a row it is either (1) being fed somewhere else; (2) hunting; or (3) sick. If you can eliminate (1) and (2) as possibilities, take the cat to a veterinarian.

Here is a sample test for obesity: you should be able to feel your cat's ribs, but not see them. If you can see the ribs, the animal is too thin; if you cannot even feel them, it is too fat.

Nutrition
See also Feeding.

Although not much is known about the cat's exact nutritional requirements, it is obvious that a well-balanced diet is essential to its health. This is especially important for the house cat, who is completely dependent on its owner for food.

Cats are complete carnivores; as such they need large quantities of fat and protein (much more, proportionally, than dogs) and few carbohydrates.

Commercial Pet Food

Pet owners have raised healthy cats without prepared food for thousands of years, but it cannot be denied that commercial pet foods make the average cat-owner's life much easier. They are also safer than hunting, since mice and other prey could contain tapeworm or other parasites.

It is well worth paying a few extra pennies for good-quality cat food, if only to ensure that your pet is not eating a mixture that is mostly cereal (or in some cases, sawdust). Most countries require that cat foods labeled 'complete' or 'balanced' be able to support a normal adult animal as its sole source of nourishment.

Variety, however, is no problem with the profusion of pet foods on supermarket shelves today, and it is desirable for several reasons.

From a nutritional point of view, cats cannot get all the nutrients they need from one food source – even fish. Also, while dry cat chows contain more ash than moist canned foods (ash is believed by some to contribute to cystitis in cats), they help reduce the accumulation of tartar on the cat's teeth. A large portion of dry food can be left out, too, without fear of its spoiling if you have to be away from home for any length of time.

Another very important reason for variety is that cats' eating habits are established very early in life. If the cat becomes accustomed to many different types and textures in its food it will be much easier for it to accept special diets which may become necessary when the animal is older or ill.

A normally active adult cat should thrive on one-half to one can of moist food a day, chow (and water) to snack on, table scraps, grass, and whatever else can be found during a day of wandering.

Fresh Food

If you prefer to prepare your cat's food yourself, a few logical rules should suffice.

Meat can be eaten raw (except pork); avoid spicy or cured meats like ham and salami, and be sure to provide a good balance between beef, lamb, horse, and chicken. Fish should be cooked and the bones ground if possible. Vegetables should always be cooked as well. Many cats cannot digest egg whites easily, but hardboiled egg yolks are good occasional diet supplements. Skim milk is better for cats than whole.

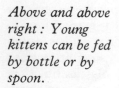

Above and above right : Young kittens can be fed by bottle or by spoon.

Essential Nutrients

Cats' nutritional needs are not too different from humans'; a balanced diet for a cat contains the proper amount of all five major groups of nutrients (proteins, fats, carbohydrates, vitamins, and minerals).

Proteins are composed of various combinations of about twenty different amino acids, and are needed for body building and repair. An adult cat needs almost twice as much protein as a dog does; Dr Patricia P Scott of the Royal Free Hospital School of Medicine (London, England) hypothesized in a 1971 report that cats use protein, not only for growth, but to produce energy as well (most other animals get their energy from carbohydrates). Proteins are found in muscle meat (beef, lamb, pork, chicken), milk (which many adult cats cannot tolerate in large amounts), fish, cheese, and eggs.

Fats are a source of energy and heat. They also help keep the cat's skin and hair in good condition. Good sources of fats are cheese, butter, bacon and bacon grease, and moist cat food which usually has vegetable oils added to it.

Carbohydrates (sugars and starches) are another energy source, and are not essential in a cat's diet. Most cat foods contain cereal; small amounts of

Other Pets

There are so many stories of devoted friendships between dogs and cats that it hardly needs saying: there is no reason why the two species cannot live together in near-perfect harmony.

This is especially true if the animals have been brought up together from childhood. Introducing a cat (especially a mature one) into a home where there is already an adult dog (or vice versa) requires more tact and patience, as the two work out territorial disputes, jealousy, competition for food, and so on. Your own reading of your dog's character and temperament will have to tell you whether you can acquire a cat at all or if it should be a kitten or an adult. In any case, as with children, you will have to keep a sharp eye out until the two have come to some sort of truce based on mutual respect. Go as slowly as necessary; trying to force the friendship never works. You may even have to keep the two in separate rooms for awhile until they get used to the idea of another animal in the house.

Birds are a different story. About the best you can do is keep the cage out of reach and away from launching pads as much as possible, install a cat-proof latch (if any have been invented yet), and allow the bird out only when you are certain that the cat is outdoors. Some cats become accustomed to pet birds and virtually ignore them; others never give up the hunt.

Pet mammals (hamsters, gerbils, mice, etc), fish, and small reptiles will probably be irresistible. Again, cages should have strong locks; aquariums should be covered with heavy glass, and terrariums with heavy wire mesh.

Sanitation

Litter boxes are absolutely necessary for house-bound cats, and it is a good idea to keep one handy for outdoor cats as well.

Aluminum or stainless steel litter trays are more expensive than plastic, but they are more durable, are easier to keep clean, and do not absorb odors. The box should be large enough for the cat to turn around in, and should be at least two inches deep.

The pan should be placed somewhere that is accessible but private, and out of the way of household traffic and children.

A commercial litter, sand, or gravel is the best for the sanitary pan. Sawdust, peat moss, peanut shells, or shredded newspaper can also be used. Litter should be about two inches deep.

cooked carbohydrates such as potatoes, bread, or noodles will do no harm if the animal enjoys them.

Vitamins are needed to build up resistance to disease and to help regulate various body processes. Cats who already have a balanced diet do not usually need vitamin supplements, though pregnant cats are often given supplemental Vitamin D (helps build strong bones and teeth). Supplemental niacin is sometimes prescribed by veterinarians for cats with tongue or gum problems.

Minerals are essential in minute quantities, and again, cats usually get what they need from their regular diet.

Above left: A Sable Burmese tastes the water of a neighborhood pond.
Above: Cats use a litter tray with almost no training at all.
Top: This Tabby seems to have become a close friend of the King Charles Spaniel.

A dirty litter pan will begin to annoy your cat long before it annoys you. Litter (or at least the soiled litter) should be removed and replaced every day. The pan should be washed once a week with hot water and detergent. Perfumed detergents and disinfectant sprays will probably annoy the cat and can make it stop using the pan altogether. Read the labels on disinfectants carefully to make sure they are safe.

Training

Many people believe that cats cannot be trained at all. In a sense this is true. Cats are certainly as intelligent as most other animals, but they are not about to be coaxed, teased, or especially threatened into doing what you want them to do. Nor will they go out of their way to behave in a certain way just to please you.

Dr Benjamin Hart notes that cats are the only animals except for primates who learn by observation. Cats who have had many opportunities to watch others open a latched door, for example, often figure out how to do it themselves.

Cats can, however, be manipulated into the sort of behavior you desire if they believe it is in their own best interests. The quality required to implement this manipulation is confidence. And remember that there is no such thing as 'uncatlike behavior' – if you do not train your cat it will certainly train you.

Especially in the beginning, use a high-pitched voice to get the cat's attention (Ears, page 30). Physical maltreatment should be avoided. Often effective with other pets, it usually only makes a cat want to fight back or escape.

Collars and Other Accessories
Cats will tolerate collars, leashes, and harnesses only if these were introduced when they were kittens. Sometimes, however, they are a necessity – for example, if you live in a community that requires cats to wear identification.

Collars can be very dangerous (Hazards, page 213). The best kind to buy is an all-elastic safety collar that is not tight enough to choke the animal and not so loose that it falls off or catches on protruding objects.

If you want to use a leash, buy one of leather, with a swivel hook, and let the cat smell it and play with it a bit before attaching it to the collar. With patience, and the knowledge that the cat will probably never walk sedately at your side for more than a few steps, you and your pet will eventually

come to a compromise where you allow it the freedom to wander back and forth while it walks when you want to walk instead of balking.

Harnesses are usually used for walking larger cats such as ocelots. They should be snug but not tight. If necessary, pad the straps that go across the chest.

Coming When Called
Teaching your cat to come when you call will save you an incalculable amount of aggravation when it is time for feeding, grooming, or locking up for the night.

The procedure is a simple one. Get the cat's attention by calling its name (a falsetto voice will probably work best). Then offer it an irresistible treat – a sardine, brewer's yeast tablet, bowl of chocolate ice cream, or whatever. When it comes over to you, give it the treat and a lot of praise.

After many iterations you will have established a Pavlovian reaction and the cat will come running whenever it hears its name. It is not a good idea to tap the bowl on the floor as you call; you will never be sure which of the sounds the cat associates with the food – and it is uncomfortable standing outside at midnight, in the dead of winter, desperately tapping on a little plastic bowl.

While this technique works with many cats, many others will refuse to be manipulated. Even the experts fail sometimes. Confidence and persistence still give you a pretty good chance of success.

Obeying the House Rules
Whenever you acquire a new cat it will have to learn the 'house rules' – that some chairs or sofas are off limits, that the dining room table and kitchen counter are forbidden territory, that furniture is not for scratching nor drapes for climbing nor plants for eating, and so on.

Scolding is often enough to let a kitten know that it has misbehaved. If that does not work, a sudden loud noise is often effective – hand clapping or smacking a table with a rolled-up newspaper. The next stage might well be a toy squirt gun or spray water bottle. If a cat persists in clawing carpets or drapes, it may be necessary to trim its front claws.

Some misbehavior stems from *your* failure to provide acceptable alternatives. For example, a cat needs to sharpen its claws, and in the absence of a scratching post will generally use the nearest chair or carpet. Kittens are easily trained to use a post; with older cats a little catnip on or around it will help attract the animal.

*Left: A Cream
Persian has been
allowed to use this
ladder as a
scratching post.
Left, below: This
Tabby has been
taught how to beg
most appealingly.
Bottom, center: A
Sable Burmese
does not seem to be
bothered by the fact
that he is on a lead.
Far right, center:
Cats learn very
quickly how to open
doors that have
been left slightly
ajar.
Far right, bottom:
This Abyssinian
mother and her
kittens have taken
to their cat basket
quite well.*

Boredom is another reason for mis-behavior. Be sure that the cat has some things around that can provide permissible diversions. Paper bags, empty thread spools, and stuffed socks are good, safe, inexpensive playthings.

Some cats misbehave to punish their owners – usually in a way nicely calculated to infuriate them. (I once had a cat who would mess in the middle of the bath mat whenever she felt she had been unfairly scolded or had not been given enough attention.)

Again, confidence and persistence must be your watchwords coupled with vigilance and *consistency*. You cannot expect a cat to be anything but confused if you allow it to sleep in a certain chair one day and reprimand it for doing so the next.

Litter Box

It is very easy to teach a cat to use a litter tray. Since cats instinctively prefer to urinate and defecate in a sandy place where they can cover up their excreta, they will usually take to the litter pan almost immediately.

Mother cats usually teach their kittens to use a litter tray, but sometimes a kitten will get confused, or find what it thinks is a better spot – a large potted plant, for instance. A few days spent keeping a close eye on the kitten, picking it up and placing it in the sanitary pan at the first hint of trouble, should solve the problem.

If an older cat starts refusing to use the pan, make sure the litter is clean and that the pan is placed somewhere accessible, yet private. Male cats sometimes refuse the tray when they are sexually aroused, and some sick cats cannot use it. In these cases, keep the cat in one room with newspapers on the floor.

Cats have been taught to use the toilet successfully. One procedure, described by Benjamin L Hart in an article for *Feline Practice* (and reprinted in *Cat Catalog*) is as follows.

1 Keep the regular litter tray in the bathroom until the cat is used to the location.

2 Remove the regular tray and make a new one. Cut a cardboard rim the size of the toilet seat, cover it with clear plastic material, and attach it by wires to the underside of the seat. When filled with litter, the toilet seat is the edge of the 'litter box' and the plastic is the bottom. Of course, this means that the humans in the house must use another toilet for awhile.

3 The cat should be used to its new litter box in a few days, and will probably already be balancing itself on the toilet seat (since the plastic bottom feels very insecure). At this point, reduce the amount of litter by about half.

4 Over the next few days, continue to reduce the amount of litter, making holes in the plastic for urine to drip through, until finally you remove all the litter and the plastic. If you remove the litter too quickly and the cat stops using the toilet seat, go back to an earlier stage and go through the removal process again.

5 Expect the cat to fall in at least once. This may then mean that you have to go back to litter-and-plastic and go through the training process all over.

6 Some cats try to switch to the bathtub. Keeping an inch or two of water in the tub for a few days is an easy way to discourage this practice.

Cats and House Plants

Keeping both house cats and house plants at the same time can be a problem – as anyone who has come home from work to find their favorite *Coleus* chewed to a frazzle knows only too well.

No one is quite sure why cats eat plants. Boredom, say some. As roughage, or as an enemic, say others. Whatever the reason, it is something that is best stopped, not only to spare the feelings of the harassed cat/plant lover, but because many popular house plants are very poisonous to cats. Plants to watch out for include ivy, philodendron, daffodil and hyacinth foliage, Christmas cherry, and mistletoe.

No determined cat worth its salt will be foiled by elementary tricks like arranging plants close together (just knock a few pots off to make room on the shelf) or hanging them from the ceiling (great practice for the running high jump!) But spray repellants from pet stores will deter most cats.

Another solution, that does not deprive the cat of its late afternoon snack, might be to give it its own plants to munch. Grass seed is readily available and easy to grow, but many cats prefer meatier plants like wheat or oats. Have two or three pots growing in rotation so that a supply is always available.

For cats (especially kittens) who prefer your large plant tubs to their litter tray, try a repellant, or perhaps a layer of heavy pebbles with a dash of cayenne pepper.

Tricks

Cats *can* be taught to do tricks – if they feel like it and decide that there is something in it for them. The best technique to use is called 'shaping' – which simply means reinforcing the behavior you want.

For example, suppose you want to teach your cat to sit up. Wait until it comes up one day and puts its paws on your lap. Say 'sit up' in a pleased tone, perhaps moving your knees away and letting it balance with its front paws on your palms. Then reward it immediately. Continue this repetition of command and reward for closer and closer approximations to sitting up unassisted. After the cat has the idea, do *not* reward it for sitting up without the command.

When the trick has been well learned, you can begin rewarding the animal every other time it performs, then every third, every fourth, and so on, until you are rewarding on a random basis about every ten times. This will actually make the reinforcement stronger.

This same technique can be used to teach your cat to shake hands, fetch, or perform any other trick (that is not too undignified).

Below: A wicker basket is probably one of the lightest and least expensive cat carriers available on the market today. However, should your animal contract a disease which is contagious, these cases cannot be properly disinfected.

Travel

It is best not to feed a cat during the eight hours immediately before a trip. If you will be traveling for more than one day, plan to feed it in the evening so it will have time to digest its food before you resume the journey. Remember, cats can go 24 hours without food or water, and plan your feeding schedule accordingly.

If your cat is used to wearing a collar, attach a tag carrying information such as your name, your home address and destination. The same information should appear on whatever container the cat is traveling in.

Cars

It is almost certain that at some point you will want to transport your cat by car, if only to the veterinarian. Short trips when the animal is young make subsequent traveling much easier.

Cats in cars should always be confined in a large, well-ventilated, securely fastened box or carrying case. Many an accident has been caused by a nervous cat suddenly jumping on the driver.

Never leave a cat in a sealed car in summer when temperatures can be as much as 30° or 40° higher inside the car than out. On long trips in hot weather, give the cat small amounts of water at frequent intervals to prevent dehydration and heat stroke.

Cats have varying reactions to motion-sickness pills and tranquilizers, so use them with caution and only when absolutely necessary.

Airplanes

Every airline has a different set of regulations concerning animals. Make sure you call well ahead of time, both to alert them and to find out about any documents you might need (such as a health certificate or record of immunizations).

If you are traveling abroad, check with consulates; many countries (like Great Britain) and some States (like Hawaii) have entry restrictions and quarantine periods.

Unaccompanied cats travel by air freight. If you are traveling with your cat some airlines will permit it to ride in the passenger compartment as long as it stays in its carrying case; others will insist that it goes as checked baggage (at an extra charge).

Trains

American trains will not carry unaccompanied cats and regulations vary in Europe. Most companies insist that the cat travel

Above: Two other types of cat carrier both of which can be easily cleaned and are very light. Immediately above is a clear plastic-glass cat kennel with air holes at each end for ventilation. The advantage of this one is that the cat can see out. The top kennel is made out of fiberglass and is perhaps the strongest and most durable of cat kennels. Both types can be disinfected.

in the baggage car, in a suitable box, and charge a nominal amount for it.

Buses

Some bus lines accept cats; others (notably Trailways and Greyhound in the USA) do not.

Ships

Most passenger lines have special kennels where animals are kept and cared for by their owners. Charges for this service, however, are often exorbitant.

Moving to a New Home

Be sure to put the cat in its carrier before the moving men arrive. If it becomes frightened and runs away you could have a difficult time finding and catching it.

At the new home, keep the cat indoors for a few days until it is used to its new surroundings. Cats have a very strong homing instinct, so be quite sure that it accepts the move before allowing it to roam outside.

Vaccinations

Your veterinarian should be consulted about a vaccination program for any new kitten.

Cats get their first rabies vaccination when they are three to six months old, and some veterinarians advise a yearly vaccination after that.

It is also important that the cat be vaccinated against feline enteritis (distemper). Immunization programs vary, but the most usual time for the first vaccination is when the kitten is six to eight weeks old. This vaccination should be repeated every year.

Diseases and Other Ailments

Following is a brief summary of the major diseases and ailments common to cats. Your veterinarian is the proper person to make a final diagnosis and prescribe treatment, and should be notified whenever you suspect serious trouble.

Above: A veterinarian applies disinfectant to a cat's eyes.

Signs of Trouble

Bad Breath. If you are sure that your cat's bad breath is not caused by fish or other foods with an offensive smell, take it to the veterinarian. Bad breath can be a symptom of decayed teeth, a urinary disorder, or roundworm infestation.

Bloating. A distended abdomen can be caused by cystitis, heart trouble, tumors, or dropsy.

Cloudy Eyes. Can indicate ulceration or other serious eye ailments. Take the animal to the veterinarian at once.

Constipation. Can mean that the cat is not getting enough exercise or lacks roughage in its diet. Try switching to dry cat food for a day or two; if the condition does not improve, try a mild laxative (such as a teaspoon of mineral oil) with its food. If these methods do not work, take the animal to the veterinarian; constipation can also be caused by hairballs or a tumor.

Convulsions. There are many reasons for convulsions, ranging from nervousness or fright to constipation, parasite infestation, poisoning, uremia, a brain injury, or eclampsia (if the cat has recently given birth). If your cat has frequent convulsions, it should be seen by a veterinarian. (See also, Convulsions, page 232.)

Coughing. Can indicate toxoplasmosis or pneumonia.

Diarrhea. True diarrhea is a watery bowel movement (as opposed to a soft one). It can be a sign of excitement, poor diet, or parasites. If adding starchy food (cooked rice or macaroni, or cottage cheese) does not help after a day or two, see your veterinarian. Bloody diarrhea, which can be caused by tumors, parasites, or disease, should receive immediate attention.

Difficulty in Breathing. Gasping and shortness of breath can signify pneumonia, toxoplasmosis, or heart trouble.

Difficulty in Urinating. Frequent straining attempts at urination or blood in the urine are symptoms of cystitis. Get the animal to the veterinarian without delay, especially if you have a male cat; toms can die within 24 hours if the urinary tract is blocked.

Dragging Hindquarters. This can be something as simple as feces caught in the hair around the anus or at the base of the tail. It can also indicate tapeworms, or an infection of the anus or anal glands.

Drastic Change in Behavior. If a cat that is usually friendly suddenly turns violent and savage, or just as suddenly becomes very quiet and hides under the bed, refusing to come out, be careful. Cats rarely get rabies, but when they do it is usually the furious kind. A cat with rabies usually shouts in a deep, hoarse voice that is not at all like its usual one. (See Rabies, page 222.)

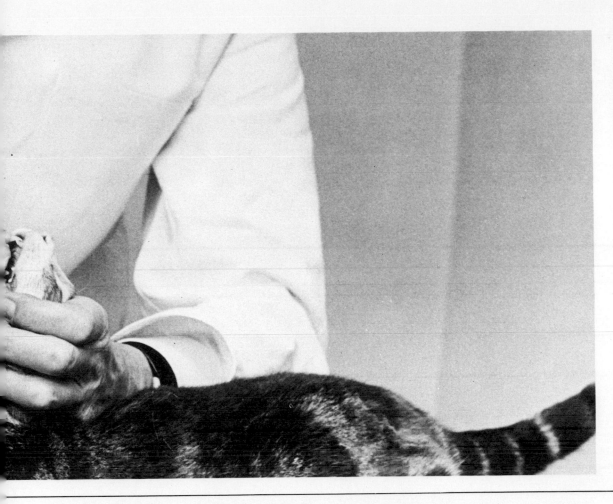

Left:
Administering a
pill to a cat. First
get a good hold on
the animal and
then hold the head
steady and press
gently on the edge
of the jaw. When
the mouth opens
throw the pill as
far down the throat
as possible and then
hold the mouth
shut. Stroking the
throat or blowing in
the cat's face will
make him swallow.

Drinking Too Little. A cat that sits with its head hanging over the water bowl, but not drinking, is exhibiting one of the most noticeable symptoms of distemper. This behavior can also indicate a kidney disease.

Drinking Too Much. This can indicate diabetes, kidney trouble, cystitis, or a uterine infection.

Drooling. Can be an indication of poisoning, or of a virus infection (such as pneumonia or a cold). It can also mean that a foreign object has been lodged in the mouth and should be removed immediately.

Dry, Dull Coat. Can indicate that the cat has tapeworms, and is also a symptom of distemper.

High Temperature. A temperature over 102°F indicates that something is wrong – either because of disease or a parasite infestation. A temperature below 101°F is also a sign of trouble.

Listlessness/Weakness. If the cat becomes listless and weak, suspect anemia, heart trouble, or perhaps a parasite.

Loss of Appetite. A cat can decline two or three meals and still be healthy, but if it almost stops eating for four or five days, it should be taken to the veterinarian.

Loss of Weight. Severe and sudden weight loss should always be investigated; it can be caused by anemia, diseases, or parasites.

Lumps. Any lump should be examined by a veterinarian, especially if its size increases rapidly.

Nasal Discharge. Indicates a viral infection, such as a cold or pneumonia.

Pale Gums. Indicates anemia, which may in turn be caused by a variety of diseases or parasites. After an accident, pale gums can be a sign that the animal has suffered internal injuries.

Pawing at Ears. Often indicates the presence of ear mites. A lot of bad-smelling, crusted wax in the ear is usually caused by an ear canker; if the ear feels hot and there is swelling and pain, a hematoma (blood tumor) is probable. This condition requires surgical drainage.

Red, Inflamed Eyes. This can be a symptom of colds or some respiratory diseases, but is more often the result of air pollution or a foreign object in the eye (see Eyes, page 30).

Running Eyes. This condition is usually caused by a cold.

Sneezing. Either the cat has something up its nose, or it has a cold.

Vaginal Discharge. Indicates an infection of the uterus.

Vomiting. Cats vomit for many harmless reasons, but vomiting can also indicate poisoning, worms, or an infection of the liver or kidney. If the cat vomits a yellowish fluid, take it to the veterinarian as this is a symptom of distemper.

Feline Enteritis (Distemper)

Feline enteritis, panleukopenia, feline leukopenia, or distemper – whichever name is used – is a highly infectious disease that kills thousands of cats every year, often in epidemics that sweep through cities in spring and early summer.

Distemper is a viral disease, and a cat can catch it simply by entering a room or cage where an infected cat has been kept. The incubation period (between the time the animal contracts the disease and the time the first symptoms appear) is four to ten days, and the disease progresses with amazing rapidity; the cat can be dead within 48 hours.

Thus it is important to get the animal to a veterinarian quickly if you suspect distemper. It is a difficult disease to diagnose, but symptoms include vomiting (often a yellowish or greenish fluid), a high temperature, crying out in pain, and severe diarrhea. Cats with distemper often sit with their heads hanging over their water bowl, making little or no attempt to drink. Later the cat becomes thin, weak, and loses hair from its tail; its coat becomes dull and often stands on end; and it becomes dehydrated.

Only a very few cats ever recover from distemper. Cats can, however, be vaccinated against the disease.

If your cat has distemper the veterinarian will probably give it antibiotics to ward off secondary infections and send it home. This is because there is a very great danger of the disease sweeping through his entire establishment, and also because hospital care is very expensive without much hope of recovery.

Your major task will be to prevent the animal becoming dehydrated (feeding liquids with an eye dropper if necessary) and later, if it survives, building up its strength first with baby food and then with more substantial fare. But be prepared for the worst – very few cats survive.

Rabies

Rabies is not common in cats, but they can and do contract it by being bitten by a rabid animal – dog, fox, coyote, or bat. Whether or not a cat then develops the disease depends on the location of the bite (bites on the face or legs are most dangerous) and its severity.

Cats rarely have 'dumb' rabies – they are far more likely to have the furious form. The animal becomes very nervous and excited, biting and scratching everything in its path; its pupils dilate and it has difficulty swallowing. It drools copiously and shouts in a deep, hoarse voice.

Then the cat loses its appetite, drinks with difficulty (hence the other name for the disease – hydrophobia), and eventually goes into convulsions. It will usually die three to seven days later.

Obviously, you cannot assume your cat has rabies simply because it hisses or scratches someone. But if it undergoes a complete personality change, becoming in effect a wild animal, be careful. Try to keep it in an escape-proof room, keep out of its way, and call your veterinarian, the humane society, or the police. If it bites anyone, report the fact to the police or health authorities and see a doctor immediately, In fact, if you are ever bitten by a strange cat, whether it demonstrates rabies symptoms or not, first wash the wound well with warm water and strong soap and then see your doctor.

Vaccinations against rabies are available from the veterinarian.

Toxoplasmosis

Toxoplasmosis is a parasitic disease common to cats and other domestic animals all over the world. It is carried in the feces, nasal discharge, and saliva of infected animals and can be transmitted to humans.

The disease is especially dangerous to unborn children. If a pregnant woman is infected her child can be born with permanent brain and eye damage if the disease is not recognized and treated in time. Since it is extremely hard to diagnose, taking measures from the very beginning is the best form of defense.

1 Do not let your cat hunt, if possible. Feed it only dry, canned, or cooked food.
2 Someone else should deal with the litter box. If that is impossible, wear gloves and wash your hands well immediately after you handle the box.
3 Always wear gloves when gardening.
4 If you have a sandbox, cover it when the children are not using it, and keep a sharp eye out when they are.
5 Do not eat raw or rare meat.
6 Control household pests (flies and cockroaches).

Symptoms of toxoplasmosis in the cat include loss of appetite, fever, cough, loss of weight, and difficulty in breathing. If your veterinarian does diagnose toxoplasmosis, the treatment for you and your cat will usually be effective.

Right : This homemade box was originally constructed for a cat and her kittens to prevent the kittens from harming themselves by wandering too far afield. However it is also an excellent example of a temporary home for a sick cat.

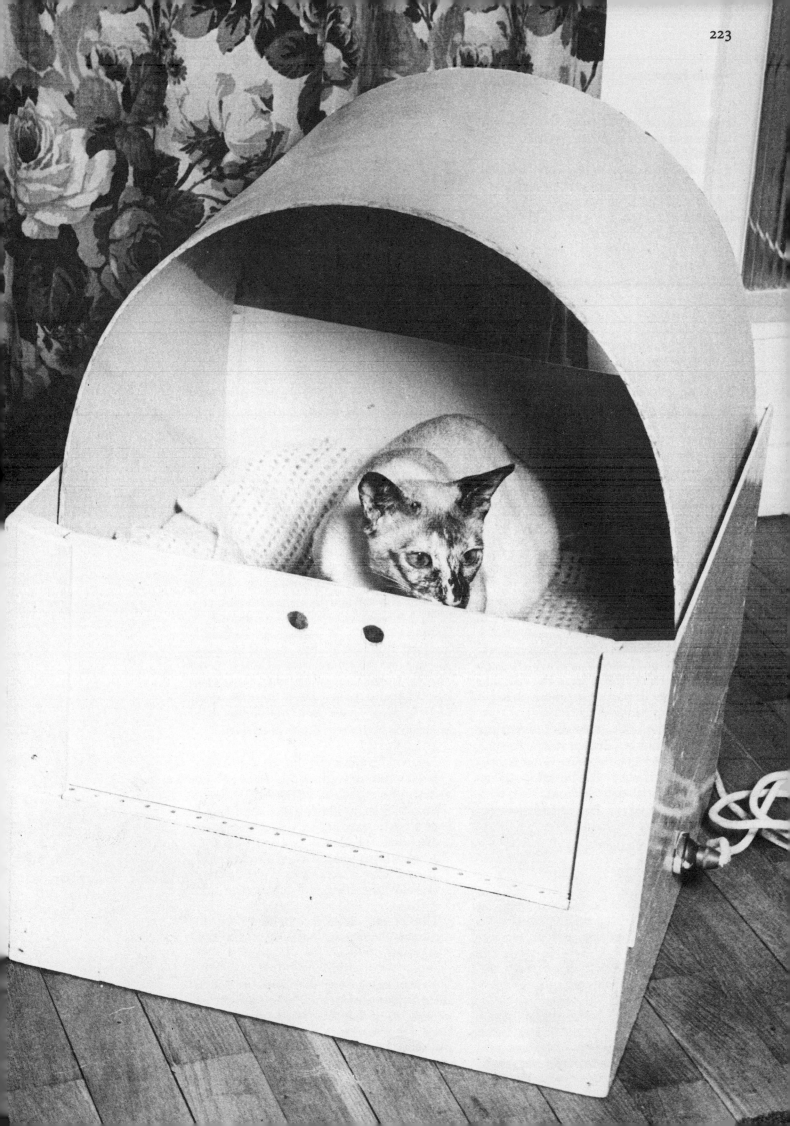

Pneumonia

As in humans, pneumonia in cats is a very dangerous disease that often occurs after the animal has been weakened by another disease such as distemper.

It is characterized by a heavy cough, followed by nasal discharge (sometimes bloody), difficult breathing, and a high temperature.

The cat probably will not survive unless you have medication from the veterinarian, but most cats respond very well to antibiotics. Keep the cat warm and get it to a doctor.

Cystitis

Cystitis is a very painful inflammation of the bladder and is common in cats. It, like pneumonia, can be either a primary infection or a complication of another disease.

Symptoms include frequent (often bloody) urination, straining to urinate, high temperature, loss of appetite, and great thirst.

If the urinary system becomes blocked, the cat will begin vomiting and become bloated. Do not wait until these symptoms appear before taking it to the veterinarian; blockage is very serious, especially in male cats.

Anemia

Anemia can be caused by poor nutrition or by disease. Since its symptoms resemble those of other diseases – listlessness, loss of appetite, vomiting – it is difficult to diagnose at home. Pale gums are sometimes an indication of anemia.

Below : This Havana is being treated for conjunctivitis by a veterinarian.

Eclampsia

Eclampsia is a potentially dangerous disease, caused by a lack of calcium in the blood, and generally occurs after a cat has given birth.

It is characterized by loss of appetite, a high temperature, restlessness, panting, a stiff walk, and convulsions. If nothing is done, these are followed by a coma, and death.

There is no way to treat eclampsia at home; the cat must be taken to the veterinarian without delay for an injection of calcium gluconate.

Cancer

Cancer of the skin, mammary glands, bones, and blood are the types most commonly found in cats.

Ear Ailments

Ear Cankers

Ear cankers can be caused by parasites or an infection. They cause wax to form in itchy, uncomfortable crusts. You can wash off the crusts with water and mild soap and swab the area with mineral oil to make the cat more comfortable.

Hematomas

Blood tumors or hematomas form between the skin and the ear cartilage and cause swelling and pain. Take the cat to the veterinarian to have the hematoma drained.

Ear Mites

This common problem can lead to serious ear trouble. (For further information see Ear Mites, page 227.)

Eye Ailments

Conjunctivitis

Redness and tearing in the eye, called conjunctivitis, is usually caused by irritation from smoke, dust, fumes, or a speck. You can wash the eyes using an eye dropper and a solution of one teaspoon boric acid to one pint water, boiled together and cooled until tepid. Squeeze a few drops into the corners of the eyes. If the condition has not improved after a day or two, take the cat to the vet.

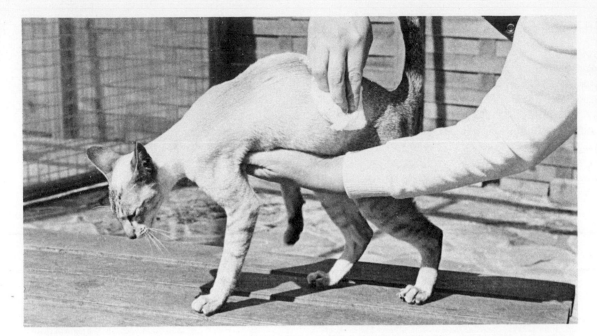

Left : Cleaning a cat's coat regularly will help prevent skin diseases and will help the owner become aware of an infection or skin condition at an early stage of development which will aid treatment.

Keratitis

Keratitis is an inflammation of the cornea, or an ulceration that has usually been caused by an injury. Symptoms are sensitivity to light and sometimes a bluish-white clouding of the eye. The inflammation is treated in the same way as conjunctivitis; a cat with ulcerative keratitis should be seen by a veterinarian.

Skin Ailments

Skin problems not caused by parasites can take a long time to cure, mainly because most of them can be caused by any one of a number of things – finding which one is often a process of trial and error.

Allergies

Allergies to foods, plants, etc. often take the form of dermatitis, itching, or skin sores. It is as long and complicated a process to find out what a cat is allergic to as it is to track down human allergies.

Baldness
(alopecia)

Baldness sometimes occurs without any apparent reason. Treatment, however, depends on finding the cause which could be a thyroid or pituitary gland malfunction, a kidney disease, a parasitic infestation, a dietary deficiency, or even just friction from lying on a hard surface.

Dandruff

All too familiar to most humans, dandruff with its dry skin and grayish-white scales is common to cats as well. Daily grooming improves the cat's appearance. Some basic causes might be a lack of fatty acids in its diet, too many baths and/or too strong a soap, or dry heat.

Dermatitis

This is a catch-all term which is applied to a combination of scaling skin, loss of hair, and intense itching. The itching can get so bad that the cat rubs itself raw against the furniture. Among the many suspected causes are allergies, parasites, insect bites, freezing, and too much sunlight. If bathing with warm water and mild soap followed by an application of calamine lotion does not help, or if the condition recurs frequently, seek advice from your veterinarian.

Eczema

Symptoms of eczema include itching, pustules with a bloody discharge, scabs, and dandruff. The causes are varied, and similar to those of other skin ailments (faulty diet, allergies, parasites, etc.). Treat eczema as you would dermatitis, and call the veterinarian for diagnosis and further treatment.

Impetigo

This particular skin disease is very contagious to other animals and to humans; its characteristic pustules break easily and spread the infection all over the body. Wearing rubber gloves, dust the pustules with an antiseptic powder; do not let children handle the animal.

Parasites

All animals, including man, are plagued with both external and internal parasites at one time or another. Good sanitation and a knowledge about the life cycles of the parasites are your best weapons; while completely eliminating them is almost impossible, control (by breaking up the life cycle) is not difficult.

Fleas

Fleas are small, hard-shelled insects that can jump great distances. Most prefer the warmest parts of the body; in the cat's case these are the chest, neck, the base of the tail, although sticktight fleas prefer less hairy areas (such as around the eyes or ears).

Female fleas lay vast numbers of eggs (as many as 500 in a lifetime) in rugs, furniture, blankets, between floorboards, or outside in sand and dirt. Adult fleas emerge from protective cocoons in about two weeks if the temperature is above freezing; the entire life cycle takes about a month.

Besides being dreadfully annoying, some fleas carry tapeworm eggs, and some can even carry bubonic plague or typhus organisms. Thus it is important to control them.

Defleaing the Cat

It is not difficult to deal with fleas; safe flea powders are available at most stores.

The easiest and most effective way to deflea a cat is to use a cat bag or towel. Smear vaseline around the eyes. Dust the cat's body and place it in the bag for 15 minutes. The fleas will move to the head, which you can then dust very carefully avoiding the eyes, nose and mouth.

Remove the bag, stand the cat on newspaper, and comb out the fleas. Burn the paper. This whole process may have to be repeated once a week for a few weeks, and periodically after that.

Defleaing the House

Eliminating fleas on the cat itself is, of course, only one battle in the war. You should also dust, spray, and vacuum the house, paying special attention to rugs, furniture, cracks and crevices, and the cat's sleeping place.

Defleaing the People

Cat fleas *do* bite people – and the bites bother people more than they do cats, as anyone who has spent the summer with ugly, itching red swellings on their legs can tell you. Unfortunately they do not bite all people, and sometimes the sufferer's biggest problem is convincing a skeptical spouse or roommate that he or she is being bitten at all.

Cat fleas, however, do not actually live on people, so eliminating them from the cat and the house usually solves the problem nicely. In the meantime, here is one hint born of bitter experience: do not wear tight trousers and if all possible *go barefoot* around the house. Fleas are most likely to bite the lower legs, and would much rather snuggle up inside a wooly sock than hop about on bare skin.

Ticks

Ticks are eight-legged, hard-shelled arachnids that can go for long periods without food and live through widely varying extremes of temperature and climate.

They were once a problem only in the country, but they are moving rapidly now into cities and suburbs. Adult ticks climb up on weeds or grass; when a victim (cat, dog, sheep, cow, or human) passes by, it fastens on, burrows into the skin, and gorges itself on blood.

Ticks are very dangerous parasites; they carry diseases that attack both cats and people. They sometimes inject a toxin that can affect a cat's neuromuscular system, and generally debilitate their host. The skin often becomes inflamed or an abscess forms where the tick has burrowed in.

If there are only a few ticks on the cat, they can be loosened with vinegar, alcohol, or nail polish remover. Then, using blunt-edged tweezers, you can carefully and gently *slide* them out. Do not use your fingers; it is difficult to pull out the entire tick, and you could be exposing yourself to disease.

Commercial tick dips are more effective than powders for cats that have many ticks. Use the same procedure as when bathing the cat (see Bathing, page 225).

Make a concentrated effort to rid the house and grounds of ticks too; it will not be easy. Use a commercial tick spray on every possible hiding place you can think of. Ticks can hide almost anywhere and are exceptionally strong.

Cat Flea (ctenocephalides felis).

Cat tick (ioxides).

Below: The harvest mite (trombicula autumnalis).
Bottom: Ear mite (otodectes cynotis).

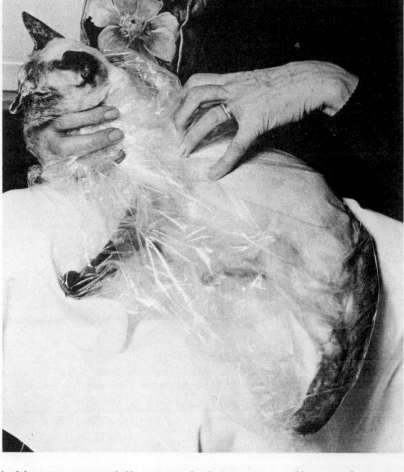

Ear Mites

Ear mites are frequently seen on cats. These small parasites work their way down into the outer ear. They cause a large amount of crusty wax to form, and are very irritating.

A cat that is continually shaking its head or pawing its ears, or holds the ears abnormally flattened, is likely to have ear mites. These pests should be eliminated by a veterinarian. If you want to help the cat in the meantime, you can soften the built-up wax with a cotton swab dipped in diluted hydrogen peroxide. After you have removed the wax, apply a light vegetable or mineral oil. You will prabably need someone to hold the cat down during this operation.

When the cat shakes its head some of the ear mites fly out. Thus you will probably have to disinfect the house if you do not want a recurrence of the problem.

Mange Mites

There are two kinds of mange mites: *demodetic* and *sarcoptic*. Only a veterinarian can make a positive distinctive diagnosis.

Symptoms of demodetic mange include:

bald spots, especially around the eyes; reddened skin; thick, hard spots on the skin; and excessive shedding. Another type of demodetic mange is characterized by very red skin, a bloody discharge and a disagreeable smell. Demodetic mange mites have also been found in the liver, spleen, lungs, and other organs. Once there they are difficult to eradicate.

Sarcoptic mange is evidenced by thick, dry skin, itching, loss of hair, and scabs. It usually begins on the head, but can also appear on the body.

Lice

Lice are small wingless insects that spend their entire life on their host – which can be any warm-blooded animal, including man. They do not jump like fleas, but are transferred by direct contact, either with the cat or with cat hairs that contain the eggs.

Cats can be deloused using the technique described for defleaing (page 226). If you have children you will probably have to delouse them too (using a slightly different technique). It is important to eliminate lice; they can cause severe anemia in kittens and, on occasion, typhus or trench fever in humans.

Above and center top : Fleas can be annoying to cats and humans alike. One way to deflea a cat is to put the cat in a plastic bag (except for its head) and add flea powder (see text). Below : The common cat louse (felicola subrostrata).

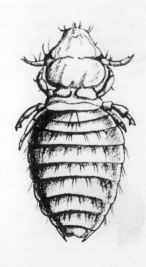

Ringworm

Ringworm is not caused by a worm at all, but by a parasitic fungus. It is very contagious; always wear rubber gloves when handling a cat you suspect has ringworm, and try to prevent children handling it at all.

When a cat has ringworm it loses its hair in patches; these patches then develop round or oval lesions with scabs and crust. These can be either circular scaly areas or just small, red, swollen spots.

Iodine (tincture or ointment) works well with ringworm; apply it after washing away the scabs with warm water and mild soap. You can also buy an oral medicine for ringworm.

Favus

Favus is similar to ringworm – it too is caused by a fungus and is highly contagious. Favus causes honeycombed crusts on the head and paws. It is treated the same way as ringworm, taking the same precautions.

Roundworms

Roundworms (or ascarids) are the most common internal parasite found in cats. Cats pick them up by coming into contact with feces from infected cats; when the cat licks its paws the worms travel to the stomach, then circulate through the bloodstream, into the lungs and esophagus. and eventually wind up in the intestines, where they mature.

Signs of a roundworm infection are a bloated abdomen, thin body, dull coat, sweetish breath, and diarrhea. Often you can see the worms in the cat's vomit or feces.

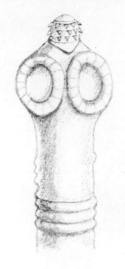

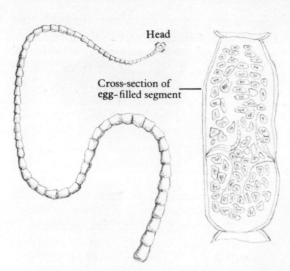

Above : Tapeworm dipylidium caninum). *On the left of the picture is the head of the tapeworm showing the hooks and suckers which it uses to attach itself to the walls of the intestine.*

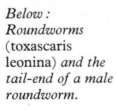

Below : *Roundworms* (toxascaris leonina) *and the tail-end of a male roundworm.*

Since the roundworm larvae circulate through the blood, kittens can become infected while they are still in the uterus. It is therefore a good idea to take the veterinarian a sample of the kitten's feces when it is about four weeks old.

These parasites do not usually infect humans, but there have been cases of roundworm infections in children.

There are several commercial worm medicines available on the open market, but it is best to use them under a veterinarian's supervision. Worming is a dangerous process, and one that can kill a kitten as easily as it kills the worms.

Tapeworms

Tapeworms are another very common feline parasite. They live in the cat's intestines, and grow to a length of one to two feet.

Tapeworms are not as harmful as other worms, but if there are many of them they can completely block the intestines. Certain evidence of a tapeworm infestation is seeing the eggs on the hairs around the anus (they look like small grains of brown rice) or in the feces. Cats with tapeworm often drag their hindquarters along the ground (this can also indicate infected anal glands); more general symptoms are a dull coat, vomiting, nervousness, and sometimes convulsions.

As with roundworms, the patent medicines available are effective, but dangerous. It is difficult to prevent your cat getting tapeworm, but eliminating fleas and cooking all fish thoroughly will reduce the possibility.

Hookworms and Whipworms

Hookworms are a common problem, especially in hot, humid climates. Like tapeworms, they circulate through the bloodstream on their way to the intestines, and thus can infest kittens before birth. Early symptoms include anemia, listlessness and loss of weight, and bloody diarrhea. Later, symptoms that resemble more serious diseases appear – high temperature, coughing, and discharging from eyes and nose. The hookworms themselves are too small to be detected except by a veterinarian.

Whipworms, which infect the cecum and colon, often must be removed surgically. Symptoms include inflammation of those areas, pain, loss of weight, diarrhea, and vomiting. There are no external signs since the worms 'sew' themselves into the tissues of the cecum.

Protozoa

There are two main types of microscopic intestinal parasites that infect cats: *coccidia* and *giardia*. Both coccidiosis and giardiasis are characterized by loss of weight and bloody diarrhea. Positive diagnosis can only be made in the laboratory.

A cat, injured in a car accident, is resuscitated by a veterinarian.

First Aid

The first rule of first aid is 'Don't panic.' Keep cool, and talk quietly and reassuringly to the cat. Remember that it is likely to be nervous and in some pain; you will probably have to restrain it, and may well need another person to assist you.

Artificial Respiration

There are two methods for administering artificial respiration.

In the manual method, stretch the cat out on its side with its legs extended front and back. Pull out its tongue so that it will not interfere with breathing. Then, with your hands on the cat's chest, push down, release, wait . . . push down, release, wait . . . in a rhythmic sequence.

For the oral (or mouth-to-mouth) method, clean the cat's face. Close its mouth. Inhale; put your mouth over the muzzle; and exhale. Remove your mouth and allow the chest to deflate. Repeat rhythmically, about six times per minute.

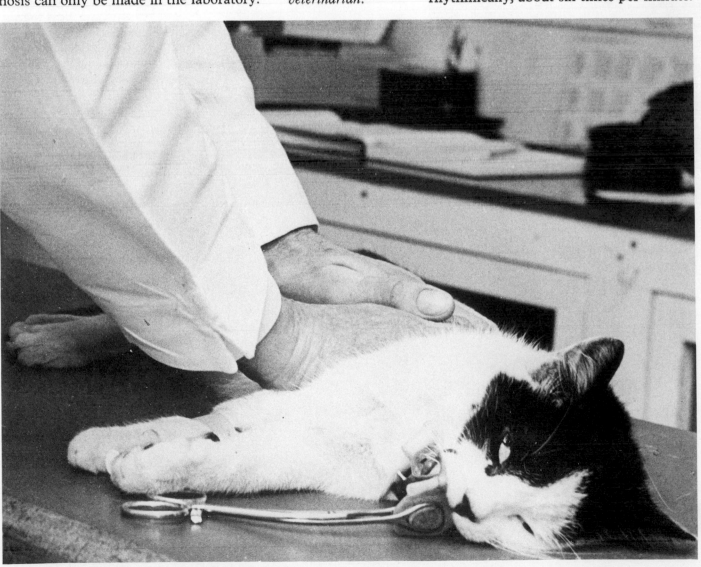

Do not give up too quickly when using either method. If the animal responds, it will begin taking slow, shallow breaths and gradually increase their rate and depth. As soon as the cat revives, treat it for shock and get it to a veterinarian.

How to Lift and Transport an Injured Cat

If the cat is conscious, the easiest (and safest) way to lift it is by the scruff of the neck, supporting its hindquarters with your other hand. This allows you to hold it away from you if it is nervous and excited and likely to scratch. If any bones have been broken, apply splints before picking the cat up.

If there are no broken bones the cat can travel to the veterinarian in a box or cat bag. Cats with broken bones or more serious injuries should be wrapped in a blanket.

If the cat's hindquarters are paralyzed and you suspect a fractured pelvis, place it gently on a board and have someone keep it still.

If you suspect internal injuries, wrap the animal's body with strips of cloth, like a girdle, before carrying it to the veterinarian.

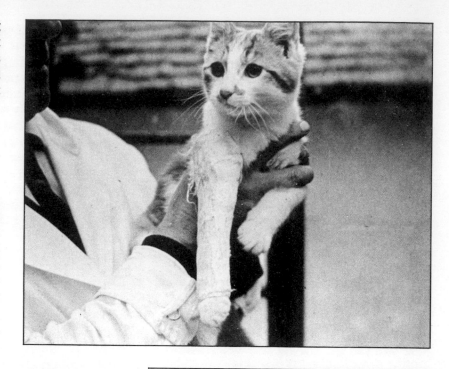

Above : A vet carries a cat with a cast on its foreleg. Below : Administering anesthetic to cats is similar in many respects to administering it to human beings.

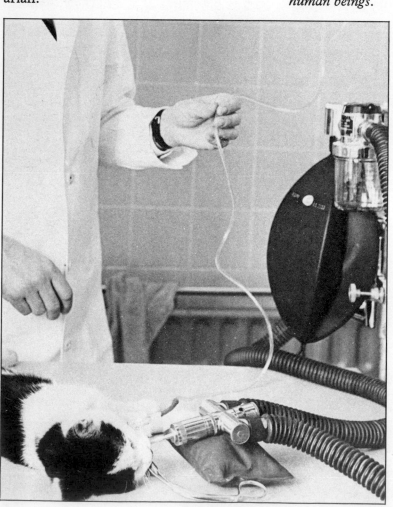

A First Aid Kit and Medicine Chest for Cats

The basic list below contains many items found in medicine chests for people. However, for obvious reasons, it is best to keep the cat's medical supplies for its use alone.

Absorbent cotton
Adhesive tape
Antiseptic powder or spray
Calamine lotion
Eye dropper
Hydrogen peroxide
Insect powder for fleas, ticks, and lice
Mineral oil
Vaseline (Petroleum jelly)
Rectal thermometer
Roller bandages
Scissors (small, with blunt ends)
Small, squeeze-type medicine bottle or baby syringe (for giving liquid medicine)
Spoon
Sterile pads
Tweezers (blunt-ended)

Your veterinarian will probably be able to suggest other useful items.

Automobile Accidents

Never leave an injured cat unattended while you go for help. First, slide it onto a blanket or coat and drag it out of traffic, on to the side of the road. Apply pressure bandages to control bleeding if necessary; check for fractures and apply splints if possible; treat the animal for shock, and rush it to the veterinarian. Grayish gums can be a sign of internal injuries.

Bites and Stings

Bites from other cats can be very dangerous; the small punctures close up quickly and can turn into abscesses. Wash the wound well with hydrogen peroxide, as soon as possible. If the bite abscesses, the safest thing to do is take the cat to the veterinarian. Often cats will lance their own abscesses, but it is not always effective, and there is a much greater chance of infection.

Dogs usually rip or tear when they bite; treat the bites as described in the section on Bleeding immediately below; large wounds may require stitches.

Cats are seldom bitten by snakes, but if you live in a poisonous snake region you should know how to deal with the emergency.

If you can get the cat to a veterinarian within an hour do so. If that is not possible, tie a cloth or handkerchief around the animal's leg, about two inches above the bite. Loosen it for a few seconds every 15 minutes to allow some circulation or if the leg gets cold.

Next, sterilize a sharp knife in a flame and make a one-inch 'X' through each bite. Remember – your cat's life may depend on your acting quickly and decisively. Then apply suction – but *not* with your mouth.

Suction kits are a good investment if you live in an area that contains poisonous snakes. If the swelling around the wound spreads to the constriction band, move the band up two more inches, make a new cross-cut, and apply suction again. Treat the cat for shock and get it to a veterinarian as soon as you can.

Insect stings can be removed with tweezers if you can see them. Cold packs help reduce pain and swelling; calamine lotion relieves itching. If the cat shows signs of an allergic reaction, take it to the veterinarian.

Bleeding

Cats treat many of their own cuts and scratches by licking them. You can treat cuts the cat cannot reach by clipping away the hair around the wound and applying an antiseptic.

Even heavy bleeding can usually be stopped by applying firm, direct pressure, using a sterile pad or a clean handkerchief or towel.

Only use a tourniquet in very serious cases, and remember to loosen it for a few seconds every 15 minutes so as not to cut off all blood circulation. Get the animal to the veterinarian as soon as possible.

Cats treat their wounds themselves by licking them.

Burns

Burns require immediate attention. When treating them, be careful not to touch the burned area with anything that is not sterile; you should not even breathe on it. *Never* use an antiseptic on a burn.

Keep cold water or ice on the burned area for about 15 minutes. Then apply a burn ointment, petroleum jelly, or if these are not available a sterile pad soaked in strong tea. (Do not use tea on large burns, since too much tannic acid can damage cell tissue.)

If the burn is severe, put a sterile pad over the ointment; put a clean cloth over the pad; and then wrap bandages around the whole area before taking the animal to the veterinarian.

Choking

You will need a helper to hold the cat if you have to dislodge a bone or other object from its throat. While your assistant holds the cat (wrapped in a coat or blanket), hold the lower jaw with your left hand and tilt the head back. Holding the cat's mouth open, work quickly to move the bone with your right hand. The animal may need treatment for shock.

Convulsions

Cats having convulsions have enlarged pupils, foam at the mouth, are very excited and run wildly around, and then lie still, with jerking legs.

The most important thing to do is prevent the animal injuring itself. Move it away from furniture after wrapping a heavy blanket around it. If it has recently given birth, or if you suspect it has eaten poison, take it to a vet immediately.

Drowning

After rescuing a drowning cat, turn it upside down to drain out any water; then place it on its side and use artificial respiration until it revives. Treat for shock if necessary.

Electrocution

Cats can be electrocuted by electrical appliances and live wires. If a wire is lying on top of the cat, lift it off with a broom handle or dry stick. If the cat is on top of

the wire, use the stick or a dry board to scoop the animal up and off the wire. Use artificial respiration until breathing resumes; then treat the cat for shock and for burns, if any.

Eye Injuries

To remove specks of dirt or other foreign objects from the cat's eye, roll one corner of a clean handkerchief and carefully remove the speck. You will need to use a cat bag or have someone else act as your assistant to hold the cat down. After you have removed the speck, wash the eye with a few drops of warm water and apply an eye ointment.

If the cat's eyes are inflamed due to dust or pollution, wash them with a warm solution of boric acid. Use an eye dropper and put a few drops in the corner of each eye; when the cat blinks the solution will be distributed over the entire eye. Then apply an eye ointment. If the inflammation has not subsided in a day or two, consult your veterinarian.

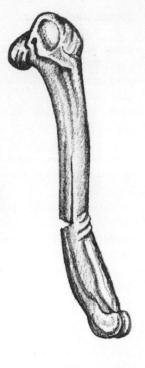

Fractures

Swelling and an inability to move the broken part characterize simple fractures (in which the bone is broken through) and 'green stick' fractures (in which the bone splinters but does not snap entirely). In the case of compound fractures you can see the bone sticking out through the skin.

You can improvise an emergency splint using cardboard or even rolled up newspaper. Place the splint carefully against the broken leg or tail so that it extends beyond it. Then fasten it with strips of bandage or adhesive tape, above and below the break.

If the cat's hindquarters are paralyzed it may have sustained a fractured pelvis. Place the animal on a board and have someone hold it still while you get it to the veterinarian.

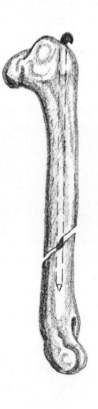

Heat Stroke

The most common cause of heat stroke in cats is being left in a hot, closed car. Symptoms are heavy, labored breathing, prostration, an increased pulse rate, a glassy-eyed stare, and sometimes vomiting.

Put the cat in a cool place and wet it down with cold water, especially the head. When it begins to stir, give it a teaspoon of black coffee.

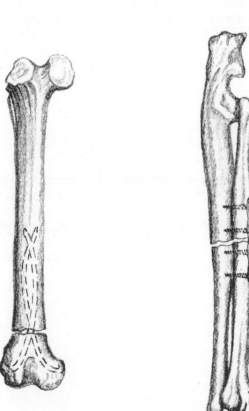

Above: A small kitten laps up some fresh milk.
Top three center illustrations show the different types of bone breaks which can occur. l to r: a greenstick fracture, a clean break, a break with splinters.
Center three illustrations show how bones can be mended. l to r: single pinning, double rush-type pins for the fracture of a femur and a bone plate repair of the radius and ulna.

If you do not know what the poison was, check first to see if the cat's mouth is burned. If it is, give the animal milk or beaten egg whites.

If the mouth is not burned, induce vomiting by giving the animal a teaspoon of hydrogen peroxide. If the cat has not vomited within five minutes, the dose can be repeated once more (but only twice in total). If you do not have hydrogen peroxide, you can use a strong mustard solution, salt water, or a teaspoon or two of salt placed on the back of the tongue. After the cat has vomited, give it milk or beaten egg whites.

In any case, get the animal to a veterinarian as soon as you have administered first aid. If that is impossible, a dose of activated charcoal will adsorb the poison and prevent it being absorbed by the body. This measure should only be taken in extreme emergencies, however.

Shock

Any severe injury will probably bring on shock, caused by lack of blood in the brain. The animal should be treated for shock as soon as you have taken care of stoppage of breath, serious bleeding, fractures, etc.

The cat in shock will be prostrate and semi-conscious; its eyes will be glassy and vacant; its breathing shallow and irregular; its pulse rate slow; and its temperature low.

It must be kept warm with a blanket, coat, or sweater wrapped *all* around it. Lowering the head will help return blood to the brain. Take it to the veterinarian as soon as you can.

Poisoning

The most important thing to remember in poisoning cases is that you must work fast.

Symptoms of poisoning include pain, vomiting, trembling, convulsions, and, in the case of acids or alkalis, a burned mouth.

If you know what kind of poison your cat has eaten, follow the directions on the label for administering antidotes.

Daily Care of the Sick Cat

Although cats can be very difficult patients, competent loving home care is often the best way to speed recovery.

If you are unlucky enough to have a very sick cat to care for, your veterinarian will be able to provide support, advice, and if necessary training to supplement the guidelines that follow.

The Sick Room

When your pet is very sick or badly injured, things will be easier for you and more comfortable for the cat if you can set up a clean, efficient sick room area.

Ideally, this area should be quiet and away from family traffic, but in a place where the cat can see the other members of the household. It should be warm, airy but not drafty, and easily cleaned. It is often a good idea to carpet the area with layers of newspaper.

The sick bed itself can be a washable blanket or a box of clean litter. Have a small table nearby for medicines and supplies (which should be locked up, however, if there are small children around).

Taking the Cat's Pulse

To take the cat's pulse, find the femoral artery, which runs down the inside of the hind leg. When you can feel the pulse, count the beats for 15 seconds, then multiply by four. A normal pulse rate is between 100 and 130 beats per minute.

Taking the Cat's Temperature

Always use a rectal thermometer to take a cat's temperature. Shake the thermometer down and coat the bulb end with vaseline. Put the cat on a table and clamp its body between your arm and your body. Lift its tail and insert the thermometer about one inch into the rectum. Keep it there for about three minutes; remove it, wipe it clean with cotton, and take the reading.

Normal temperature for an adult cat is between 100.5 and 102.5°F. (It is usually lower in the morning and higher in the afternoon and evening.) Kittens' temperatures are usually slightly higher.

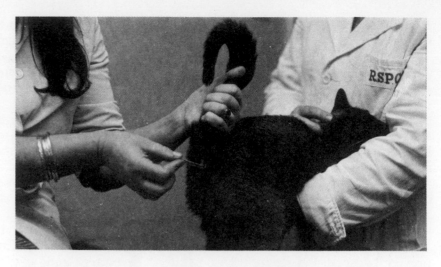

Above : Cats' temperatures are always taken with a rectal thermometer.

Giving the Cat Its Medicine

The easiest way to administer liquid medicine is with a small squeeze bottle or baby syringe, though a spoon will do as well. Until you get the hang of it, an assistant to hold the cat would also be useful. Hold the cat on a table, with its head level. Then pull the loose skin away from one corner of the mouth and squirt or pour the medicine into the pouch that forms. Release and hold the mouth closed until the cat swallows.

There are several tricks to getting a cat to take a pill or capsule. The first two are obvious: see if the animal will accept it without a fuss, or try slipping the medicine into its food.

If neither of these works, wrap the animal in a towel and hold it on your knees. Place your thumb and index finger at the corners of the mouth and push in, at the same time tilting the head backward. As soon as the mouth is open drop the pill in as far back as possible. Hold the mouth closed and stroke the cat's throat until it swallows. Rubbing its lips with a wet finger or suddenly blowing in its face are other ways to promote swallowing.

Feeding

You may have to forget the rules and pamper a sick cat if you want it to eat at all. It is worth doing, since the animal must eat if it is to recover. Experiment until you find the best foods to stimulate its appetite. If it cannot keep solid food down put it on a liquid diet for a few days.

If the cat must be hand-fed, give it liquids the same way you administer liquid medicine. You can place soft foods directly on its tongue.

A starchy diet (boiled rice, cottage cheese, etc.) will usually help control diarrhea.

Special Care for the Incapacitated Cat

A cat that cannot move about at all needs special attention. Since it cannot get to the litter box, it will have to lie on a washable blanket, or you can even put on a make-shift diaper. The blanket or diaper will have to be changed and cleaned whenever soiled.

You will also have to keep the cat's body clean if it cannot do it itself. Wash soiled areas with warm water and soap, combing out matted hair if necessary.

Turn the animal several times a day to prevent bedsores and strain.

If the cat becomes constipated, and your veterinarian forbids a laxative, an enema may be necessary.

Giving the Cat an Enema

Giving an enema is a nasty job that many people prefer to have the veterinarian handle. Sometimes that is not practical, however, and so the procedure is described below.

If the cat is reasonably active, it will probably object strongly to the entire process; unless you are experienced you will need someone to help you.

Administer the enema in a laundry tub or bathtub. Use a regular enema bag with a small nozzle (or, for kittens, a rubber syringe), and an enema solution of warm water and mild soap.

Fill the enema bag and smear the end of the nozzle with petroleum jelly (taking care not to plug up the openings).

Let a little of the solution run out to clear out any air. Insert the nozzle about two inches into the cat's rectum. Hang or hold the bag about a foot above the animal's body, and open the clamp. Keep the pressure low (by lowering the bag if necessary) and watch for signs of discomfort that would indicate that the cat's colon is full.

Keep the solution in the colon for a few minutes. Then quickly remove the nozzle, and the feces and enema will be expelled.

The Elizabethan Collar

A collar, made of an eight-inch circle of cardboard with a hole large enough for the cat's head cut out of the middle, may be necessary to prevent the animal pulling off its bandages or licking off ointment. The inside of the collar can be padded.

Below: A homemade Elizabethan collar – it may not be beautiful but it does stop the cat from aggravating its wounds or licking off ointment.

Care of the Older Cat

Cats are arbitrarily considered 'old' at nine years, and most live for ten to fifteen years. Some have been known, however, to live twice that long, making them the longest lived small domestic animal.

Old age in cats, like old age in people, varies with the individual. Some elderly cats are spry and alert, while others become ill and senile while they are still comparatively young.

Giving the older cat a quiet, comfortable home, a warm, dry bed, and a good, nourishing diet is one of the most important things you can do. Diet, especially, should be carefully watched. Older cats get less exercise, and easily become overweight. They are also prone to tooth trouble, constipation, and diseases like nephritis and diabetes which require special diets.

Regular grooming will make the old cat feel more comfortable, will help keep it free from parasites that could sap its strength, and will make it look younger and healthier.

Old cats suffer from many of the same ailments that affect old people, including arthritis, cataracts, and deafness. Otitis (an inflammation of the ear) and nephritis (an inflammation of the kidneys) are common. Dropsy, diabetes, pancreatitis, and metritis (an inflammation of the uterus) are other diseases that affect elderly cats. They are also likely to develop tumors and cancer.

Some changes in behavior are inevitable. Old cats are creatures of habit, and will not tolerate drastic changes in their lives. Many become much more sensitive to changes in temperature. They often become jealous of children or other pets, and need reassurance that they are still loved and wanted.

At some point, if the cat becomes seriously ill and is in great pain, you will have to make an unenviable decision about whether or not to put it to sleep. The phrase is not just an euphemism; your veterinarian will simply inject an overdose of anesthetic, and the cat will drift off to sleep and not wake up – a peaceful way to pass from this world.

Most city health authorities will not allow you to bury your pet in the back yard. Information about facilities for cremation, or pet cemeteries, is available from your veterinarian, or from local newspapers or pet magazines. Your local humane society will probably also be happy to help you.

Genetics and Breeding

Selective breeding is, of course, of interest to professional breeders and cat fanciers who are interested in showing their pets.

For those who require in-depth knowledge, there are several excellent and informative books devoted entirely to the subject of cat breeding. The following discussion will serve as an introduction to some of the basic principles involved for those new to cat breeding or for anyone who wants to mate their cat with some foreknowledge of the results.

Cat Genetics

Nearly 100 years ago an Austrian monk named Gregor Mendel discovered the basic hereditary principles that determine how certain characteristics are passed from one generation to another. These principles have been used by cat breeders to produce the fine purebred cats seen today.

Genetics is a very complex science. Simply put, each cell in a cat's body contains the genes that control inherited characteristics, strung like beads on nineteen pairs of chromosomes. During mating the egg and the sperm cell each divide to form two cells with nineteen individual chromosomes; then cells from the two parents combine to form new cells that

Below : Cats should have a dry and comfortable place to sleep.

contain nineteen pairs again – this time with one strand from the father and one from the mother.

If you know the genetic history of both parents you can construct a simple matrix (called a Mendelian checkerboard) to help predict what the litter will look like. Capital letters indicate dominant genes and small letters recessive ones.

For example, suppose you are mating a short-haired mother (S) with a long-haired father (l).

SS x ll   **Mother**

		S	S
Father	l	Sl	Sl
	l	Sl	Sl

Since the mother can only pass on S genes and the father only l, each of the kittens will have one of each. Since short hair is dominant over long, the kittens will all have short hair, but will carry a recessive long-hair gene.

Now, suppose we mate two of the kittens.

Sl x Sl   **Mother**

		S	l
Father	S	SS	Sl
	l	Sl	ll

We find that of the four kittens, one is a pure short-hair, two appear to have short hair but carry recessive genes for long, and that one is long-haired.

Note that each parent carries two genes for each characteristic.

Breeding for Various Characteristics

Color breeding can become very complicated. White is usually dominant over all other colors, and red dominates everything except white. Black and tabby do not dominate each other: you can breed black cats and tabbies and find some of each in the resulting litter. Black dominates all colors except white, red, and tabby. Sex has some bearing on color. For example, males can only carry one red gene; therefore, the mother must also have a dominant red gene if the kittens are to be red. Usually, only females have tortoiseshell markings. Tortoiseshell males are almost always sterile on the rare occasions when they appear. Sometimes genes will combine to produce diluted colors, such as gray (diluted black) or cream (diluted red).

Length of hair is not as difficult a problem. Short hair is dominant over long hair. If you fill out the matrix, you will see that two short-haired cats may produce long-haired kittens, but two long-haired cats cannot produce short-haired kittens.

Breeding for a specific *eye color* is still very chancy, since not as much research has been done in this area.

Disposition cannot be reliably bred, since health and environment play such a large part in determining the animal's behavior. Mating two placid, docile animals may increase the odds that their kittens will be calm and easy going, but by no means insures it.

Of course, you can breed for many other traits: size, shape of tail, and so on. But it may take many more than one or two matings to get the set of characteristics you are looking for, as any breeder can tell you.

Breeding Abnormalities

Crossed eyes (squint) is an inherited trait that frequently occurs in Siamese cats.

Deafness, when it is present from birth, is often associated with white, blue-eyed cats – which is not to say, however, that all white, blue-eyed cats are deaf. Breeders are finding this a very difficult trait to eliminate.

Extra toes (polydactylism) is inherited as a dominant trait. It is often prevalent within rather strictly defined areas. For example, almost twelve percent of the cats in the Boston, Massachusetts area have extra toes, while in New York City they represent only 0.2 percent and in Philadelphia, Pennsylvania 0.5 percent of the feline population.

Folded or flopping ears is an inherited trait that appears when the kitten is about one month old. Some breeders are attempting to develop this trait, much as dog breeders have deliberately exaggerated differences in the canine breeds.

Kinked tails were once common among Siamese cats; today breeders have almost entirely eliminated the trait, although it is apt to recur when they least expect it. In fact, kinked or shortened tails are not rare in any breed, though it is sometimes hard to tell whether it is a result of heredity or an accident during birth. Short tails are controlled by a recessive gene. Kinked tails have a much more complicated genetic story which is not even thoroughly understood today.

Split feet are caused by a dominant gene. The split in the middle of one or both front feet can also be accompanied by other abnormalities such as double claws, the absence of toes, or malformed pads.

Choosing a Mate

If your main interest is to produce several tiny replicas of your pet, then simply choose a mate that matches your cat in size, color, and temperament.

If yours is a purebred cat you will probably want to mate it with another purebred of the same breed.

If you intend showing the kittens, you will need to know the standards for its breed and carefully select a mate with a genetic background that will combine with your cat's to produce kittens as near that standard as possible.

How to Mate Your Cat

There is more to mating a purebred cat than immediately meets the eye.

If you are offering a male as a stud, setting the price is usually your prerogative; you can ask for either cash or a kitten (or kittens) from the litter. There should be a written agreement between you and the owner of the female, stating (1) that you do not guarantee conception; (2) whether or not there will be a return service if the female does not conceive; (3) that your cat is in good health; and (4) the precise terms of payment. If the payment is to be a kitten, be sure to specify its sex and the age at which you will claim it. You should also require a health certificate for the female cat.

If your cat is a female, be sure that you co-sign an agreement as outlined above. Purebred cats are often very valuable, and the issues raised by the setting of fees and the rights of the owners have often led to arguments, and even court cases.

Below: Seal point Siamese kittens wander only a short distance from their mother at this age.

*Far right:
Chestnut Brown
and Lilac Oriental
(or Foreign)
kittens and their
mother.
Right: A Siamese
mother licks her
new-born kittens.
Notice that the
eyes of the kittens
have not yet
opened.*

Terms Commonly Used in Genetics and Breeding

The definitions below, brief as they are, encompass most of the key concepts in genetics and cat breeding.

Alleles
Alternate forms of a gene that are not completely dominant or recessive. The tailless characteristic of Manx cats is a good example of the result of an allele.

Breed
A group of cats which have characteristics in common that set them apart from other cats.

Chromosomes
The rod-shaped structures in a cell that carry the genes.

Cross-breeding
The mating of a purebred cat of one breed with a purebred cat of another.

Dominant gene
A gene for a given characteristic which will suppress the gene for the opposite characteristic and appear in the offspring. (For example, short hair is *dominant* over long hair.)

Genes
The basic units of heredity, made up of deoxyribonucleic acid (DNA), which determine all inherited characteristics.

Genetics
The science, or study, of heredity.

Genotype
The genetic make-up of an animal, as opposed to its outward appearance.

Grade breeding
The mating of a purebred with a mongrel, or mixed-breed cat.

Heterozygous
Describes an animal that carries both a dominant and a recessive gene for a given characteristic. For example, a short-haired cat that carries genes for both short (dominant) and long (recessive) hair.

Homozygous
A 'double dose' of a gene for a given characteristic. For example, a short-haired cat that has received short-hair genes from both its parents.

Inbreeding
The mating of cats that are closely related (father/daughter, brother/sister, etc.). This type of breeding is used to concentrate desired characteristics and does not always produce monstrosities, but it is best not to try it unless you have had a certain amount of experience; some undesirable traits can be accentuated at the same time as the ones you are looking for.

Line breeding
The mating of cats that are more distantly related, such as cousins. You can spot line breeding by the appearance of the same name in several generations in a cat's pedigree. This is the most reliable and commonly used breeding system.

Mutation
A spontaneous change in the chemical structure of a gene, leading to the production of a new hereditary trait.

Outbreeding
The mating of unrelated cats of the same breed.

Phenotype
The outward appearance of a cat (as opposed to its *genotype*).

Purebred cat
A cat whose parents were both of the same breed.

Recessive gene
A gene which remains latent in the presence of a dominant gene.

Reproduction in Cats

Unaltered cats need sex in a way that is often incomprehensible – and sometimes frightening – to humans. Females in heat who are kept away from males, often rub their hindquarters on the floor and yowl as if they were in pain. They are, but the pain is psychological, not physical. There is evidence to show that depriving an unaltered cat of sex for long periods can impair both its emotional and physical health, and some veterinarians believe that preventing purebred females from breeding until their show years are past might well be a contributing factor to their sterility in later years.

Behavior of the Female

The average female cat matures sexually when it is six to eight months old. North of the equator there are two main times when cats come into heat: late winter (January to March) and spring (May and June). Many cats also go into heat in the autumn. There are four stages in the female's reproductive cycle.

1 *Proestrus* is the first stage, when the uterus and vulva are preparing for mating.
There is a discharge during this phase.

2 *Estrus* is the period when mating can occur, lasting for four to ten days. At this time the cat is very affectionate, rolling on the floor, rubbing against people and furniture, and often calling for a male at the top of her voice. Catnip often produces this same behavior, but there has not been enough research on the subject to determine the exact reasons why.

3 *Metestrus* is the stage when if there has been no mating, the uterus and vulva begin to return to normal.

4 *Anestrus* is the name of the period when the reproductive organs are inactive.

Behavior of the Male

Toms usually mature at about ten or eleven months. Many will simulate sexual activity when they are much younger, but this is simply play/practice to prepare the kitten for his future adult role.

Toms often travel comparatively large distances to find available females. If there is a female in heat in the neighborhood the tom will often cry and try to get out. He is also likely to spray the room with urine, as an advertisement of his presence and great ability. The smell thus produced is extraordinarily offensive to humans.

Kittens are not usually weened until they are about four weeks old.

Mating

A tom will investigate (and spray) an area carefully before he begins to court a queen; males, more than females, need to feel that they are in familiar territory. He then circles the queen carefully and, if there are several toms, fights will break out. The female has the final say in the matter, however, and the victor may not be the first to mate with her. There is evidence to show that females display distinct preferences and no small amount of discrimination, although they may mate with several toms (and indeed become pregnant by more than one) during any given estrus cycle.

The queen crouches, rubs against the ground, and treads with her feet. The male then grips the back of her neck; she raises her hindquarters; he mounts her, inserts his penis, ejaculates, and withdraws, all in only a few seconds. As they ejaculate males utter a deep grunt and females emit a unique high-pitched cry. As the female cries out she pulls away and takes a thoroughly discourteous swipe at her unfortunate lover. Then the two relax, clean themselves, and likely as not begin all over again. Some couples have been known to mate as many as ten times in an hour.

Contraception

Neutering (spaying or castration) is the obvious solution to both undesirable sexual behavior and the production of the thousands of unwanted kittens that are born every year.

Spaying is the removal of the female reproductive organs: both ovaries, the Fallopian tubes, and the uterus. The operation generally takes about fifteen minutes and the cat usually stays in the hospital overnight. Within a few days it has completely recovered and has lost all interest in sex. The operation should be performed before the animal first comes into heat – probably at about four months.

Castration, or removal of the testicles, is the most common method of neutering males. It is a simple operation, and cats are often allowed to go home the same day. If the animal is castrated when it is between five and six months old it may never display some of the coarser tomcat behavior. With older cats, spraying and roaming may stop immediately or wear off gradually.

Drugs which will prevent conception in females are being developed in both England and America. Most of those that originally appeared on the market, however, have been withdrawn. Your veterinarian can give you further advice.

Many people believe that a neutered cat becomes fat and lazy, and that a neutered male is more apt to develop a blocked urinary tract. Neither is true. Neutered cats generally require fewer calories, and therefore less food, but the solution to the problem is to avoid overfeeding, not to refrain from neutering. The urinary tract becomes blocked in many male cats, but it has to do with the narrowness of the male urethra, rather than with whether or not the cat has been castrated.

Pregnancy and Birth

Pregnancy

The gestation period in cats is about nine weeks. After about five weeks you should be able to feel the kittens by gently feeling the queen's abdomen (palpating) for lumps, which gradually grow larger. The abdomen becomes swollen during the fifth or sixth week. The mammary glands are enlarged during the last two weeks, although if the cat is having her first litter her nipples may become prominent after the first two weeks.

In false pregnancy (*pseudocyesis*), the cat shows all the physical and behavioral signs of pregnancy. If you suspect a false pregnancy either because you cannot feel any lumps or because the delivery date is long overdue, consult your veterinarian. Kittens become visible on X-rays after the 38th–40th day.

Most cats require little special care during pregnancy. The pregnant cat will eat more, and your veterinarian may prescribe a vitamin supplement, but most doctors advise against making any major changes in diet.

As the end of pregnancy approaches the queen becomes more and more sedentary. Then as the time for delivery nears, she will become very restless. This is the time to watch carefully to see that she does not decide to have her kittens in your shirt drawer or some other unsuitable place.

Although there is no guarantee that the cat will use it, you can provide a box, lined with cloth or newspaper, for the delivery. Remember that most cats prefer isolation and privacy at this time, and put it in an appropriate spot. You can cut an entrance for the mother, leaving a rather high lip at the bottom to keep the kittens from climbing out.

If you have a long-haired cat, trimming the hair around the anus, vagina, and breasts will be a help. You might also have a few basic supplies on hand in case there is an emergency. Scissors, strong thread, small clean towels, and petroleum jelly could all prove useful.

Birth

Labor contractions start slowly, and gradually increase in speed and intensity. The first kitten should appear about an hour after strong, purposeful contractions have begun; if it has not appeared after eight hours of labor there is something wrong and you should call your veterinarian.

The kitten will appear head first (about sixty percent of the time) surrounded by a grayish, semi-transparent birth sac. The umbilical cord attaches the sac to the placenta (afterbirth). The mother will immediately begin licking away the membrane (this is important, since the kitten cannot breathe while its nose and mouth are blocked) and eating the afterbirth which breaks the umbilical cord in the process. No one knows why animals eat the placenta; some think it is to remove all traces of the birth so it will not attract predators, and others think that it is a temporary source of food, until the mother can leave the kittens.

Other kittens will appear at intervals ranging from ten minutes to an hour; often there are longer delays with smaller litters. Sometimes there is a lag after the first two or three kittens that can last as long as twelve hours. The average litter is three to five kittens.

Queens rarely need assistance in carrying out their maternal duties, but it is just as well to keep an eye on the births and be prepared to help if necessary. The situations you are most likely to encounter are described in the following paragraphs.

If the mother fails to break the birth sac and lick the kitten clean, you will have to do so without delay. Pick up the kitten and membrane in a clean towel, stretch the membrane near the kitten's head, and gently rip it with a hooked finger. If the kitten does not begin gasping for breath, hold it carefully and firmly and swing it, head down, to clear mucus from its nose and mouth. Give the kitten back to the mother; if she will not lick it clean, towel it dry.

If the mother does not sever the umbilical cord, tie a tight knot around it with strong thread, about three inches from the body, and cut it with scissors on the side of the knot away from the kitten.

Above:
A Chinchilla
kitten begins to
hunt.

Try to keep count and make sure that a placenta follows each kitten. If the placenta is not expelled it can interfere with the birth of the next kitten or, if it is retained at the very end, can cause a severe infection as it decomposes. Using a clean towel, grasp the broken cord that will be hanging out of the vagina, and gently pull the afterbirth out.

Breech births (the kitten appearing rear first) are so common that they are considered normal for all intents and purposes.

If a kitten is stuck in the vagina, call your veterinarian, who will be able to tell you whether to perform the delivery yourself or bring the animal in. The former is much more likely, since it can be dangerous to move the mother at this point. If no veterinary advice is available, scrub your hands well, lubricate your finger with petroleum jelly, and try to insert it in the vagina, moving it around the kitten and nudging it forward. Pull the kitten out slowly and gently, in a downward and outward direction, holding it by the shoulders (not the head).

A greenish-black discharge during labor, or a greenish-yellow one following birth should be reported to the veterinarian immediately.

Care of the Kittens

Generally, mother and children should be left strictly alone for the first week. The mother will need peace and quiet, and a lot of food to keep her milk supply at an adequate level.

The mother will begin weaning the kittens when they are around four weeks old. You will then have to provide supplemental food; finely chopped (raw) beef, baby cereal with milk, and baby food are all good. The kittens should be weaned and housebroken by the time they are six weeks old. Begin the kittens on four meals a day, gradually cutting down to two (or one, if they prefer) by the eighth month.

Broadly speaking, kittens are healthy if they eat and sleep a lot and do not cry too much. Conjunctivitis is one common problem during kittenhood; another, which is more dangerous, is diarrhea which can cause the animal to become seriously dehydrated.

At six to eight weeks, take the kittens to the veterinarian for a check-up, inoculations, and if necessary, worming. Remember particularly to inoculate your kittens against feline enteritis.

Below: Motherhood: Kittens are dependent for several weeks.

Photography

by Irvin J Sattinger

Cats make natural subjects for the enthusiastic amateur photographer. All you need is a cat and a camera and the pictures almost take themselves. Kittens grow into cats at an alarming rate but the youthful antics of the developing kitten are recorded for posterity on film. The following pages outline a few suggestions which should allow the inexperienced photographer to get the most out of his time and film and to make the most out of his opportunities.

With some luck and finesse the results of the amateur can approach those of the professional photographer. There is little that the professional can do that the amateur cannot approximate with the right attention paid to detail and technique.

General Rules

Obviously the rules for taking good photographs apply equally well to animal photography as to any other type of photography. Below are some general guidelines to aid the amateur photographer.

1 Equipment

Good photographic equipment is desirable but modest equipment is quite satisfactory as long as it is in good working order and clean. For detailed photographing of cats, a good close-up or portrait attachment can be an advantage and will help to bring out the singular markings of the cat's fur, its eyes and so on.

2 Lighting

Natural, balanced lighting is best for all photos but flash pictures may be necessary for action shots or for taking pictures where natural lighting is not available (for example, if the cat is posing under the table or behind a chair).

3 General Procedure

Of course, the right selection of film, accurate focussing and correct exposure all contribute to excellent results. Proper procedure always gives the best results.

4 Composition

Finally, good composition is the hallmark of excellent technique. Try to keep irrelevant structures and articles from appearing too often (if at all) in your photographs.

Types of Cat Photographs

1 The Portrait

The portrait is meant to define the owner's perception of his pet. In most cases the cat will be resting, sitting or even sleeping and, as cats do a lot of this sort of thing, opportunities for good pictures are plentiful. The 'subject' can be posed and arranged, the background can be controlled and manipulated, and there is plenty of time to make camera and lighting adjustments.

As a general rule, for portrait photographs it is a good idea to locate the camera at the same level as the cat either by descending to its level or raising the cat to yours. In this way distortion is minimized. Close-ups enhance the detail of the picture and accurate focussing and exposure will bring out the texture of the cat's fur and the contour of its body. Grooming the cat in advance is, needless to say, part of the ritual.

Portraits should capture the essential personality of the subject whether it be human or feline. To achieve this result, it helps to study your cat and try to understand the animal as best you can. Is your cat's basic personality haughty, aggressive, sultry, friendly, mischievous . . . or an intricate combination of some or all of these plus many others? With understanding and care and with an eye open for your cat's moods, the amateur photographer can obtain innumerable pictures which will give the outsider an in-depth profile of his/her cat's personality.

2 Typical Cat Antics

There are certain actions and reactions which are typical of all members of the feline family. For example, most domestic cats stretch in the same way, arch their backs, yawn so wide as to almost engulf their faces, wash themselves, scratch their ears and so on. To capture these moments on film the order of the day is patience, preparation and perseverance. With care and time the novice cameraman should

Right:
Amateurs can achieve this degree of professionalism with a bit of perseverance and patience. This photograph of a Seal Point Siamese was taken against a white wall.
Below: With proper cropping the floodlamp in the center of the picture would not show. It has been included here to show how its use has countered the strong backlighting from the sun outside and left the characteristics of the Siamese cat clearly defined. Had the flood-light not been used the cat would appear underexposed and featureless.

Usually the action (or reaction) occurs when the animal is confronted by a new stimulus or situation which he has not encountered before. These are the most difficult photographs to catch. Unless a standard response can be evoked on a regular basis, the photographer must wait until the animal decides to perform the 'action' on its own. Much patience is required, and the camera and the camera-man must be ready to react immediately, or even better, to anticipate the event. In the final analysis, it is often better to keep your camera loaded and instantly accessible in order to capture these never-to-be-repeated moments. Obviously the camera must be set beforehand, the range and exposure already adjusted, the flash attachment at hand and the cameraman's reflexes sharpened.

Inevitably when trying to catch a cat in a unique pose you will face the problem of deciding what to do when the cat suddenly offers you a good opportunity for an original photograph but is wrapped around an irrelevant and unphotogenic chair leg. The true amateur photographer will take the picture anyway and hope that judicious cropping may render the end product more acceptable. Even if this is not possible, the picture may not win any prizes but it does document a situation which may never repeat itself.

Occasionally it is possible to capture the once-only picture using contrived stimuli. With a certain amount of luck and a lot of ingenuity some 'moments of madness' can be repeated for the camera using a manufactured catalyst. The photographer will undoubtedly still have to be alert and quick but with the help of an assistant and some form of inducement, the special photograph can be obtained.

have a large selection of pictures of his cat performing all the 'universal' feline maneuvers.

3 Personality Pics

Every cat is also an individualist who reacts uniquely to special situations: these are the traits that separate your animal from everyone else's. Your pet's tendency to leap into the refrigerator every time the door is opened can be photographed and recorded for posterity. Some cats learn how to open the door of refrigerators which makes it necessary for their owners to devise a means of padlocking the door shut. Another cat might show an affinity for curling up in a particular bowl or box, or nibbling only African violets and so on. These are the photographs which separate your cat from all the others and should receive special attention. The best way to capture these moments on film is to keep a loaded camera readily available.

4 Once Only Shots

These 'targets of opportunity' often are spontaneous and totally original, and thus are, as often as not, missed by the camera.

Below: Someone was lucky (or well-prepared) to catch this Siamese in mid-air.

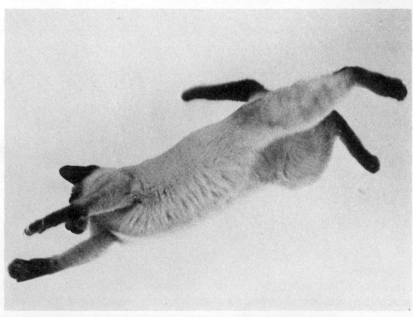

Problems and Solutions

1 Background

It is best to watch out for distracting elements that can appear in the background of what could be an otherwise excellent photograph. A newspaper with a crime headline or a vacuum cleaner or an unidentified (or even identified) human leg can completely alter the photograph and should be maneuvred out of the viewfinder unless it bears directly on the cat and its action. However it is not always possible to remove the distracting item(s) and the picture can often be salvaged by judicious cropping.

2 Flash Equipment

Obviously natural lighting is desirable but a flash may be required occasionally. A problem peculiar to flash guns or strobe lighting is that the flash itself is reflected in the cat's eyes which gives them an unnatural look and results in remarkable but not necessarily good pictures. One way to avoid this is to photograph the cat in profile rather than head-on. Another alternative is to illuminate the subject from a point other than the camera position.

3 Outdoor Photographs

Outdoor photographs can produce excellent results because of the availability of natural light and attractive surroundings and backgrounds. Haze and shade or backlighting with direct sunlight should produce the best pictures. Direct sunlight on the animal may result in a picture with harsh contrasts.

4 The Cat and Friends

If you have more than one cat then your opportunity to take good photographs is multiplied immeasurably and the proportion of good shots should increase. Cats interacting with members of the family, especially children, often provide the best pictures of both animal and child. You can catch them in familiar poses: at work, at play and at rest. The interaction of a cat with a dog, a parrot, a goldfish bowl, hamsters and so on provides fuel for another whole range of potential award-winning and pleasing photographs but be careful about inciting conflict!

Above: A reflection of his personality or is this a 'once only' shot?
Below: This Russian Blue is basking in the floodlights which have been placed overhead and on the right of the picture.

Above : Two Burmese kittens are repremanded by an irate parrot. Left : Personality Pics! This Tabby will undoubtedly get what he's begging for . . .

To Finish Up . . .

Not every picture that you take will end up a prize-winning classic. The best strategy for obtaining really good pictures is to take them in quantity. If you take enough pictures, some of them are bound to be good. And by showing only the successes to your friends, you can establish a (somewhat undeserved) reputation for excellence.

When you have assembled a large collection of photos, then you have the final task of organizing your *selection* in albums or slide trays. Note the emphasis on the word, 'selection.' Keep only the best shots. Duplication and repetition of the same poses or actions detracts from your ultimate collection. Some imagination in the arranging of the material within the album or slide collection will yield results. One way to organize material is by theme – adventures, fauna and flora, suppertime, playtime, and so on.

Cats are marvellous subjects for the camera enthusiast; photographic possibilities are limited only by the cameraman's imagination and pocketbook. Stalking your cat with camera poised can be a rewarding experience.

Index

Numbers in *italics* denote illustrations, numbers in **bold** type indicate main entry under heading.

A

Abyssinian, *21*, *22*, **50**, *50–51*, 120, *217*
    Cream, 50; Kitten, *39*, *52–3*;
        Red, *50–51*; Ruddy, *50–51*;
        Somali, 50
Accidents, Automobile, 229, 230
Acinonyx, see Cheetah
African Lion, see Lion
African Wild Cat, **52**
Alleles, 239
American Blue, see American Short-
    hair; Russian Blue
American Short-hair, **52**, *52–3*, 64, 68,
    100
Anal glands, Infection of, 220
Anatomy, 27
Andean Cat, see Mountain Cat
Anemia, 221, **224**
Anestrous stage, 35
Angora, **52–4**
Anus, 35; Infection of, 220
Appetite, Loss of, 221
Archangel, see Maltese; Russian Blue
Art, Cats in, 23
Artificial Respiration, **229–300**

B

Bali Tiger, see Tiger
Balinese, *47*, **54–5**, *54–5*
Bay Lynx, see Bobcat
Behavior, Drastic change in, 220
Bengal Tiger, see Tiger
Bi-colored Long-hair, see Bi-colored
    Persian; Colors and Patterns
Bi-colored Persian, **56**, *56–7*, 60
Bi-colored Short-hair, see Colors and
    Patterns
Birman, **58**, *58–9*
Birth, 242
Bites, 231
Black, *20*, 39, 82
Black-footed Cat, **60**

Black Long-hair, see Black Persian
Black Panther, see Leopard
Black Persian, **60**
Black Short-hair, **60**, *60–61*
Black Smoke, 41
Black Smoke Short-hair, see Smoke
    Short-hair
Bleeding, 231
Bloating, 220
Blood, 33
Blue, 39, 159
Blue American Short-hair, see
    American Short-hair; Russian Blue
Blue Burmese, see Burmese
Blue Chinchilla, see Chinchilla
Blue Colorpoint, see Himalayan
Blue-Cream, 44
Blue Cream Burmese, see Burmese
Blue Cream Long-hair, see Blue Cream
    Persian
Blue Cream Persian, **62**, *62–3*, 64
Blue Cream Point, see Colorpoint
    Short-hair; Himalayan
Blue Cream Short-hair, **64**
Blue Exotic Short-hair, 64
Blue Japanese Bobtail, 64
Blue Long-hair, see Blue Persian
Blue Lynx Point, see Colorpoint
    Short-hair
Blue Manx 'Longie,' see Blue Short-
    hair
Blue Oriental Short-hair, 64
Blue Persian, **64**, *64–5*, 92
Blue Point, see Colors and Patterns;
    Himalayan; Siamese
Blue, Russian, see Maltese; Russian
    Blue
Blue Short-hair, **64**
Blue Smoke, 41
Blue Smoke Persian, see Smoke
    Persian; Colors and Patterns
Blue Smoke Short-hair, see Smoke
    Short-hair
Blue Tabby, see Colors and Patterns;
    Tabby
Blue Tortie Point, see Colorpoint
    Short-hair
Blue Tortoiseshell and White, see
    Colors and Patterns (Dilute
    Calico); Calico
Bobcat, *64–5*, **68**, *68–9*
Bobtail, see Japanese Bobtail
Bombay, **68–70**
Bones, 28–9; breaks, *233*
Brain, 32; injury, 220
Breath, Bad, 220
Breathing, difficulty, 220
Breed, 239
Breeding abnormalities, see Genetics
    and Breeding
Breeding, see Genetics and Breeding
British Blue, 64, **70**, *210*
British Cream, see Cream Short-hair

British Short-hair, 52, 64, **70**, *70–71*
Bronze Mau, see Egyptian Mau
Brown Burmese, see Burmese
Brown Tabby, see Colors and Patterns;
    Tabby
Brown Tabby Persian, *192–93*
Brown Tabby Short-hair, 192–93
Burmese, 70, *72–3*, **74**, *76–7*, 120, 128,
    247: Blue, 64, *74–7*, **78**, 80; Blue
    Cream, 62, **78**, see also Colors and
    Patterns; Brown, see Sable;
    Champagne, **78**; Champagne
    Tortie, **78–9**; Chocolate, see
    Champagne; Cream, **79**, Lilac, see
    Platinum; Platinum, **80**; Platinum
    Tortie, **80**; Red, **80**; Sable, **80**;
    Tortoiseshell, **80**
Burns, 232
Bush Cat, see African Wild Cat

C

Caffre Cat, see African Wild Cat
Calico Cat, **82**, *82–3*; long-hair, *44*;
    short-hair, *44*, 82
Cameo, **84**; Cameo Shaded, *39*, *84–5*;
    Cameo Smoke, *84–5*; Cameo
    Tabby, 42, 85
Canadian Hairless, see Sphynx
Cancer, 224
Canker, 221
Caracal Lynx, **86**, *86–7*
Carrier baskets, *217–19*, *222*
Caspian Tiger, see Tiger
Castration, **241**
Cat, Choice of, 210
Cat Fanciers' Association (CFA)
    Championship competition, 54;
    standards, 39, 52, 70, 74, 82, 158
Cat shows, 18–19; CFA, 112; Crystal
    Palace, 18; Madison Square
    Garden, 19
Central American Jaguar, see Jaguar
Champagne Burmese, see Burmese
Champagne Tortie Burmese, see
    Burmese
Chartreux, 64, 70, **89**, *88–89*
Chat Sans Poils, see Sphynx
Cheetah, 30, *48*, **90–91**, *90–91*
Chestnut Brown Foreign, *239*, also see
    Havana Brown
Chinchilla, 52, **92**, *92–3*, *94–5*, *96–7*,
    210, *242*; Blue, 92; Silver, 39
Chinese Desert Cat, **97**
Chinese Tiger, see Tiger
Chocolate Burmese, see Burmese
Chocolate Cream Point, see Colorpoint
    Short-hair
Chocolate Lynx Point, see Colorpoint
    Short-hair

Chocolate Point, see Colors and
    Patterns; Siamese
Chocolate Self Long-hair, see
    Himalayan
Chocolate Tortie Point Burmese, see
    Burmese
Choking, 232
Chromosomes, 230
Cinnamon Oriental Short-hair, *121*
Circulatory system, 33, *34–5*
Classic Tabby Pattern, 42
Claws, 30
Clouded Leopard, **98**, *98–9*
Coat, Dry, dull, 221
Cold, 221
Collar, Elizabethan, 235, *235*
Colorpoint Long-hair, see Himalayan
Colorpoint Patterns: Blue Point, 47,
    64–5; Chocolate Point, Lilac
    (Frost) Point, Seal Point, 47; see
    also Colorpoint Short-hair
Colorpoint Short-hair, **101–102**:
    Solid Color Point; (a) Red Point, (b)
       Cream Point;
    Lynx Point; also known as Silver
       Point Siamese, Shadow Point, and
       Tabby Colorpoint Short-hair,
       100–101 (a) Blue Lynx Point,
       (b) Chocolate Lynx Point, (c)
       Lilac Lynx Point, (d) Red Lynx
       Point, (e) Seal Lynx Point;
    Parti-color Point; (a) Blue Cream
       Point, (b) Chocolate Cream Point,
       (c) Lilac Cream Point, (d) Seal
       Tortie Point, (e) Tortie Point
Colors and Patterns: **39–47**
    (a) Solid Colors: Black, Blue, Cream,
       Red, White, 39;
    (b) Shaded: Chinchilla Silver,
       Shaded Cameo or Red Shaded,
       Shaded Silver, Shell Cameo or
       Red Chinchilla, 39;
    (c) Smoke: Black Smoke, Blue
       Smoke, Red Smoke, 41;
    (d) Tabbies: Classic Tabby Pattern,
       Mackerel Tabby Pattern, Blue
       Tabby, Brown Tabby, Cameo
       Tabby, Cream Tabby, Red Tabby,
       Silver Tabby, 42;
    (e) Parti-colors: Bi-colour, Blue-
       Cream, Calico, Dilute Calico,
       Tortoiseshell (Tortie), 44
Conjunctivitis, 224, *224*, 243
Constipation, 220
Contraception, 241; drugs, 241
Convulsions, 220, 232
Copper, see Supilak
Copulation, 35
Cornish Rex, **102**, **105**, 120; see also Rex
Cornish Si-Rex, *102–103*
Cougar, see Puma
Coughing, 220
Cream, 39

Cream Abyssinian, see Abyssinian
Cream Burmese, see Burmese
Cream Persian, 20, *104–105*, **105**, 217
Cream Point, see Colorpoint Short-hair
Cream Short-hair, *104–105, 106–107*, **107**
Cream Tabby, see Colors and Patterns; Tabby
Cross-breeding, 239
Cymric, **107**
Cystitis, 220, 221, *224*

D

Desert Cat, Chinese, see Chinese Desert Cat
Desert Cat, Indian, see Indian Desert Cat
Devon Rex, **108**, *108–109, 110–111,* 120
Diabetes, 221
Diarrhea, 220, 222, 243
Digestive System, 35
Dilute Calico, see Calico; Colors and Patterns
Diseases and Other Ailments, 220–36; Signs of trouble, 220–21 (see also separate entries) Distemper, see Feline Enteritis
Domestic Cats, 15, 17, 24
Dominant gene, 239
Drinking, too little, 221; too much, 221
Drooling, 221
Drowning, 232

E

Ear Ailments, *224*; Cankers, 224; Hematomas, 224; Mites, 221, 227
Ears, 30; Pawing at, 221
Eclampsia, 220, *224*
Eggs, 35
Egyptian Cat, see African Wild Cat
Egyptian Mau, **112–15**, *112–13, 114–15, 152–53*; Bronze, *18*, 115; Silver, 115; Smoke, 115
Electrocution, 232
Elizabethan collar, 235, *235*
Enema, Administration of, 235
Esophagus, 35
Estrous cycle, 35
European Wild Cat, 52, *106–107*, **116**, *116–17,* 141
Excretory system, 35
Exotic Short-hair, 85, **116**; see also Colors and Patterns; Exotic Short-hair (blue), 70

Eye Ailments, **224–25**; Cloudy Eyes, 220; Conjunctivitis, 224, 243; Keratitis, 225
Eye Injuries, 232
Eye Structure, 31
Eyes, **30**; Care of, *220*; Red, Inflamed, 221; Running, 221

F

Fallopian tubes, 35, 241
Favus, 228
Feeding, **213** (see also Nutrition, 213–15); in sickness, 234
Feline Enteritis (Distemper), 221, **222**
Female Cats, 35
Female Reproductive System, 35
Fertility, 35
Fever (teething), 35
First Aid, 229–33, see also separate entries
First Aid kit, 230
Fishing Cat, 119
Flame Point, see Himalayan
Flat-headed Cat, 119
Fleas, 226, *226*; defleaing Cat, 226, *227*; house, 226; people, 226
Folklore and Myth, Cats in, 20
Foreign Black, see Oriental Black
Foreign Lilac, see Oriental Lavender
Foreign Short-hair, 120
Foreign White, see Oriental White
Fractures, 232
Frost Point, see Colors and Patterns; Siamese

G

Genes, 239
Genetics and Breeding, 236–39; Terms commonly used in, 239 (see also separate entries)
Genotype, 239
Geoffroy's Cat, **120**, *121*
German Rex, **122**
Glands, 30
Golden Cat, Temminck's, see Temminck's Golden Cat
Grade breeding, 239
Grant, Colonel Walter, 52
Grooming, **211–12**: Bathing, 211; Brushing and Combing, 211, *211*; Claws, 211–12, *213*; Eyes, 212, *213*; Ears, 212, *213*; Teeth and Gums, 212
Gums, 35; pale gums, 221

H

Hair, 30
Hairless Cat, see Mexican Hairless;
    Sphynx
Havana, 120
Havana Brown, **122**, *122–23*, **125**,
    124–25, *224*
Havana Foreign, see Havana Brown
Hazards, *212–213*; Collars, 213;
    Electricity, 213; Enclosed Places,
    213; Heights, 212–13; People,
    213; Poisons, 213
Heart, 33, *32–3*, 220, 221
Heat Stroke, 232
Hematoma, 221
Heterozygous, 239
Himalayan, 55, *100–101*, **126–28**; Blue
    Point, 47, *64–5*; Blue Cream
    Point, 128; Chocolate Point
    Himalayan, *126–27*; Flame Point,
    128; Seal Point, *47*; Tortie Point,
    128
Himbur, **128**
Hindquarters, Dragging, 220
History, Cats in, *17–19*
Holophoneus, 17
Homozygous, 239
Hookworms, 228

I

Inbreeding, 239
Incapacitated Cat, Special Care for, 235
Indian Desert Cat, **128**
Indian Lion, see Lion
Indian Tiger, see Tiger
Indo-Chinese Tiger, see Tiger
Insect bites, 30
Internal injuries, 221
Intestines, 35

J

Jaguar, **130–31**, *130–31*
Jaguarondi, **132**, *132–33*
Japanese Bobtail, **132**
Javan Tiger, see Tiger
Joints, 29
Jungle Cat, **135**, *134–35*

K

Kaffir Cat, see African Wild Cat
Keratitis, 225
Kidney disease, 221
Kittens: Birth of, *34–5*, 242; Care of,
    214, 233, 238, 240, 243, 243; Sex
    determination, 35, *34–5*
Kodkod, **135**
Korat, 64, 120, **135**; Korat Cat Fanciers'
    Association, 135

L

Laxative, 220
Leopard, 20, **136–37**, *136–37*
Leopard Cat, **141**, *140–41*
Leopard, Clouded, see Clouded Leopard
Leopard, Snow, see Snow Leopard
Lice, 227, *227*
Lilac Burmese, see Burmese
Lilac Cream Point, see Colorpoint
    Short-hair
Lilac Lynx Point, see Colorpoint
    Short-hair
Lilac Oriental, *239*
Lilac Point, see Colors and Patterns;
    Siamese
Lilac Self Long-hair, see Himalayan
Lilac Tortie Burmese, see Burmese
Line breeding, 239
Lion (African and Indian), 20, *129*;
    142–43, *142–45*
Lion, Mountain, see Puma
Lips, 35
Listlessness, 221
Literature, Cats in, *21–3*
Little Spotted Cat, see Tiger Cat
Liver, 35; infection, 221
Long-hair, see Persian
Lumps, 221
Lungs, 33, *32–3*
Lymph Nodes, 33
Lynx, Bay, see Bobcat
Lynx, Caracal, see Caracal Lynx
Lynx, Northern, see Northern Lynx
Lynx Point, see Colorpoint Short-hair

M

Mackerel Tabby Pattern, **42**, 52, 112
Magpie, see Bi-colored Persian; Colors
    and Patterns
Maine Coon, **147**; Maine Coon Cat
    Club, 147
Male cats, 35

Male Reproductive System, 35
Maltese, 64, **147**
Manchurian Tiger, see Tiger
Mange Mites, 227
Manx, *146–47*, **147–48**; Short-haired, 107
Manxamese, **151**
Marbled Cat, **151**
Margay Cat, *150–51*, **151–52**
Mate, arrangements and choice of, 238
Mating, 241
Mau, see Egyptian Mau
Medicine, Administration of, *221*, 234
Medicine Chest, 230
Mendel, Gregor, 236
Mendelian checkerboard, 237
Mexican Hairless, **152**
Mites: Ear Mites, 224, *226*, 227; Harvest Mite, *226*; Mange Mites, 227
Moon Cat, see Sphynx
Mountain Cat, **152**
Mountain Lion, see Puma
Mouth, 35
Muscle structure, *26*
Music, Cats in, 23
Mutation, 239

N

Nasal discharge, 221
Nervous System, 32
Neutering, 210, **241**
Northern Lynx, 68, **152**, *152–53*, *206–207*
Nose, 30
Nutrition, *213–15* (see also Feeding, 213); Commercial Pet Food, 214; Essential Nutrients, 214–15; Fresh Food, 214

O

Ocelot, *128–29*, **154–56**, *154–55*
Ocicat, **156–57**; Dark Chestnut, 157; Light Chestnut, 157
Odd-eyed White, see White Persian; White Short-hair
Older Cat: Ailments, Care of, Diet, 236
Orange-eyed White, see White Persian; White Short-hair
Oriental Black, see Oriental Short-hair
Oriental Lavender, *80–81*, *134–35*, **157**, *160–61*, see also Oriental Short-hair
Oriental Short-hair, *80–81*, 120, *121*, *156–57*, **158–59**, *158–59*, see also Siamese

Oriental White, **159**
Ounce, see Snow Leopard
Outbreeding, 239
Ova, 35
Ovaries, 35, 241
Ovulation, 35

P

Pads, 30
Pallas's Cat, **160**, *160–61*
Pampas Cat, **160**
Panther, see Leopard
Panther, Black, see Leopard
Parasites, 220, 221, *226–29* (see also separate entries)
Parti-colored Persian, see Bi-colored Persian; Calico; Colors and Patterns; Persian; Tortoiseshell Persian
Parti-colors, see Colors and Patterns
Paw, *30*
Pedigree cat, Choice of, 210
Peke-Face Persian, **163**, *162–63*
Penis, 35
Persian, 55, 56, 107, **164**, *164*; Blue, *64–5*; Blue Cream, *62–3*
Persian Tiger, see Tiger
Pets, cats with other pets, 215
Phenotype, 239
Photography, 244–47, *244–47*
Placenta, 242
Platinum Burmese, see Burmese
Platinum Tortie Burmese, see Burmese
Pneumonia, 220, *224*
Poisoning, 220, 221, **233**
Polydactylism, 148, **237**
Pregnancy, 35, *241–42*; False, 241
Prostate gland, 35
Protozoa, 229
Pulse, 234
Puma, **166–67**, *166–67*

Q

Queen, 35

R

Rabies, 220, *222*
Ragdolls, **168**
Recessive gene, 239
Red, 39
Red Abyssinian, see Abyssinian

Red Burmese, see Burmese
Red Lynx Point, see Colorpoint Short-
    hair
Red Persian, see Solid Red
Red Point, see Colorpoint Short-hair;
    Himalayan
Red Self, see Colors and Patterns;
    Solid Red
Red Smoke, 41
Red Tabby, see Colors and Patterns;
    Tabby
Reproduction in Cats, 240–43
Reproductive cycle, 240
Reproductive system, 35
Respiratory disease, 221
Respiratory system, 33, *32–3*
Rex, *122–23*, **170**, *170–71*, *210*
Ringworm, 228
Roundworms, 220, **228**, *228*
Ruddy Abyssinian, see Abyssinian
Rumpie, see Manx
Russian Blue, *39*, 64, 120, 147, **172**,
    172–73, *246*
Rusty-Spotted Cat, **174**

S

Sable Burmese, *21*, *215*, *217*, see also
    Burmese
Sand Cat, **174–77**, *174–75*
Sanitation, 215–16
Scottish Fold, **177**, *176–77*
Scottish Wild Cat, *116–17*, see also
    European Wild Cat
Scrotum, 35
Seal Lynx Point, see Colorpoint Short-
    hair
Seal Point, see Colors and Patterns
Seal Tortie Point, see Colorpoint Short-
    hair
Sebum, 30
Seminal fluid, 35
Senses, 30
Serval, **178**, *178–79*
Sex determination, *32–3*, 35
Sexual Behavior of the Female, 240;
    of the Male, 240;
    Maturity, 35, 240
Shaded Cameo (or Red Shaded), see
    Cameo; Colors and Patterns
Shaded colors, see Colors and Patterns
Shaded Silver, 39, 52
Shaded Silver Long-hair, **181**, *180–81*
Shaded Silver Persian, see Colors and
    Patterns; Shaded Silver Long-hair
Shadow Point, see Colorpoint Short-
    hair (Lynx Point)
Shell Cameo (or Red Chinchilla), see
    Cameo; Colors and Patterns
Shock, 233

Short-hair, see American Short-hair;
    British Short-hair
Siamese, 50, 54–5, 100, 159, **182–187**,
    182–183, 239, 245: Blue Point,
    185; Chocolate Point, 185; Kitten,
    48, *74–5*; Lilac Point, *34–5*, 185,
    184–85; Seal Point, *25*, *47*,
    184–85, *186–87*, 187, *238*, *244*;
    Tabby Point, *47*
Siberian Tiger, see Tiger
Sick Room, 234
Silver Mau, see Egyptian Mau
Silver Persian, see Chinchilla
Silver Point Siamese, see Colorpoint
    Short-hair
Silver Tabby, see Colors and Patterns;
    Tabby Persian; Tabby Short-hair
Si-Rex, see Devon Rex; Rex
Si-Sawat, see Korat
Skeleton, 28–9, *28*
Skin, 30
Skin Ailments: Allergies, Baldness,
    Dandruff, Dermatitis, Eczema,
    Impetigo, 225
Skull, *32–3*
Smilodon (saber-tooth tiger), 17
Smoke Cameo, see Cameo; Colors and
    Patterns
Smoke Long-hair, see Smoke, Persian
Smoke Mau, see Egyptian Mau
Smoke Persian, 41, **187**, *186–87*,
    188–89; Blue Smoke Persian, 188
Smoke Short-hair, **188**
Sneezing, 221
Snow Leopard, **188**, *188–89*
Solid Color Point, see Colorpoint
    Short-hair
Solid Colors, see Colors and Patterns
Solid Red, *168–69*, **188**
Somali, **188**
Spaying, *210*, **241**
Sperm, 35
Spinal cord, 29, 32
Sphynx, **191**
Spleen, 33
Spotted Cat, *42*, *190–91*, **191–92**
Spotted Cat, Little, see Tiger Cat
Spottie, see Spotted Cat
Stings, 231
Stomach, 33, 35
Stumpy, see Manx
Sumatran Tiger, see Tiger
Supilak, **192**
Swamp Cat, see Jungle Cat
Swimming Cat, see Turkish Van Cat
Swiss Mountain Cat, see European
    Wild Cat, 192

T

Tabby, 20, *42*, **192–95**, 215, 217, 247:
Blue Tabby Persian, 192; Brown
Tabby Long-hair, *42*; Brown
Tabby Persian, 192; Brown Tabby
Short-hair, *194–95*, 195; Red
Tabby Persian, 192; Red Tabby
Short-hair, 195; Silver Tabby
Persian, 192; Silver Tabby Short-
hair, *42*, 195
Tabby Colorpoint Short-hair, see
Colorpoint Short-hair (Lynx
Point)
Tabby Point, see Colorpoint Short-hair
Tail, 29
Tapeworms, 220, 221, **228**, *228*
Teeth, 35; Baby teeth, 35
Temminck's Golden Cat, **195**
Temperature; high, 221; how to take,
234, *234*
Testicles, 35, 241
Thompson, Dr Joseph C, 74
Ticks, 226, *226*
Tiger, **196**, 198: Bali, 198; Bengal,
196–97, 198; Caspian, 198;
Chinese, 198; Indo-Chinese, 198;
Javan, 198; Saber-tooth, 17;
Siberian, 198; Sumatran, 198, *199*;
White, 198, *198*
Tiger Cat, **201**, *200–201*
Tongue, **30**, 35
Tonkinese, **201**
Tortie, 201
Tortie Point, see Colorpoint Short-
hair; Himalayan
Tortoiseshell, 44
Tortoiseshell Burmese, see Burmese
Tortoiseshell Cameo, see Cameo
Tortoiseshell Persian, **202**, *202–203*
Tortoiseshell Short-hair, **202**, *202–203*
Tortoiseshell and White Long-hair, see
Calico
Tortoiseshell and White Short-hair,
200–201, see also Calico
Toxoplasmosis, 220, *222*
Training, 216–18, *216*
Travel, 219
Tumors, 220
Turkish Angora, see Angora
Turkish Van Cat, *25*, **202**, 204–205

U

Umbilical Cord, 242
Uremia, 220
Urinary disorder, 220
Uterus, 35, 341; infection of, 221

V

Vaccinations, 219, 222
Vagina, 35; vaginal discharge, 221
Van Cat, see Turkish Van Cat
Vertebral column, *32–3*
Virus infection, 221
Vomiting, 221
Vulva, 35

W

White Persian, *162–63*, *165*, **205–6**;
Blue-Eyed, **205**, *204–205*; Odd-
Eyed, *39*, **205**; Orange-Eyed, **206**
White Short-hair, *25*, **206**; Blue-Eyed
White, **206**; Foreign or Oriental,
18; Odd-Eyed White, **206**;
Orange-Eyed White, **206**
White Tiger, see Tiger
Wild cat, 25
Wild Cat, African, see African Wild Cat
Wild Cat, European, see European
Wild Cat
Wild Cat, Scottish, see European Wild
Cat

Z

Zibeline, see Burmese

Picture credits